Dear Abby,
I'm Gay

Dear Abby, I'm Gay

*Newspaper Advice Columnists
and Homosexuality in America*

ANDREW E. STONER

McFarland & Company, Inc., Publishers
Jefferson, North Carolina

ISBN (print) 978-1-4766-8496-3
ISBN (ebook) 978-1-4766-4310-6

LIBRARY OF CONGRESS AND BRITISH LIBRARY
CATALOGUING DATA ARE AVAILABLE

© 2021 Andrew E. Stoner. All rights reserved

No part of this book may be reproduced or transmitted in any form or by any means, electronic or mechanical, including photocopying or recording, or by any information storage and retrieval system, without permission in writing from the publisher.

Cover image © 2021 Gustavo Frazao/Shutterstock

Printed in the United States of America

*McFarland & Company, Inc., Publishers
Box 611, Jefferson, North Carolina 28640
www.mcfarlandpub.com*

Table of Contents

Preface   1

Introduction   3

1. "Your Problems"—Ann Landers   9
2. "Dear Abby"—Abigail Van Buren   23
3. "Helen Help Us!"—Helen Bottel   39
4. "Ask Dr. Brothers"—Dr. Joyce Brothers   50
5. "The Worry Clinic"—Dr. George Crane   62
6. "Mary Haworth's Mail"—Mary Haworth   87
7. "Dear Meg"—Margaret Whitcomb   102
8. "Ask Beth"—Elizabeth Winship   108
9. "Tell Me About It"—Carolyn Hax   124
10. "Dear Prudence"—Herb Stein, Margo Howard, Emily Yoffe and Mallory Ortberg/Daniel Lavery   135
11. "Ask Amy"—Amy Dickinson   149
12. "Since You Asked"—Cary Tennis   163
13. "Savage Love"—Dan Savage   171
14. Other Columnists—The Rev. Dr. Martin Luther King, Jr., Miss Manners (Judith Martin), Cullen Moore, Dr. Walter C. Alvarez, Lew and Joanne Koch, the Rev. Billy Graham, Dr. Michael Fox, Dr. Lawrence E. Lamb and Lori Gottlieb   184

Chapter Notes   201

Index   215

Preface

The rationale for reviewing the words of America's newspaper (and later online) advice columnists regarding homosexuals and homosexuality is based in the desire to help answer the question of how and why historic and societal attitudes and beliefs about homosexuals have been formed. There are many explanations for the acceptance—or lack thereof—of lesbian, gay, bisexual, transgender and queer people in our society, many of them based in (and inextricably linked to) issues of religion, politics, race, gender and class. But none of these societal influences by themselves exists in a vacuum, and the role mass media plays in reflecting, examining and interpreting views on homosexuality is critically important. So what role did these columns play throughout the latter part of the twentieth century and into the early portion of the current century in forming ideas and opinions about the homosexual in America? Was the advice offered helpful in advancing the rights and placement of LGBTQ people in modern society, or did their words slow progress toward more equality? A further consideration must be given to the public and mediated nature of the advice given—advice printed in the daily newspaper or online as opposed to private conversations where heartfelt worries and concerns are shared with someone else. The advice given, presumably meant to assist the person asking for help, also served the broader audience of readers consuming the information shared and advice given, cascading its influence far and wide. There is no systematic or scientific attempt here to measure some of the impact of advice columnists on issues related to homosexuality, but rather to highlight and reflect upon the words given as a guide to understanding the evolving nature of our understanding of and acceptance of one another.

Introduction

In the era when the daily newspaper served up an eclectic variety of content, from politics, business, crime, sports, recipes, and comic strips, the advice column quickly became one of the most popular features of most dailies. And while newspaper readership has continued to spiral downward in recent years, the popularity of asking an old "agony aunt" for advice hasn't waned—it's just moved to a new location, online.

For many millions of Americans, advice columns served the important dual function of providing advice to those seeking help, *and* providing a stimulating, interesting peek into the lives of the people around us. They also often provided the first mention of homosexuals outside of newspaper police reports where gays were presented as a criminal threat, or in mid-century "security sweeps" of the federal government where the loyalty of gays was placed in doubt. The influence of advice columns could be wide and impactful, as more than 100 million readers regularly read one of the columns in their heyday.

Advice columnists of all types took up the subject of homosexuality as early as the 1930s and demonstrated positions that varied from empathy and compassion to damnation and scorn. Traditional lovelorn columnists and those offering psychological or social advice were among the first to step into the discussion, but many have followed, including astrologists, evangelical religious leaders and even veterinarians. In all instances, advice columnists seemed to reflect—and sometimes lead—American attitudes toward their LGBTQ brethren.

Not only did the columnists themselves offer varying views on homosexuality, readers were not shy in offering their own viewpoints. As the topics and advice contained in the columns continued to evolve, readers could show disgust and approval.

One mother, writing to the venerable Ann Landers in 1974, declared, "I am wondering just how far the publisher will let you go before they decide to throw your column out of the newspaper. I am sick

Introduction

and tired of trying to beat my teenagers to the front porch to see if your column is fit for them to read. I refer specifically to some of the trash you have printed on homosexuality and venereal disease."[1]

Such views contrasted widely with a reader thanking "Ask Beth" impresario Elizabeth Winship as she retired from her column in 1998: "I grew up in a small town as a gay teen. Reading the letters in your column [in the 1980s] from other gay teens, along with your reassurance and frank and honest information, helped me realize that I was not some freak of nature, helped me through one more day, and I believe, may have saved my life."[2]

As author Diane Anderson-Marshall noted, the gay kid writing to "Ask Beth" represented "the voice of the coming [teen] age Gen Xer" and credited Winship with offering a forum where a gay person (or their parents) could ask a question without being portrayed as being "weird or stupid."[3]

Of course, it wasn't always so. Newspapers and mass media in general were unfriendly territory for homosexuals for much of the twentieth century. Many a gay man or lesbian woman scanned newspapers or books for the word "homosexual" in a sometimes-desperate search for community beyond their own closet. Police blotters provided the most regular place where a gay person could find mention of their kind, but only in the context of being a problem (even a criminal one) in search of a solution.

The only notable exceptions were occasional psychological or social discussions of the homosexual as "a deviate" where emphasis upon their differences from "the heterosexual norm" were highlighted, and the entire issue of a gay or lesbian sexuality was confined to the perspective of a problem needing an answer.

Even when newspapers attempted to cover homosexuals as either victims or perpetrators of crime in a coy or shielded way with broadly worded news stories, they were subject to criticism. In his 1941 essay about the coverage of homosexual issues in newspapers, sociologist F.A. McHenry argued that newspapers should be more explicit in their coverage of homosexuality, particularly gay men as perpetrators and victims of crime, that a "clear attitude of mind toward the problem of homosexuality" was as necessary as previous media focus on the dangers of sexually transmitted diseases, such as syphilis.[4]

Little progress was noted by 1966 when *Time* magazine examined homosexual communities in some of the nation's largest cities, referring to the gay lifestyle as "a pathetic little second-rate substitute for

Introduction

reality, a pitiable flight from life." *Time* noted that while homosexuals may be deserving of fairness, compassion, understanding and (mental health) treatment, it quickly added: "But it deserves no encouragement, no glamorization, no rationalization, no fake status as minority martyrdom ... and above-all, no pretense that it is anything but a pernicious sickness."[5]

Life magazine continued the "problem perspective" when discussing homosexuality, declaring it in 1971 as the "most shocking, and to many Americans, the most surprising liberation movement yet." America's coffee-table magazine noted the topic of homosexuality was "rarely mentioned in print before today" and in some ways represented "a direct assault on laws and customs."[6]

There is no question that homosexuals were at least hoping advice columns could serve an ideological function regarding the place and understanding of LGBTQ people in America. Further, given that advice columns were read by millions of readers, but a much smaller subset of people ever wrote to the columnists seeking advice, the columns' primary function clearly was one of satiating reader curiosity and nosiness about others.

As historian Joanna Scutts noted, writing to a newspaper advice column doesn't make a large amount of sense for people actually needing help. "It makes no practical sense to write to a newspaper for advice on an urgent problem, given the days and weeks that will elapse between the questioner sending the letter and the columnist publishing a response," Scutts wrote.

Scutts concluded, as do many, that the "draw" of the advice column is not really about getting an answer to a problem or input on a situation, but about "readers' voyeurism and moral theorizing." She suggested that because readers take such delight in their responses to the problems presented—whether it manifests as empathy, judgment, mockery or scorn—the advice column becomes an artifact of "how secular authorities take over from religious ones."[7]

Scutts's point covers why readers enjoy the column, and helps explain why the individual advice given in any particular column was often far less important than the overall topic being introduced. Could it be that some of the issues raised were not so much a question, but an issue in need of airing?

This text attempts to review the hundreds of gay-related letters submitted to the newspaper advice sages over time that help reveal that the writers were often already decidedly settled on matters of

Introduction

sexuality. Their issue more often than not appears related to how they are accepted—or rejected—in the greater society. As a result, the letters give the writers (and perhaps the columnists as well) a chance to make their case again about the inequity, and pain, associated with the rejection homosexuals have known throughout the decades in American culture. It is here that we encounter the ideological—or even political—function advice columns have played in the navigation of gay people in America, and the understanding of Americans of their gay counterparts.

Scutts takes a related view—readers continue to "defer to expertise, but they crave empathy." Noting that a person writing for advice is under no obligation to accept or reject the advice given, she says "the therapeutic act of framing a dilemma, of sharing a problem, keeps the advice seekers writing—and the rubbernecks reading."[8]

Marilyn Coleman and Lawrence Ganong took up advice columns in their volume *The Social History of the American Family*. They noted the columns served as a "consistent, mainstream, widely available public forum" for discussions of problems of all types, and "were staples of lifestyle sections of newspapers and were meant to entertain and to inform." And while the columns were widely popular for more than a century, "little scholarship has been devoted to them. Communication researchers have typically focused on front page news, and the content of lifestyle or women's sections of newspapers or women's magazines, where advice columns usually ran, has rarely been studied."[9]

Among the issues not studied, but evident, are the relative advancement in the level of sophistication offered in advice columns. "Late 20th century advice columnists raised the standards of earlier columnists by incorporating information that they [solicit and] include from medical, mental health and other professionals with their common-sense wisdom," Coleman and Ganong wrote.[10]

Scutts posits that some of the earliest columnists—Hearst "newsroom gals" turned columnists Beatrice Fairfax and Dorothy Dix—were qualified only as a result of "the stamina and emotional resilience to avoid being overwhelmed by the suffering of others. Expertise or qualifications were not really the point."[11]

In 1920, Hearst editor Arthur Brisbane called on his "newsgirl" Fairfax to write the "Advice to the Lovelorn" column. Fairfax, whose real name was Marie Manning, was a seasoned reporter for more than 20 years, but initially lacked in enough letters to feed a daily column. Undeterred, Fairfax reportedly had to make up out of whole cloth the

Introduction

letters in the first installments of the column because of a lack of letters received from readers.

Eventually "Advice to the Lovelorn" became so popular, Hearst syndicated it to newspapers across the country via its King Syndicate. While the pen name "Beatrice Fairfax" remained, Manning was eventually replaced by other writers who continued the column for many years.[12]

"Dorothy Dix Talks" (originally offered by *The Daily Picayune* in New Orleans in 1896) started off as a "women's column" and was written by pioneering female journalist Elizabeth Meriwether Gilmer. Discovered by William Randolph Hearst, the "Dorothy Dix" column was transformed into an advice column in the 1920s and became so popular—with an estimated 60 million readers—it was eventually anchored at *The New York Post* and provided regular competition to the existing "Advice to the Lovelorn" column.[13]

As journalism historian George H. Douglas noted, "Both Fairfax's and Dix's columns concentrated their efforts on matters of the heart" and attracted an almost exclusively female readership. After World War I a wider array of issues were covered, and more men began to read (and write to) the columnists. Regardless of the wider range of topics covered, homosexuality remained a strictly "off limits" topic for either column. It was, after all, still the era of homosexuality existing as "the love that dare not speak its name."[14]

Jack Craemer, long-time publisher and editor of *The San Rafael Independent Journal* in Marin County, California, offered a column in 1967 about the notion of newspaper advice columns. He noted that during the Hearst era of dominance in journalism, advice columns won a seedy reputation for the advice (and mostly gossip) they doled out. "During the late 1940s and early 1950s, lovelorn advice columns probably fell to their lowest level of disfavor," Craemer wrote. "Then along came a couple of smart twin sisters [Ann Landers and Dear Abby] ... who quickly became the hottest thing in advice columns [with] readership surveys according them top spots on the scale of popularity with readers."[15]

Not surprisingly, the rise of the Internet has promoted a greater democratization of advice columns. Anyone with a computer and a willingness to solicit and respond to queries can do so, and as a result, advice has become increasingly segmented and specialized. Today one of the most widely-read advice columns, "Savage Love" by Dan Savage, not only takes up the issue of homosexuality as part of its regular fare, it

Introduction

is written from an entirely homocentric point of view reflecting Savage's commitment to living out as a proud gay man. Further, one contemporary columnist, Daniel Lavery, sitting at the helm of the popular online column "Dear Prudence," took readers along with him as a transgender person transitioning from a female gender identity (as Mallory Ortberg) to a male gender identity.

Regardless, as journalist Hannah Finnie noted recently, "though advice columns have changed significantly over the years, one aspect has remained the same: the delicate balance columnists must strike between engaging with an individual letter-writer and appealing to a wider audience."[16]

Finnie's note serves as a telling precursor to an amazing exchange "modern day" advice columnist John Paul Brammer wrote about regarding a heart-breaking letter received from a gay man from Uganda, a part of the world where his sexuality, if discovered, could result in his imprisonment or death. "Being gay is illegal in my country," the young man wrote. "I could be attacked or killed if I come on too strong."[17]

Interestingly, Brammer disclosed later that he declined to answer the query in his column from the gay African man. "A responsible advice columnist is aware of the limitations of the medium, and acts accordingly (even if the resulting piece would have garnered a lot of clicks)," he wrote. "This advice seeker did not need counsel from an openly gay media professional living in Brooklyn.... Whatever advice I gave would be inextricably linked to a privileged Western experience of gayness. What if, because of me, he came out, and doing so put him in danger?"[18]

Brammer's experience also emphasizes the "new frontier" for advice columnists—their letters and responses not limited to 800 words or less—and not limited to just subscribers of any particular publication. In addition, several contemporary columnists have begun to "group source" replies to queries received on all topics, reflecting the democratization of media and the desire for symmetrical interaction between readers and experts.

From this examination of advice columns, we hopefully learn the expected framework of how Americans understood their homosexual compatriots, but also how attitudes and feelings toward them continued to evolve and expand. The advice columns effectively illustrate the journey of homosexuals from residing in a problem perspective to more sympathetic portrayals of lesbians and gays as legitimate members of the family and society.

CHAPTER 1

"Your Problems"
—Ann Landers

The undisputed queen of newspaper advice columns was Ann Landers—whose real name was Esther Pauline "Eppie" Friedman Lederer—and became for decades the standard by which all other advice columns were measured. No other column reached as many readers as Ann Landers—including the column of her twin sister—or had as much social impact.

Quoted widely, author of best-selling books and a frequent television guest, Lederer was awarded honorary degrees from 33 U.S. colleges and universities, and for just under 50 years influenced generations of Americans on a wide array of issues. At its peak, her "Your Problems" column was published in more than 1,200 newspapers worldwide, and had an estimated daily readership of 90 million readers. Her success, Lederer believed was "because [the readers] don't consider me a stranger. I'm the lady next door, their best friend, the mother they couldn't communicate with before, but now they can. Most of all, I'm a good listener."[1]

Described as "frank, feisty and funny," Lederer—or Landers—always seemed to have a ready answer for readers asking for her help—or at least had the experts lined up to help her answer questions. In fact, she enlisted the help of a personal friend, U.S. Supreme Court Justice William O. Douglas, as part of her "audition" for the column in order to answer a question about how a reader should handle walnuts from a neighbor's tree littering their yard. Lederer landed the "audition" in 1955 after sharing a train ride with a top editor at *The Chicago Sun-Times* who said he was in search of a new writer for their "Your Problems" advice column.

Lederer admitted she had no particular expertise or experience in dolling out advice, but did possess a lot of Midwestern common sense that held appeal. The *Sun-Times* editor, Larry Fanning, who hired her, noted, "This girl has something beyond mere shrewdness—a quality very close to genuine wisdom.... It's some kind of inherited thing."[2]

The daughter of Russian immigrants from Sioux City, Iowa, she was born in 1918 just 17 minutes before her identical twin, Pauline Esther "Popo" Friedman (who later claimed the persona of "Dear Abby"). She was known throughout her life as "Eppie" and for years maintained a fierce competition (both personal and professional) with her sister. After Lederer and her husband moved to Chicago, she began seeking work to help support her family and the advice column landed in her lap at an opportune moment—her sample responses for *The Sun-Times* editors helping her beat out 30 other applicants for the job.

Esther Pauline "Eppie" Lederer—better known to millions of Americans as "Ann Landers"—shown here in a 1961 publicity photograph. Lederer died in June 2002 at age 83 (Library of Congress Image LC-USZ62-111600).

Advice columns may have been silly or vacuous pursuits for some, but for Lederer it was serious business from the start. "If I had to leave the column for even a day or two," Lederer/Landers shared, "I know I'd feel anxious about it."[3] Allowed to hire secretaries to handle the quickly growing flow of letters rolling into her Chicago office, Landers readership quickly bested more established columnists (such as Dorothy Dix or Mary Haworth). She briefly enlisted the help of her sister "Popo" in answering some letters just prior to the younger twin moving to California and soon landing her own advice column on the pages of *The San Francisco Chronicle*.

The intrusion of "Popo" into Landers' established role as an advice column set off a years-long feud between the sisters that was reported on by no less than *Time* and *Life* magazines. The hard feelings between the two seemed real, though their editors (and syndication managers) seemed happy to exploit the feud in order to gain attention and interest in the columnists. In April 1958, *Life* magazine ran a lengthy report on

Chapter 1. "Your Problems"

the battle between the "Twin Lovelorn Advisers," noting, "There is nothing communal in their efforts. From the fierce rivalry between them, in fact, it sometimes appears that they are using U.S. journalism as a personal battlefield and its hundreds of newspapers as personal artillery in what must be the most feverish female feud since Elizabeth sent Mary Queen of Scots to the chopping block."[4]

In the *Life* magazine report, it became clear the hardest feelings were held by Landers who may have had reason to resent her sister's intrusion on her turf. Beyond that, Abby had enjoyed more personal successes than did Landers—Abby married a wealthy business tycoon (founder of Budget Rent-A-Car company) while Landers labored as the wife of a middle-management business salesman. As *Life* magazine noted, "For years, Ann says, she has been trying to escape twinhood and to prove that she is an individual in her own right. For years, Abby says, she's been trying to get her twin back."[5]

The race to become America's most popular advice columnist did nothing to enhance the bond between the sisters—Landers being the first to accuse her sister of being "imitative" of her efforts. Beyond that, the battle between the Friedman twins "is a curious battle for newspapers, for neither can't help selling the other's column. As soon as a newspaper buys one, its rival in town is virtually forced to buy the other to match reader interest."[6]

Landers could be direct in her criticism of her sister and her claims that she never intended to "one up" her sister. "That's her fantasy," Landers said in 1958. "She's just like a kid who beats a dog until somebody looks, and then she starts petting it."[7]

The rivalry aside, Landers said she distinguished herself as not just someone who would sit and hold a friend's hand while they cry, but instead urge them to get on with solving their problems. "Just getting people to write problems down is part way to solving them," she said. "They can think about the problem, then they can cope with it in a more objective way."[8]

Landers also said she put more thought than others into the letters she selected for publication from the thousands received. "I look for letters that teach something, or that people can relate to," she said. The contrast with Abby was particularly sharp—"Dear Abby" featuring often much shorter replies to readers than Ann Landers' more thoughtful and lengthy replies. Landers also said she made it her practice to "be with people smarter than I am. That's how I learn. If you hang out with people not as smart as you are, you won't learn anything." That value drove her to frequently give column space to experts on a variety of human and social issues.[9]

It wasn't as if, however, Landers was not known to turn a smart or funny retort—perhaps most famous for telling readers to "mind your own beeswax" instead of "mind your own business," or advising someone to "wake up and smell the coffee." When she felt she had been in error in one of her replies, Landers readily rolled out a prescribed personal punishment of "fifty lashes with a wet noodle."

She said she followed an early editor's advice who told her, "Baby, you gotta remember what [the readers] tell you is happening to them, not to you. You have to learn to separate yourself from the people who have the problem."[10] In interviews and profiles, it's clear Landers viewed her column as a journalistic pursuit, and not entertainment. However the column was classified, it was big business with *The Sun-Times* eventually selling the "Your Problems" column and the Ann Landers franchise to their cross-town rival, *The Chicago Tribune*, and its powerful national syndicate.

Writing a column for 46 years, Landers admitted that her views on various issues evolved—perhaps most notably around marriage when her own marriage ended in a heartbreaking divorce in 1975 at the height of her popularity. In an interview five years after her marriage ended, Landers said she handled "the major tragedy of my life" as she would have advised a reader to do, with kindness and by talking to others for help.[11]

On the issue of homosexuality, Landers advanced more slowly than did her sister, Abby, holding on to pronouncements about whether gays were sick, deviant or suffering emotional or mental imbalance for many years.

Her slow advance on the issue was clear even up until near the end of her career as the issue of same-sex marriage began to gain support and interest. She wrote in 1996 that she supported legal rights for gay couples (such as home ownership, taxes, hospital visitation rights, employment), "but that is as far as I want to go. I define marriage as a union between a man and a woman." She seemed prepared for the renewal of criticism she would receive "from you gay-rights folks," but added: "I have been supportive of [the gay rights] movement for many years, have withstood a great deal of criticism in the process and have risked the wrath of some editors and publishers. I cannot support same-sex marriage, however, because it flies in the face of cultural and traditional family values we have known for centuries. And that's where I draw the line."[12]

Chapter 1. "Your Problems"

Twenty years earlier, in 1976, she was also on the opposing side of the advancement of gay rights taking exception to a decision by the American Psychiatric Association to no longer classify homosexuality as an illness or emotional disorder. Landers highlighted that "many psychiatrists refused to accept the decision" of the APA and "made it abundantly clear that the APA does not speak for all its members. My principle consultants disagreed with the decision and that's where I stand."[13]

She reminded her readers, "I fought for the civil rights of homosexuals 20 years ago and argued that that they should be regarded as full and equal citizens. However, I do NOT believe homosexuality is 'just another lifestyle.' I believe these people suffer from a severe personality disorder. Granted, some are sicker than others, but sick they are, and all the fancy rhetoric by the American Psychiatric Association will not change it."[14]

Landers had arrived early on the discussion of homosexuality—the very first column featuring the subject coming in an October 1959 column in which a reader wrote concerned that her teenage brother was in danger by continually hitchhiking. "The other night my brother told me (as if it were a joke) that he hitched a ride with a man who turned out to be a homosexual," the reader reported. "It was then I decided to write you this letter. Please print it. It may save a life." Landers seemed to agree with the inherent "danger" someone might face accepting a car ride from a homosexual, adding, "Riding with a stranger can be an invitation to disaster and I hope your letter will alert those who haven't given serious thought to the repercussions."[15]

The theme of "how to deal with those homosexuals" was present in Landers' next letter on the topic appearing in February 1961 from a Detroit man whose wife forbid him to invite an openly gay—and effeminate—childhood male friend to their home for any reason. The gay man was described as "brilliant, talented, well-thought of and popular [and] has done well in a creative field, is a sparkling conversationalist, a deep thinker and a thoughtful, kind person."[16]

Ann compared the homosexual friend to a person with polio. "You wouldn't snub a friend because he was crippled by polio, would you? Well, your boyhood friend is an emotional cripple." While noting that the man may have many fine adult qualities, "he is a case of arrested development." She said, "Many homosexuals lead useful lives and enrich society through their creative activities. Homosexuals of past decades have contributed handsomely to the arts and sciences. A person so afflicted, if he behaves in a socially acceptable manner, should not be insulted or snubbed." In the end, however, Ann sided with the man's wife and reminded the reader that his first obligation was to her, and not his friend.[17]

The breakthrough nature of the letter openly discussing homosexuality—with at least an attempt at compassion on Landers part—did not go unnoticed by her readers (and the editors and publishers who ran her daily column). In a March 1961 column, Landers wrote a "Dear Readers" entry noting, "During the five and a half years that I have been writing the Ann Landers column I've received hundreds of letters which dealt with homosexual problems. I have counseled these readers through the mail. In February, the first letter on homosexuality appeared in print. So far as I know, every client newspaper ran it. Not a single publisher or editor phoned or wrote to complain."[18]

She added a cautionary note. "The reaction from readers, however, was mixed." She decided, as a result, to run a sampling of the responses, such as a letter from a Madison, Wisconsin, reader thanking her "for the first sympathetic, intelligent and understanding words I have ever seen in a newspaper on the problem of homosexuality. This is the most misunderstood aspect of life in our country—and it will remain so until others muster their courage and present the facts."[19]

Another letter from a Cleveland, Ohio, reader declared they were "thoroughly disgusted with Ann" and that "the idea of a woman in your position standing up for queers! Why should normal people put themselves out to accommodate these oddballs?" A Chicago reader appeared to agree, telling Ann, "You're all wet. Anyone who associates with a swishy gay is suspect. I say, let 'em alone. They have their own circles and prefer one another's company anyway." A Houston reader asked, "Have you gone off your rocker? I hid the newspaper today so my 16-year-old son wouldn't see your column on pansies. A father has enough trouble with his teenage kids these days without answering questions on *that* subject. Doesn't anybody censor your material?"[20]

Homosexuals themselves wrote in to thank Ann—one man from St. Louis saying, "thank you for saying a kind word about homosexuals. We need it. I have died a thousand times for being the way I am. I'd give my right arm to be like other men. God only knows why we are different. It is a terrible cross to bear." A "former homosexual" from Detroit also thanked Ann, reporting that through the help of a psychiatrist he was able to be married and become a father and offered that those "whose condemnation is most violent [against homosexuals], the ones

Chapter 1. "Your Problems"

who are least tolerant of homosexuals, are not quite sure of their own masculinity."[21]

The concept of being a "former homosexual" or "cured homosexual" seemed to catch Landers' attention and was the subject of many letters to follow, including one just a day after addressing the reaction of her readers to a column on a homosexual topic. The letter writer detailed being the son of a single mother who encouraged (or at least allowed) him to play with dolls as a boy and dressed him up. After spending "a small fortune" for psychiatric care for seven years, "I was one of the lucky ones who found the road back to normalcy. But when I think of how close I came to a completely different life, I shudder."[22]

Declaring that homosexuals were "tragic figures" and often "victims of sick parents" causing them to suffer from mental illness, he nonetheless argued for "understanding and not ridicule" of homosexuals. His concluding thoughts, however, were easily overwhelmed by the loathsome language used to discuss his own sexual orientation (and that of others). Ann ran the letter with no comment of her own offered.[23]

Just two days later, Landers ran another letter from a homosexual man who expressed suicidal feelings because years of psychiatric treatment had yet to "cure" him from being gay. Ann urged the man not to "bum rap" psychiatry and to recognize how it had at least helped him to see what a problem being a homosexual could be. "Psychiatry is not voodoo magic," she said. "It cannot transform the severely disturbed into contented, integrated personalities merely because they surrender themselves to the couch several times a week." She encouraged the man to go back into psychiatric care and told him, "Of this you can be certain: Living means constant change.... Your letter is proof that you are better equipped than you realize to 'battle against the futility of everything.'"[24]

Not surprisingly, "overbearing mothers" were frequently discussed as either a cause, or at least a risk of causing a young boy "to grow up to be a homosexual." One father wrote that his wife insisted on setting his 10-year-old son's hair in curlers, "dress him in fussy clothes and put lipstick and nail polish on him. She thought it looked cute." The father told Ann, "I am seriously concerned because he likes to dress up in his mother's clothes and he'd rather play with girls than boys."[25]

Ann declared, "You have a real problem now. Children who are treated as if they were members of the opposite sex often grow up to be homosexuals. Both your wife and your son need professional help." Her other suggestions? Consider adopting a female child "so your wife will stop trying to make a girl out of her son," and take the boy on fishing trips and introduce him to sports.[26]

Weeks later another mother wrote in to defend the practice of putting curlers in her son's hair—defending it because it made him look good. Ann seemed to have some fun at the mother's expense, taking lightly the possibility of the boy being subjected to physical abuse. "I don't know everything," Ann wrote, "but I do know that an eight-year-old boy should not be sitting under the dryer in the beauty shop next to his mother. If this All-American boy goes to Little League practice with curlers in his hair, you'd better teach him how to fight."[27]

Many parents seemed quite convinced that there were many outside influences that could lead their child to becoming a homosexual. The "discovery" of anything homosexual would often send panicked parents to Ann. One mother wrote that her son, popular with the girls and a good athlete, had a stash of male pornography in his room. Her letter prompted another from a young man whose own stash of gay porn had been discovered by his father. The young man advised Ann, "No amount of family doctoring or friendly counseling is going to make any difference," he wrote. "My father found my collection of nude males when I was 15 and two years of doctors and psychologists left me a nervous wreck."[28]

The young man appealed to Ann—and all parents—to try to accept a son's homosexuality as normal as someone who wears dentures. "The best thing the desperate mother can do for her son is to leave him alone and help him cope with life as it is," he concluded. Ann disagreed, writing, "I have heard from thousands of homosexuals these past years and most of them are unhappy, frightened and lonely. They long to lead normal lives and ask me if psychiatry can help…. I always recommend therapy, however, [knowing] that while it might not produce a cure, it does help the homosexual to accept himself."[29]

As Ann's views on homosexuality seemed to progress, she printed an interesting letter verbatim in November 1972 from a reader describing themselves as "a homosexual, a lesbian, a closet queen, a fairy princess, a butch number and a fruit. I am your brother, your sister, your son, your daughter, your nephew, your niece, husband, wife, friend and neighbor." The writer shared, "I live in fear of being found out. I might lose my job, my family, my friends, and in some states, my freedom. I am not a child molester, rapist or a sex maniac."[30]

The writer shared, "I am a person who is different and therefore, in

Chapter 1. "Your Problems"

some states, I am considered a criminal. I don't ask the world to embrace me, but I hope the day comes when I and others like me will no longer be persecuted for being a member of a minority group."[31]

The desire for gay rights—for homosexuals to live in the fullness of the freedom others enjoyed—was a regular theme in letters Landers chose to print. One letter writer from Chicago wrote after witnessing a portion of the 1973 Gay Pride Parade in the city. "I never saw anything like it in my life," the writer noted. "Some of the costumes were out of this world, sequins, feathers, tights, black leather, whips and chains…. There was much cheering and singing, 'Two-four-six-eight, is your husband really straight?'" The writer concluded, "If these people are normal and healthy, then I want to be sick." Ann just added, "I hope you know that not all homosexuals look and act that way, and what you describe sounds like the lunatic fringe. Many homosexuals are soft-spoken, dignified people."[32]

A clear majority of the letters to Ann Landers regarding homosexuality had to do with male homosexuality, and not lesbians. Ann explained she was not engaged in any sort of slighting of the problems of gay women, saying that any of her advice for any homosexual man would apply to a lesbian woman. A 1971 letter from a lesbian attempted to address Ann's lack of consideration of gay women.

"I am a homosexual woman and I do not want to be a man," the woman explained. "I have the body of a female. My emotions are those of a homosexual woman. I am not sick, in fact I am healthier than most straight women who insist on hanging the 'sick' label on me."[33]

She asked Ann and her readers to understand that lesbians "do not want a man or a straight woman, or even a bisexual woman. And most of all, I do not want to be bothered by curious straight people who view me as a freak or a conversation piece."[34] Another gay woman wrote, "The principal desire of lesbians is to be accepted as human beings, to be allowed to hold jobs, to be paid commensurate with their abilities, and to be left alone by straight people who view them as freaks."[35]

The "danger" of young women "falling victim" to homosexuals and marrying them without understanding the true sexual orientation of their husbands came up as early as 1964. A reader wrote begging Ann to publish her letter "for the sake of all the young and innocent people" needing the advice. She detailed how her niece was going through a divorce after having two children with her husband, only to have him declare that he was leaving her for another man. "We are heartsick and bewildered," the woman wrote. "How could this girl have avoided this tragedy? What are the danger signals? And please tell me why homosexuals *want* to get married?"³⁶

Ann replied that some homosexuals married because "they yearn to be normal and mistakenly believe marriage will 'straighten them out,'" and that they want wives and children "as a cover, a cloak of respectability." Ann seemed less certain about any "warning signals" young women should watch out for, other than advising against having "chummy best pals" around too often during the courtship or engagement. A young bride-to-be should "also be wary of a fiancé who insists on several nights out 'with the boys' or 'the boy.'"³⁷

Two women who wrote to Ann were dealing with the "aftermath" of the divorce from their homosexual husbands. In one case, the man's parents wanted to get back expensive wedding gifts they had given the couple when they were first wed (Ann disagreed, encouraging the woman to keep her gifts), and another where an ex-wife was trying to keep her husband's sexual orientation a secret (despite the divorce). She asked Ann to share with her readers, "When people announce they are splitting up, family and friends should accept their decision and leave them alone. Why must they know all the details before they can accept a divorce?"³⁸

Dozens of letters were published over the years by Ann on the topic of heterosexual women seemingly trapped or tricked into marrying a homosexual man. The letters came either from women dating or engaged to a man they knew or suspected was a homosexual, or from married women who discovered such after matrimony. The perspective of the letters was always in the favor of the women, except for one early letter from a gay man. The young man said he wanted to offer yet another reason why a homosexual man, such as himself, would marry a woman.

"I married a woman knowing full well I was a homosexual," he wrote. "In simple language, I did so from the unbearable pressure from well-meaning family and friends. I was 29, good looking, well built, and successful in my profession, and frankly, quite content with my life as it was."³⁹

He noted that his "homosexual drives" were low-key and "I had none of the manifestations generally associated with homosexuality. I managed to keep that side of my life so well disguised that family and friends suspected nothing. Finally, I was so bedeviled by the relentless pressure to get married that I decided to do it."⁴⁰

While the young man's letter offered at least the perspective of a gay person, it added troubling details that furthered ideas that homosexuals

Chapter 1. "Your Problems"

were treacherous people. "The girl I married was charming, bright and totally unaware of what she was getting into," he wrote. "She is now in a private mental hospital as a result of two years with a louse who used her for his own purposes." Readers, apparently, were left to jump to the conclusion that a relationship with a gay man could or would drive a woman into a mental hospital (with no other causes or reasons given). Ann's reply was limited to thanking the man for sharing and trying to help others.[41]

As Prentice-Hall prepared to release Landers' new book in the spring of 1964, *Ann Landers Talks to Teenagers About Sex*, her "Your Problems" column was transformed into a 10-part series in which Landers took up various sexual issues raised in her book. The eighth entry dealt with "what you should know about homosexuals." For its time, the book and dedicating the column to issues entirely sexual was provocative, for certain. As a result, Landers felt a need to defend inclusion of the idea of homosexuality—"clearly a hot potato"—in the book "because my mail tells me that thousands of teenagers are either abysmally ignorant or have wildly cockeyed notions about the subject. They need constructive information, but they don't know where to get it."[42]

She detailed how many letters came in from teenagers worried that they might be homosexual because of their attraction to members of the same sex—and some of them were even driven to suicidal thoughts. While acknowledging "I am neither a physician or a psychiatrist," she insisted "I think I can help substitute dangerous ignorance and anxiety. And I hope to dispel some of the anxiety resulting from a problem which too long has been swept under the rug."[43]

Ann said the letters from teens she received centered mostly on personal fears about one's sexuality, came from teens between 14 and 19 years old, and were more than 70 percent of the time from young men—almost all of the boys "are tortured with guilt and self-hatred. They live on the razor's edge, terrified that someone may learn they aren't like everybody else." Some of the boys who wrote to her, she reported, were even worried that if another boy flirted with them that this may somehow mean they are a homosexual and don't even know it—"or they wouldn't attract queers." She said such fears were groundless.[44]

A great deal of the column that followed spent time defining exactly what a homosexual was and was not, and even more space was spent exploring the conflicting views on what "caused" some people to have homosexual feelings. Landers went out of her way, however, to distinguish between homosexuals and child molesters. "It is not true that all homosexuals are child molesters or that they are constantly making attempts to 'ruin' young boys by introducing them to their way of life," she wrote. "Most homosexuals stick closely to their own circle of friends and mind their own business. Child molesters are psychopathic personalities, a serious threat to society and they should be institutionalized and treated."[45]

Landers seemed content at this point to simply open the discussion without drawing any major conclusions, offering: "Most homosexuals yearn to be normal. And these are the ones whose heartbreaking letters cross my desk daily. Twisted and sick, through no fault of their own, they want desperately to be like everyone else…. Very little in the way of a 'cure' exists, but a great deal exists in terms of adjustment. Psychiatric therapy can help."[46]

She ended the column with a gentle call for compassion to any teenagers reading, asking heterosexual readers to "be thankful you have been blessed with healthy, normal sex drives, and remember that not all boys and girls are so fortunate. When you encounter people who are 'different,' remember that their lives are probably unbelievably difficult and that they are faced with enormous problems of adjustment. You can help by understanding."[47]

Thirty years before the battle to allow gays to serve in the U.S. military, the issue was a bit reversed with some men trying to use the military's ban on homosexuals to keep from being drafted. In 1964 and '65, Landers published a variety of letters about the Selective Service draft that was underway to provide enough American troops for military combat in Southeast Asia to defend South Vietnam from Communist invasion.

One letter writer, identified as a 23-year-old "west coast man" said he had been honest with the draft board about being a homosexual and was promptly given a 4-F release from induction. Interestingly, another 23-year-old man who had received release from the draft because of a heart murmur wrote to complain that "the day that letter appeared in print, five people asked me if I had read Ann Landers' column and they looked at me funny. It just so happens that I am not *funny*." He recommended that Ann "stop causing trouble" and "check yourself into an old folk's home."[48]

The girlfriend of a young man trying to avoid the draft also wrote in, explaining that he had purposefully lied to the draft board about being a homosexual in order to avoid being called into service. Ann warned that "Phil" was in for a few upcoming surprises because of his

Chapter 1. "Your Problems"

act of deception. "He will be called in for a psychiatric examination and asked for a letter of verification from his physician [about his alleged homosexuality]," Ann reported. "Then he will be questioned by a psychiatrist who will determine from his answers that he is lying. Phil could be charged with fraud, which might mean time in the cooler or he could be inducted promptly."[49]

Another man wrote concerned that his 4-F status—based on his honest answers about his homosexuality—might cause others to learn his secret. "I have managed to keep my homosexuality well concealed," he wrote. "Even my parents are unaware of it. Will they be informed of my rejection [by the military]?" Landers tried to reassure the man that a letter regarding his status would remain part of his "permanent history" with government agencies (which future employers could ask to see) but that parents would not be informed.[50]

One GI who had not avoided the draft wrote weeks later to ask Ann, "Where were you when I needed you?" and declared if he knew claiming to be a homosexual could have kept him out of active duty, "I would have cheerfully kissed the draft board doctor." Ann seemed to get the joke, but reminded the young man that the military might have discovered the lie and he'd have been on his way to a military jail, or active duty, "faster than you could say, 'My high heels are killing me.'"[51]

A variety of less-serious topics ran through the Ann Landers column, including parents worried that if a father kissed his son too much he might become a homosexual, or in reverse, mothers worried that fathers lacking affection might create a gay child; wives of men who secretly liked to dress in women's clothing, with worries they might be gay; effeminate behavior in young boys and adolescents; a woman unwilling to have a child because her husband's family-tree had a homosexual in it; and whether one's cat or dog could be homosexual.

Among the less serious issues were whether gays could somehow secretly recognize one another. Landers affirmed the idea in response to a 1971 letter saying, "I have been told that perceptive homosexuals have a built-in radar system when it comes to sensing the presence of their own kind. I believe this is true. The signals may be ever so faint, but they are discernable to one who is alert."[52]

Homosexuality remained a "hot button" issue for many readers who readily took on Ann Landers whenever the subject was raised. One reader wrote, "I am wondering just how far the publisher will let you go before they decide to throw your column out of the newspaper. I am sick and tired of trying to beat my teenagers to the front porch to see if your column is fit for them to read. I refer specifically to some of the trash you have printed on homosexuality and venereal disease."[53]

The reader accused Ann of "putting ideas into the heads of kids" and that she continued to make parenting difficult for many. "I resent it." Ann didn't blink, defending her attempts to educate on a variety of subjects and firing back: "From the sound of your letter, your kids need to read my column because I don't think you are emotionally mature or well enough informed to give them straight answers."[54]

Vitriol could come from both directions, left and right, as a March 1973 letter from "a former reader" indicated: "I refuse to address you as 'Dear Ann Landers' because you are an empty-headed, ignorant, meddling fool. For years I have read your column and believed you were a friend of homosexuals. A few days ago you turned on us like a jungle animal and exposed your hypocrisy and ignorance. I am shocked and outraged that you would call us 'sick' and describe homosexual activity as 'unnatural.'" In her defense, Ann offered comments from a variety of readers who supported her viewpoint.[55]

Landers' viewpoint, however, would come full circle as she told an interviewer near the end of her life, "Early on, I knew nothing about homosexuality. Later, I became sympathetic because I understood they were born that way. I believe I have helped them in their struggle for acceptance."[56]

Ann Landers—"Eppie" Lederer—died in her Chicago home on June 22, 2002, at the age of 83. Per her wishes, no one new was appointed to take over the "Ann Landers" persona. However, Creators Syndicate announced that two of Landers' editors, Kathy Mitchell and Marcy Sugar, would continue on with a new column known as "Annie's Mailbox." The last Ann Landers column ran on July 27, 2002.

Chapter 2

"Dear Abby"
—Abigail Van Buren

As was the case with her twin sister "Ann Landers," Abigail Van Buren, author of the "Dear Abby" column which premiered on the pages of *The San Francisco Chronicle* on January 9, 1956, the real-life person behind the column was hidden by a pen name. Officially, Pauline Esther "Popo" Friedman Phillips was "Abigail Van Buren," a name Phillips made up when she approached the newspaper's editors telling them she could write a better and more lively advice column than they were currently offering their readers.

In 1956, *The Chronicle* was like a lot of big-city dailies; it was in fierce competition for readers with their rival, *The San Francisco Examiner*. *The Examiner* was already home to the "Your Problems" column by Ann Landers via syndication, a column that was penned by Phillips' twin sister, Esther Pauline "Eppie" Friedman Lederer. The Ann Landers column was an established entity when "Dear Abby" came along and proved herself to be reliable competition—whether intentionally or unintentionally.

David Gudelunas, author of *Confidential to America: Newspaper Advice Columns and Sexual Education*, noted, "It is virtually impossible to tell the story of Ann Landers without telling the story of Abigail Van Buren."[1] Within a year of starting the column, the "Dear Abby" column was quickly syndicated nationally by McNaught, landing eventually in more newspapers than Ann Landers, but because the papers had smaller circulations, Ann had the larger readership. Abby's success resulted in "the beginning of a slowly festering resentment between the twins that would later erupt into several years of the once inseparable sisters not speaking to one another," Gudelunas wrote. "Abby" had "committed the ultimate crime—stealing her sister's spotlight."[2]

Gudelunas uncovered that Eppie ("Ann Landers") may have asked

Dear Abby, I'm Gay

her sister Popo for some help in answering some of the letters coming in as she got started. That work apparently convinced Popo ("Abby") she could do as well on her own. Abby insisted she did not use her sister's name to land an advice column, a claim Landers would dispute which "sparked a disagreement between the twins rooted in professional jealousy that lasted several years."[3]

Further angering Landers was the fact that Abby more quickly syndicated her column (placing her in direct competition with Landers). Popo also personally copyrighted the name "Dear Abby" ensuring she made millions from the name. Eppie, by taking over the already established Ann Landers column was virtually unable to lay claim to the name "Ann Landers"—perhaps costing her millions of dollars over the course of her career.

Abby's daughter Jeanne Phillips, who joined her mother in writing "Dear Abby" in 2000 (and took it over completely in 2002), said she believes her mother succeeded so quickly because she wrote pithy, quick and short responses that did not bore readers. Ann Landers was known to provide longer, more traditional answers.

As was the case with her sister "Ann Landers," Abby acknowledged her world view and resulting advice evolved over the more than four decades she wrote the column. One big change was her view that marriage was forever. "I always thought that marriage should be forever," she said. "I found out through my readers that sometimes the best thing they can do is part. If a man or a woman is a constant cheater, the situation can be intolerable, especially if they have children."[4]

Abigail Van Buren—or "Dear Abby"—the twin sister of the author of the "Ann Landers" column. Shown here in a 1960s promotional photograph for the Easter Seals campaign, "Dear Abby," whose real name was Pauline Esther "Popo" Phillips, died in 2013 at the age of 94.

The social progress of Abby's readers would also change—but take time. It wasn't until after "Dear Abby" had been in

Chapter 2. "Dear Abby"

circulation for more than a decade when the first mention of homosexuality in her column came up in September 1966. In one of her "Confidential to" notes—this time "Confidential to 'Do I have grounds?'"—without details offered—Abby "confidentially" told her reader: "You had better see your lawyer about an annulment. If you did not know before your marriage that your husband was a homosexual, your state might grant you an annulment, which might be preferable to a divorce."[5]

Her most famous reply to a reader's question about homosexuals didn't come until May 1972 when an older couple wrote concerned about the two men who had just purchased the house across the street. The men were openly homosexual partners. The letter writer exclaimed to Abby, "This was a respectable neighborhood before this 'odd couple' moved in. They have all sorts of strange-looking company, men who look like women, women who look like men, blacks, whites, Indians. Yesterday I even saw two nuns go in there!"[6]

The reader said they had reported their "concerns" to the local police department, but learned if no actual laws were being broken, the police could not act. "Abby, these weirdos are wrecking our property values! How can we improve the quality of this once-respectable neighborhood?"[7]

Abby replied simply, "You could move."[8]

It was a classic example of her sometimes tart, flinty, sharp but always witty means of reply. No doubt Abby could hear the hearty howl of her readers getting a good laugh at the expense of the bigoted letter writer.

More common, however, were letters such as the one printed in October 1969 from a wife who had learned her husband had homosexual interests, or a homosexual relationship in his past. Abby took the approach that was common at the time, "My authorities on this subject tell me that homosexuality is 'learned' and can be 'unlearned' IF (and this is a big IF) the patient is properly motivated, which most of them are not…. Your only hope is to insist that he see a psychiatrist; otherwise your marriage doesn't have a very rosy future."[9]

As if in support of Abby's counsel that women avoid marriages and relationships with men who acknowledged homosexual feelings, a December 1969 letter took an "I told you so" tone. The male lover of a man who had previously sought Abby's advice about marrying a woman—"advice that was not taken"—was reporting that things were not fine and that "the hope that all suspicions of homosexuality would disappear" was lost. The man reported he maintained a regular sexual relationship with the married "family man" and that his wife "will never give him up." The man said, "I am writing only to say that if a girl suspects a man is 'gay' but marries him anyway, hoping to change him, she is in for a big disappointment." The letter stood with no reply from Abby, a practice the spartan writer would often employ presumably when she thought the letter said all that needed to be said on the subject.[10]

The first full letter from a reader on homosexuality came in May 1967 concerning a teenage girl who was embarrassed to shower in front of other girls following a physical education class at school. The writer suggested that the young woman was only concerned because "actually, the girl enjoys the sight of these naked bodies and she has erotic feelings that shock her into repression. If I were her mother, I would look for signs of latent homosexuality."[11]

The letter, claiming to be from a physician in San Francisco, brought an unusual response from Abby. She wrote, "Your kind of reasoning might equally lead to the assumption that *you* are preoccupied with homosexuality because you are suffering from a similar problem, and have transferred your 'guilt' to the girl and her mother." It was an amazing leap to a conclusion based on scant information, but Abby concluded by adding, "I would never flatly state, simply because a girl objected to public showering, and her mother supported her in her objection, that they both need treatment."[12]

Beyond recommending treatment, Abby was more forthright in telling her readers when a marriage may, in fact, be at an end. One woman writer reported she surprised her husband at home in bed with a man, and that after 18 years of marriage and three children, she was uncertain how to proceed. Abby said the path forward was clear: "Give him up graciously," she told the woman. "He has already made a choice, either consciously or subconsciously."[13]

Later in 1967, as the ramp-up of American troops being sent to Southeast Asia to fight the Vietnam War was underway, Abby took a provocative letter from a 19-year-old gay man. He expressed concern about answering the standard military draft question about whether he was homosexual, but also did not want to lie. Abby explained to her readers that the answer to the military's question "Are you a practicing homosexual?" was used to determine whether to classify a recruit as either 4-F or 1-Y, depending upon the decision of a local draft board.[14]

"These records are strictly confidential," Abby assured, "and no one, not even the boy's parents, have access to these records. The classifications 4-F and 1-Y include men who are physically, mentally and morally

Chapter 2. "Dear Abby"

unfit for service. This includes everything from flat feet to homosexuality, so that classification reveals nothing." And while Abby may have correctly stated the classification rules, she missed the social price someone classified as 4-F or 1-Y would suffer.[15]

She added, "One cannot be assured of staying out of the service simply by answering 'yes' to such a question," and said additional screening would be involved. This would become a bigger issue in subsequent years as some young men reportedly attempted to avoid the draft by falsely claiming they were homosexual.[16]

The fear of being known as a homosexual prompted another man to write, this time disclosing that as a bachelor he had no interest in marriage, though he enjoyed dating women, but resented the assumption of others that he was gay. He asked Abby's help on what to do, and her answer reflected the brisk replies she would become known for: She advised, "quit protesting too much [and] don't make a phony fuss over women who don't turn you on. And lastly, don't give a second thought to what people say."[17]

What people said or thought about homosexuality brought one of Abby's very first defenses of gay people in 1970 in reply to a letter from a woman whose husband maintained a gay lover on the side. The writer noted sympathy for the woman and added, "The homosexual is a crippled personality in other ways than sex."[18]

Abby seemed to take umbrage at the letter, replying: "If, as you say, 'a homosexual is a crippled personality,' who can blame him? All his life he's heard he's a 'sick, perverted, abominable, loathsome creature,' or some kind of freak. He has had to live like a criminal much of the time—for fear someone would 'find out' about him. He feels guilty for having 'failed' his family. Is it any wonder the suicide rate for homosexuals is so high?"[19]

She wasn't finished, adding, "I don't know whether homosexuals can be 'cured.' My medical experts insist that if they are sufficiently motivated, they can. But almost all of my mail from homosexuals says that the most they can hope for is 'understanding' on the part of others, and the ability to accept themselves as they are, and learn to live with it."[20]

It is here where the influence of one of Abby's personal friends, Cloyd, an openly gay man who worked as her hairdresser, is likely felt. "He's like a brother," Abby said. "And he's been my hairdresser for about, maybe, 29 years. Beautiful guy and just a sweetheart, he came from a small town in Nebraska.... Never came out to his parents. He said they couldn't handle that. His mother just adored him and he was a wonderful son, just a wonderful son."[21]

There were, of course, counter arguments to the one Abby was developing. One "former homosexual man" wrote to say with the help of expert psychiatry he had overcome many years of homosexual activity and was now "cured." He said, "I am now married to a fine woman who knew about my problem, and I am living a full, normal, healthy life." Use of the terms "normal" and "healthy" were often on only one side of the discussion however—homosexuals still cast as the opposite of such human ideas.[22]

Parents were the source of many letters regarding homosexuality, including one early one in 1967 from the parents of a curious and intelligent nine-year-old girl who loved to read, including the local newspaper. "Abby, I can explain murders and riots to her, but how can I explain some of the things that she reads in your column?" the mother asked in a veiled complaint. "This week she asked me what a 'homosexual' was. She wanted to know how you get a 'venereal' disease. I told her a homosexual was a person who had a problem getting along with the opposite sex, and a venereal disease was a serious infection." The mother asked, "Must I hide the newspaper from my child? DO you really receive so many letters of this kind as to justify printing them?"[23]

Abby defended herself in her reply: "Yes, I really receive sufficient letters of 'this kind' to justify printing them. You are fortunate to have a child who loves to read, and doubly fortunate that she asks you to explain things she does not understand. Few children reach maturity without hearing a good deal about the subjects you mentioned, and what better place than home is there to learn the facts? You can 'hide' the newspaper from your child, but you cannot hide her from *the somewhat less than lovely truths of life*" (emphasis added).[24]

Three years later, however, Abby was taking a position that homosexuality was not one of the "somewhat less than lovely truths of life" when answering a mother who lamented her lesbian daughter. The woman had wrote advising a mom worried about her pregnant and unmarried daughter, "I would rather be in her shoes any day. She doesn't know what trouble is."[25]

Abby took on the reader directly—asking them to "face your situation realistically" and asked the mother to perhaps conclude that "while your lot is hard to accept, it is not the most tragic in the world. Many homosexuals live useful, happy lives. It is possible that a mother who has lost her child in death could conceivably be happy to change shoes with *you*."[26]

Chapter 2. "Dear Abby"

Readers were taking note of Abby's "defense" of homosexuals, one mother writing to thank her and saying, "I have lived in fear that one day my son might take his own life. Most homosexuals feel that they were born that way and are not the product of their environment," but added, "I hope and pray that someday there will be a medical cure for these poor persecuted individuals."[27]

A complaint letter printed by *The Greenwood Commonwealth* in Mississippi was typical. "If you'd like to save newsprint, I'd like to see the "Dear Abby" column dropped from your paper. I have become disgusted with her promoting homosexuality in her column every few days.... It seems she's going out of her way to say that homosexuals are normal and just 'different.' ... I'm all for tolerance of the sick and for getting help for them, but let's not further confuse them by trying to make them believe they are normal." The unnamed writer noted that Abby and her sister Ann Landers did not agree on the issue of homosexuality and asked that they run Ann instead of Abby. The newspaper's editor defended Abby's responses to questions on such topics and added, "You are the first and only to ask us to delete Abby. Thus, she'll stay."[28]

One reader, in Decatur, Illinois, wrote to the editor of *The Decatur Herald* proclaiming that Abby's column "lacked integrity" providing lengthy Biblical quotations, expressing dismay that Abby "could wield so much influence over young minds." A reader of *The Staunton News-Leader* in Virginia also took on Abby on the basis of scripture noting "her views are not in agreement with the Holy Bible" and that "she regards homosexuals as being God's children. Such a view will not help the problem. The homosexual is a sinner in need of a savior" and that "homosexuality is a mark of a society which has ignored God's word in order to do its own thing."[29]

Abby's posit that "one thing is certain, God made gays just as surely as He made straights" seemed to draw a particular ire from the right. A reader of *The Albany Democrat-Herald* in Oregon said, "I challenge Abby to present one Bible passage to substantiate her declaration.... If God made homosexuals, as Abby says, then He committed abomination! This, to me, is blasphemy." The letter, which went on a long tangent sprinkled with Biblical references, ironically came from a reader living in Tangent, Oregon.[30]

"Lots of papers complained," Abby said, "but they never dropped me. *The San Diego Union* had never published the word 'homosexual' in their newspaper when I started. It was a breakthrough ... they never published the word 'homosexual' unless some guy was going to jail or something."[31]

Abby understood she was breaking ground—daring "to be kindly toward a homosexual, to be understanding." Throughout her years of writing the column, "it was a steady stream of hate mail. Every time I'd run something compassionate or sympathetic [about homosexuals], I would get a lot of hate mail. It wouldn't bother me."[32]

It's unknown how much actual pressure newspaper editors may have tried to apply to Abby, but in print she was unapologetic in her support of gays and would not back down. In a February 1971 "Confidential" note to "the many readers who wrote about my refusal to put down the homosexual," she wrote: "The most burdensome problem a homosexual must bear is the stigma placed upon him by an unenlightened and intolerant society. Their sexual bent is as natural and normal for them as ours is for us. They are neither 'sick' nor degenerate. They are simply different. Mine is a plea for compassion and understanding for these misunderstood and mistreated souls. They, too, are God's children."[33]

A year later Abby penned the column she would be asked to repeat many times over—and ran many "thank you" letters from readers. The May 1972 letter came from a reader calling themselves a "Happy Heterosexual" and declared, "There is no such thing as a well-adjusted homosexual, the two terms are antonymous. Homosexuality, male or female, is a form of sexual deviation which is symptomatic of a personality disorder. By any reasonable standard of human development, homosexuality is an abnormal human condition which needs competent professional treatment. It is, in effect, a form of emotional illness."[34]

The letter summarized well the thinking of many Americans in the 1970s, and in previous eras. The crack in the idea that someone could be gay and well-adjusted and happy was still, at least in 1972, a radical idea to some. Abby took issue with the letter, asking outright: "By whose definition is homosexuality an illness? There are homosexuals who live socially well-adjusted, discreet, personally happy lives, whose homosexuality would come as a surprise to many of their close heterosexual friends."[35]

Abby said she believed "the fact that homosexuality is morally condemned by most people in our culture makes it *seem* abnormal. In other times and in other cultures, it has not always been so judged. Much of the maladjustment seen in homosexuals is due to the rejection, persecution and guilt imposed upon them by intolerant and ignorant

Chapter 2. "Dear Abby"

contemporaries. One who labels all homosexuals as sick does a grave disservice to a large segment of our population."[36]

Some readers sought to cast Abby in conflict with her twin sister, Ann Landers, because of Landers' continued use of the word "sick" to describe some homosexuals. Abby went back to her previously stated views—avoiding any comment on "another advice columnist's" views—noting, "Homosexuality is a problem because an unenlightened society has made it a problem, but I have received letters by the thousands (not just occasionally) from gay people telling me that they wouldn't be straight if they had a chance. All they ask is to be allowed to love in their own way without facing that they are 'sick and twisted.' I say, love and let love."[37]

Abby's laissez-faire attitude regarding homosexuality was winning her fans—in addition to enemies. One man wrote to tell Abby that her "enlightened attitude" about homosexuals had been a big help to him in accepting his youngest son who came out to him. "At first, I spent a lot of time worrying and wondering why." He noted that he had taken her advice to just love his son as he did his other children, and now "there is much warmth and affection between all of us…. Just as with his [heterosexual] brother and sister, I take for granted his standing by one of us if the need arose, so he can be certain we will stand by him. We are a family. What a wonderful feeling."[38]

Fear and concern expressed by parents could run deep, as evidenced by one mother who wrote concerned about the prospects of allowing a two-year-old boy to be in the presence of a gay uncle. Noting the uncle was "a fine, talented and very nice person," the mom nonetheless asked, "Do you think we should ever let him alone with our son, or would it be dangerous?" Without expanding, Abby was succinct in her reply: "A homosexual is no more likely to molest a child than a heterosexual (or 'normal') person."[39]

Another mother was battling her husband because their 12-year-old son wanted to take ballet lessons. "I have mixed feelings about this," mom told Abby. "Should I let him take ballet? Or do you think if he does he will have effeminate tendencies that would tip the scales in favor of his turning homosexual?" Abby was direct: "Let him take ballet if he wants to, and don't worry about tipping the scales. If his route is not gay, he won't take it."[40]

Keeping boys from displaying effeminate characteristics seemed to be a common theme as well (though Abby never seemingly ran a letter from a parent worried about masculine demonstrations by their female children). One school teacher even wrote asking whether there was "a school where a young man can go to 'butch up,' so to speak" since one of his middle school students acted in an effeminate way and was mercilessly teased. Interestingly, rather than addressing the bullying the boy was suffering, the teacher (and presumably his father) were interested in finding a way to rid him of "effeminate talking and broad hand gestures when he speaks."[41]

Abby said she found it sad that a teacher—or a parent—would ask such a question. "A drama coach might be helpful," she said, "however, since you have a dialogue with the father, please tell him that what his son *is* is more important than what *he appears to be*. Encourage the father to work on establishing a closer relationship with his son."[42]

In a similar vein, another mother wrote concerned about her son's desire to take up professional figure skating. She worried aloud that her son might "become a sissy" or "go gay." Letters such as this prompted replies from professional ballet dancers, ballet and skating coaches, and others who made the point that both pursuits required extensive athletic ability. One writer noted, "I knew someone who worked with Mikhail Baryshnikov who had to beat the women off with a club!"[43]

It was not only ballet and figure skating that seemed to send parents into worry about the sexuality of their sons—one mother wrote worried that her son's interest in becoming a male model was unnatural. "My husband and I have been warned by someone in the fashion industry that most of the men in the modeling profession are homosexual," she said. "Do you think our son can make it in that profession without being compromised or intimidated when he makes it plain that he is a heterosexual?" The letter reflected the predatory fear the parents held for male homosexuals—a topic that Abby seemed to miss. Instead, she focused on the fact that his sexual orientation was probably already set and that if he had not already expressed interest in other men, being around gay men would not likely change his views. "Whether a man (or a woman) is vulnerable to 'try anything' depends on the man or the woman," she added.[44]

Some letters from parents could be heartbreaking—as was one in June 1974 from a woman who had disowned her son after he left his wife and started a relationship with another man. "When he called to tell me, my world was shattered," the mother wrote. "I screamed at him over the phone, 'As far as I am concerned, you just died. In fact, drop dead. I never want to see you again!' Then I hung up."[45]

The mother was having second thoughts—noting that her son's wife

Chapter 2. "Dear Abby"

was seemingly willing to forgive him and let him go. "I am not without sin, Abby," she wrote. "Was I wrong to sit in judgment and condemn him? Should I accept him for what he is? Should I call him and apologize?"[46]

Abby went easy on the clearly heartsick parent and kept her answer short and sweet: "When we do the right thing, we feel good about it. When we do the wrong thing, we feel bad. Call him."

Some letters on the topic of homosexuality could get ridiculous—including a long string of letters about whether historic figures—such as Michelangelo or even a pet jaguar could be homosexual. Both topics prompted letters to the point by 1973 Abby declared she was done with the debate. For the record, Abby thought it was possible Michelangelo was gay, but drew the line at the possibility of a gay cat.[47] Another series of letters took up the mid-'70s parlor game of what the meaning, if any, earrings in a man's ear held.

Perhaps wanting to lighten the topic a bit, in January 1978 Abby took the tact many other columnists had and offered her readers a "true/false quiz" on homosexuality. The dozen questions ranged from whether homosexuals committed more crimes than straights, to the role of domineering mothers in "creating" gay sons, to whether heterosexual children raised by a homosexual parent would be gay. Nine "false" replies meant "you are fairly well informed" on the issue, while four or more "true" statements meant "you have a great deal to learn about homosexuality because all of the statements are false!"[48]

The "education" of her readers was seemingly needed as Abby occasionally continued to run letters from readers (often times parents) wanting to know what "caused homosexuality." By November 1978 (in a column ironically appearing in the same week gay icon Harvey Milk and San Francisco mayor George Moscone were being murdered), Abby seemed to have settled on a pat answer she repeated often: "My experts agree that homosexuals are *born*—not made."[49]

Abby frequently took time to promote the work of Parents & Friends of Lesbians and Gays (PFLAG) in helping parents cope with the reality of having a gay child. She promoted their publications to her readers and noted, "they are in a position to support and help parents."[50]

Perhaps unknowingly, Abby participated in the "forced outing" of Oliver Sipple, a decorated U.S. Marine from the Vietnam War, who stepped in and prevented Manson family-follower Sarah Jane Moore from striking President Gerald R. Ford with a bullet. Sipple was in the crowd outside a San Francisco hotel on September 22, 1975, when

Dear Abby, I'm Gay

Moore attempted to assassinate Ford, but grabbed the gun from her and caused her shot to go awry. Sipple later unsuccessfully sued newspapers and others for identifying him as a homosexual—a fact he had not yet disclosed to his family. Abby joined the chorus in a "Confidential to Hates Queers in Pasadena" note run in her column in January 1978. She wrote, "Yes, some homosexuals are capable of committing crimes, but they are also capable of heroism. How soon we forget. Not long ago in San Francisco, an acknowledged homosexual prevented the murder of President Gerald Ford at the hand of a heterosexual assassin."[51]

"Outing" someone was at the center of a troubling letter from a 16-year-old boy who said he trusted his Presbyterian minister with the secret of his sexuality, only to have the pastor call his parents and spill the beans. "I am devastated and embarrassed," the boy wrote. "Why would the minister betray me in this way?"[52]

Abby described the minister's betrayal as "shocking" and said, "It is appalling that someone so lacking in intelligence and integrity could be a spiritual leader." She urged the boy to leave that particular church, and to write a letter of complaint to the regional synod or presbytery employing the pastor. Doing so, she said, "would be performing a community service."[53]

Decades before same-sex marriage became legal in the United States, "Dear Abby" was dealing with the issue via letter from a confused reader who said she had received "an engraved invitation" to attend a "wedding" between two men ("two such people"). The writer asked, "Abby, when did they pass a law making marriage between two people of the same sex legal?" Abby clarified that no such law was on the books in any state in 1971, and added: "A celebration of love is simply a ceremony and does not constitute a legal marriage."[54]

The parents of a gay man who planned to "marry" his lover wrote to Abby to express their disgust and dismay. "Our tall, athletic, handsome son who served four years in the Navy returned to civilian life and college and 'married' an undersized, effeminate male hairdresser." She reported "the odd couple" had come to visit the family recently and were inseparable and "acting out a peculiar husband-wife relationship that was both bewildering and disturbing to us. So far, we have been polite, but what the dickens do you say to friends and relatives? We can't condone it. We love this boy, but as his parents we feel torn." Abby said, "You owe friends and relatives no explanation, so don't feel obligated to offer any. Since your son's lifestyle bewilders and disturbs you, either learn to accept it or quit seeing him."[55]

Chapter 2. "Dear Abby"

Beyond weddings, protocol was also at hand with a gay man who wrote in wondering if he should have to pay for the expenses of a female date even if she knows that she is only being invited as a "beard" or cover for the gay man. Abby was having none of this suggestion—bluntly replying, "The one who needs the favor should pick up the check."[56]

Friendships with gay men also were a topic of discussion—including an earnest letter from a 65-year-old widow who enjoyed evenings out with her openly gay hairdresser. She may not have known it, but she was writing to the right person, as Abby talked often about her own gay hairdresser who was one of her dearest personal friends.

"My hairdresser is a wonderful companion and we frequently go places together," the woman wrote. "Of course, I pick up the checks, which I suppose, makes my friend uncomfortable. But I can't see myself letting him pay and then trying to settle up with him afterward. He may not have that much cash anyway. Is there a way to handle money matters without embarrassing him?" Abby suggested that the woman arrange with the restaurants they visit to bill each person separately, or before starting the evening out, "give your escort enough cash to cover everything and at the end of the evening he can return the change."[57]

Readers even wanted to know how to properly introduce gay couples in social settings. One reader asked if they should use terms such as "lover" or "live-in companion" when introducing such couples. Abby was of the opinion that it was not necessary to explain the nature of relationships when introducing people, and that it was presumptuous to use terms such as "lover" or "partner"—and recommended using given names of people instead.[58]

Terminology was on the mind of an unnamed "Illinois State Senator" who wrote to Abby expressing his "gall" at the use of the term "gay" to describe "homosexual sexual deviates." He believed "the word 'gay' means joyous, merry, happy and cheerful … to describe homosexuality as 'gay' is a perversion in itself and I respectfully request you, Abby, discontinue the use of the word in that context." The good senator thought Abby should use the word "queer" instead.[59]

Abby took up the popular discussion of how "gay" came to mean homosexual, but concluded that many gays would be offended by the use of the word "queer." She said to use such a term when homosexuals have indicated it is offensive to them would be the same as continuing to use words such as nigger, spic, kike or wop. She noted, "When you, sir, are willing to have yourself described in print and in introductions to your family, friends, strangers, etc., as 'Heterosexual' before your name, then you may insist that gays be identified by the clinical 19th century term 'homosexual.'"[60]

Employment of open homosexuals was also an issue—a reader asking Abby, "What sort of a person would hire a male secretary?" The writer said her boss did not "seem faggy, but I've heard that sometimes this doesn't mean anything." Abby replied, "You can't tell if a man is a homosexual by his appearance, but if you really think it's your business, why don't you ask him? Homosexuals as a group are honest." She noted that many companies hire male secretaries and that there was nothing "special" or odd about it.[61]

Transsexual issues were occasionally raised in "Dear Abby," but not frequently. The very first such letter on the topic appeared in October 1974 with a male nurse writing to say, "I am miserable. All my life I have wanted to be a woman.... Abby, this secret desire to be a woman is about to destroy me. I am not a homosexual, but I'd rather be dead than to continue living like this."

Because the writer made specific reference to being a "born-again Christian," Abby noted that "the Lord created all of us, and why he made you different, I don't know. Nature sometimes makes biological blunders, as is the case when one's body does not conform with his (or her) natural feelings." She reassured the young man, "You are not alone. Don't feel guilty. One cannot help what he feels." With that, she referred the man to the Erickson Foundation to learn more about others with similar feelings.[62]

By 1982, Abby began running her very first letters dealing with the emerging AIDS crisis. In one, she printed the story of a woman who had lost her brother to AIDS and who was out to everyone prior to his death, except his grandparents. His grandparents were also under the impression that he had died of a severe case of pneumonia. "Before my brother died, he made me promise to tell our grandparents exactly what he died from," she wrote. "He begged me to fulfill it and I said I would. It's been more than a year and I still haven't told them the truth and I feel guilty because I owe it to my brother."[63]

Regardless, the young woman said she still hesitated to tell her grandparents for fear of hurting them and causing them unneeded anguish. "What do you think, Abby? What should I do?"[64]

Abby didn't waffle, noting, "You made a deathbed promise to your brother and you owe it to him to keep that promise. He had his reasons for wanting his grandparents to know the truth, and since you promised

Chapter 2. "Dear Abby"

you would tell them, I think you should. The truth never hurt anybody—only lies hurt."[65]

Another sad letter came from a gay man who said his family had now banned him from swimming in their pool even though he had not tested positive for HIV-AIDS. To add insult to injury, "My niece won't even let me hold, let alone kiss, her three-year-old daughter. My children, who are seven and nine years old, are confused about why our family members will no longer come to our house. I am heartsick over this."[66]

Abby took an official response to the letter—quoting Dr. Mervyn Silverman, the San Francisco County health officer, who assured that the response from the man's family was inappropriate and unnecessary. "AIDS cannot be transmitted by sharing utensils, hugging, holding, or swimming or any other casual contact," she quoted Dr. Silverman as saying, and said his view was confirmed by the experts at the Centers for Disease Control.[67]

Fear about AIDS transmission seemingly ran high, other letters fielded by Abby taking up whether a person should cancel their vacation to San Francisco because of "the large amount of homosexuals there," or whether a gay waiter could contaminate a food order, or even if a gay hairdresser could infect someone while shampooing a client's hair. Abby repeated the assurances she continually tried to give, and declared once again, "All gays do not have AIDS, nor have all gays been infected with the virus."[68]

She posed the question to her readers, "Who is absolutely safe from AIDS? Only couples who always use a condom unless they are in a long-standing monogamous relationship. The days of casual sex are over!"[69]

Death from AIDS was not ignored in Abby's column—a May 1987 letter coming from parents who were unsure how to handle their gay son now that his lover of more than 10 years had died of AIDS-related complications. "Here's the problem, the rest of our family does not know our son is gay, and he says he does not wish to sit down with people and pretend that life is just beautiful after having suffered the most painful and tragic year of his life. What do we do?"[70]

Abby asked the family to get over their concerns, invite their son home to them often so they could comfort him in his time of loss. The decision of whether to come out to the rest of the family rested with their son, not with the parents, Abby said. Even if such a disclosure upset some family members, she urged the parents to "make him feel welcome anyway."[71]

37

Dear Abby, I'm Gay

In 2002, Abby and her daughter Jeanne announced the column would be turned over completely to a new generation. Popo, suffering from the early stages of Alzheimer's disease, was officially retired as Abby. With advice columns becoming nearly extinct, Jeanne has continued to build "Dear Abby" (offered nationally by Universal Press Syndicate since 1980) and is now run in more than 1,400 newspapers worldwide with an estimated daily readership of 110 million.

Popo Phillips, the voice of "Dear Abby" for more than four decades, died January 16, 2013, in her Minnesota home at the age of 94. As historian Eric Marcus noted, "Abby never minced words. Biting humor was her weapon of choice. But whatever the topic, her warmth and compassion and her common sense wisdom came through, loud and clear."[72]

Chapter 3

"Helen Help Us!"
—Helen Bottel

Long-time California newspaper publisher Jack Craemer told his readers in 1967 about why his newspaper, *The San Rafael Independent-Journal*, had never carried an advice column—"then along came Helen Bottel." Craemer seemed to have little time for more popular columnists, such as Ann Landers or Dear Abby, who he said seemed to lack "a serious effort to deal reasonably with heavy personal burdens" and "the bereft person in need of serious counseling seems to be just a pawn in this game."[1]

Craemer said he had decided to run Bottel's "Helen Help Us!" column because "she genuinely tries to help people with problems, giving them good common-sense advice. This is her first and foremost concern; she leaves the wisecracks and titillation to others."[2]

Bottel was not acquainted with Craemer or his staff, but he said he had heard from many readers over the years that Bottel had responded personally to some of the letters she received. "Obviously a national columnist cannot perform personal by-mail counseling for every person with a problem," Craemer noted. "But Helen Bottel does not turn her back on anyone with a really critical problem. She just jumps in and gets to a sympathetic and helpful answer as soon as she possibly can."[3]

Bottel's "Helen Help Us!" column was distributed by King Features Syndicate throughout the 1960s and '70s and focused often on parent and child relationships and child behavior. Many of her letters came from children and adolescents and prompted Bottel in 1971 to launch her own "Stamp Out Steadying" or "SOS" campaign designed as a program to support teens who faced social pressure to steadily date just one mate.

While popular with many readers, Bottel's positions on issues related to homosexuality seemed uneven, at best. While most

ADVICE
with good humor
For adults • For teenagers

"Helen Help Us"

by
Helen Bottel

"Helen Help Us" author Helen Bottel from a 1958 newspaper advertisement in *The Minneapolis Star Tribune* (courtesy Star Tribune Media Co.—Newspapers.com).

columnists evolved on issues of homosexuality, Bottel seemed to go back and forth in her positions, making it difficult to categorize her. In her earliest days, Bottel used words such as "tolerance" for homosexuals, which reflected an attitude of something less than acceptance.

Bottel liked her niche in the world of advice columnists: "This column is for young people, their problems and pleasures, their troubles and fun," she wrote in 1966. "As with the rest of "Helen Help Us!"—it welcomes laughs but won't dodge a serious question with a brush off."[4] She also liked young people: "I am convinced young people are doing the very best they can. They aren't out to 'get' the grown folks. They don't hate their parents. In fact, many are very worried about their parents. They're worried about them smoking too much, and they're even worried because they're changing partners so much."[5]

For a short period of time, Bottel co-wrote another column titled "Generation Rap" with her daughter Suzanne (Bottel) Peppers. The mother and daughter column allowed them to offer their sometimes-contrasting responses to readers who wrote to "Dear Helen and Sue."

"Helen Help Us!" started on a lark—writing a newsletter for the

Chapter 3. "Helen Help Us!"

Parent-Teacher Association at her children's school, Bottel discovered she enjoyed writing. Finding her husband laughing over the type of advice offered in a "Dear Abby" column, she declared to herself: "'Heck, I can do better than that.' I didn't think I could, but you have to say things like that once in a while to get your husband's attention."[6]

Serious about her beliefs—and following her own "leap before you look" advice—she wrote up four sample columns. Her timing was good as King Features was looking for a new competitor to Dear Abby and Ann Landers. "I didn't even know what a syndicate was, but I sent them my entire output: four columns. They signed me up!"[7]

In a 1988 interview from her Sacramento home, Bottel said she approached her advice in a specific way—"I don't tell [readers] what to do," she said. "I just tell them what I would do if I were faced with the same problems."[8]

The life-advice Bottel gave came from some experience. She often disclosed the struggles of her own family life—a mother who battled mental illness and a father who abandoned the family when she was just two years old. "I raised myself," she said. "We were extremely poor. I have no idea how we ate. It was a small town and we were definitely the very dregs. I kind of dropped through the cracks."[9] She expanded on that idea in a 1979 interview when she noted that parents don't really have as much to do with a child's success or failure as they think they do. "Kids raise themselves a great deal," she said. "I know I did."[10]

Despite the rough start, Bottel was convinced "it had a lot to do with my becoming a successful columnist. It wasn't that I was wiser than anybody else, but I really got involved. I've always really cared."[11]

The level of care Bottel held was clear with her first letter from a gay teenager published in 1968. "I am a 16-year-old with the ugliest curse of mankind," the letter began. "I am a homosexual. I hate myself. I fight against it. I won't give in to it, but I know I am not normal. My parents don't know. I can't talk to anyone and I have no money for a doctor."

The young male writer reported his mother "has always been overprotective and neurotic" and that his father had "a violent temper." Desperate for support, the writer noted, "Please, Helen, tell me what to do before I lose my sanity."

Helen immediately tried to reassure the writer than many teens were dealing "with fears they were homosexual" and that some had suffered such fears "only to discover later they had just a temporary detour on the road to growing up." She suggested talking to the family doctor for a referral to a psychiatrist. "I'm betting one confidential talk (with a

41

Dear Abby, I'm Gay

family doctor) will set you straight—and I'm quite sure he will let you pay the bill on the installment plan."[12]

The advice that the young man may not—in fact—be gay prompted a follow-up letter from another reader. "Thank you for telling him that [his homosexuality] wasn't necessarily so—that one experience does not mark him for life," the writer noted. "Often he is lured into this by an older man who tells him he can never change. So he drifts on, hating himself and punishing himself, sure he isn't fit for a normal relationship."[13]

The writer wanted Helen to know that "there are some who are born homosexual, but I'm sure with most, the problem is psychological." He confessed he had become convinced he was gay by a homosexual friend who "made sure I kept on believing I was homosexual." He noted that his parents helped him turn away from a homosexual lifestyle—with the help of a psychiatrist. The writer, who signed the letter "Once a Freak," noted he had gone on to become "a normal, loving husband and father."[14]

Helen replied, "I hoped someone would write that homosexuals can be cured, but only if they leave off the self-loathing and ask for help. So many men—and women too—tell me they hate their lives but feel doomed because shame won't let them discuss their problem." She again urged readers struggling with homosexuality to seek professional help.[15]

The issue of whether a homosexual could "change" their sexual orientation to heterosexual seemed to percolate under the surface of the "Helen Help Us!" column through the years. Again in 1977, Helen drew the wrath of some readers after she advised a 17-year-old gay boy that if he wanted to change his sexuality bad enough, he could.

"Homosexuality is not a social problem," one reader told Helen. "Gays must learn to live with their homosexuality rather than try to change themselves to please so-called 'normals.'" The writer warned against the idea that a young man hide or suppress his natural sexual feelings, and suggested "many psychologists have found that persons they have supposedly 'reformed' are much happier in gay relationships. It's much better to show homosexuals they can lead guilt-free lives, accepting themselves for what they are."[16]

Helen took issue with the idea that "psychologists are locked into any type of behavior" rules. She suggested she did not mean to imply that the young man should seek to change, only that he should explore whether he truly wanted to be homosexual.

Despite her apparent advocacy for homosexuals to seek help—

Chapter 3. "Helen Help Us!"

including those who didn't want to embrace their sexual orientation—Helen could vacillate and sound more supportive. A gay man wrote that he was "an unashamed homosexual" but was vexed by the lack of acceptance he found in the world—and the assumptions made about him being a "sissy" or a child molester. He asked, "When will tolerance extend to us?" Helen seemed to be on board in a very brief reply, limited simply to "Such tolerance is on the way. It's long overdue!"[17]

Her brief words of "support" notwithstanding, responses from readers objecting to her position were quick to come in. One angry reader took exception to her ideas about "tolerance" and quoted various scriptures to support the idea that "tolerance" of homosexuals was not acceptable. Helen limited her reply again, this time by suggesting another scripture passage—Matthew 7:1: "Judge not lest ye be judged."[18]

Another letter of criticism took Helen to task for her advocacy of tolerance for homosexuals—among other issues. "You are a disgrace to the word parent," the writer proclaimed. "Teenagers are disturbed enough without you making them more hostile, rebellious, indifferent and disrespectful with your 'advice' that 'parents aren't always right.'" The writer, who proclaimed themselves as "a follower of the Ten Commandments," ended the hostile letter with "What the world needs is less 'broad-mined' fools like you and more parents who are followers of the Ten Commandments." Helen wasn't in a mood to back down, saying this particular reader's letter proved her point that "parents aren't always right."[19]

On the same day, "Helen Help Us!" featured a letter from the older sister of a homosexual youth who had disclosed his situation to his sibling, but was begging for secrecy. "My brother is on the dean's list at college besides holding down a full-time job," the young woman wrote. "He is the perfect picture of young manhood, though more gentle and kind than most." She wanted to know was there more she could do to help.[20]

Helen replied, "Your brother has faced his problem," and "from you, he needs tolerance, friendship, hope, and assurance that you'll stand by. I know you won't let him down."[21]

Helen also ran a letter from a young man who offered what he thought would help parents accept their gay children. Assuring that he was not "sick," the young man said he told his parents: "I will do nothing to shame you, but I hope you will follow your common sense and admit to the fact that I've got to be me." Helen thanked the young man, saying, "I hope your letter will help parents better understand their homosexual children and perhaps have less guilty feelings about 'how it all happened.' I hope they'll agree with me that homosexuality, while 'different' is not 'sick' and it is not always their 'failures' which create this kind of sexuality."[22]

Interestingly, amidst a growing number of supportive letters for gay readers, Helen did run a December 1973 column without comment from a "former homosexual" and "male prostitute." The man wrote, "I won't go into the many hurts, disappointments and sickening perversions I experienced, but I soon found out this [homosexual] life was not for me, but once in, I couldn't get straight, so I tried suicide."[23]

The writer explained he had finally found "true love" with a young woman whom he planned to marry. "I look back now on the lonely boy I was, luring men, and hating the life I led, always seeking what I thought was impossible. I thank God I weathered the storm and the search is ended."[24]

Again, "Helen Help Us!" could be hard to label at times, with Helen herself showing a lack of consistency on whether she was fully in support of homosexuals (and "tolerance" for them) or supportive of readers "sick" of hearing about gays. Helen replied oddly to an October 1974 letter from a reader who said, "I mourn for the good old days when it was okay to be shocked. Ten years ago, I felt sorry for homosexuals, and hated those stupid jokes about them. But today I wish they'd stop yammering" and said she "felt ill" about even the suggestion that many heterosexuals were actually bisexual. "I'm sick to death of the sex talk at cocktail parties," she wrote. "Look, I'm a closet heterosexual. But if I say anything, I'll be labeled a prude. What's a fed-up woman to do?" Interestingly, Helen seemed to identify with the writer, encouraging her to "say something" and noted, "I think you'll find a lot of followers, including me!"[25]

Similarly, a troubling December 1974 letter from the mother of a gay man seemed to warrant no more serious a reply from Helen then to suggest the woman seek counseling to better understand her son. The letter detailed the financial and personal success the gay man had achieved, "but despite our offers to help him overcome his deviate ways, he acts like he despises us. His meanness makes our old age miserable."[26]

The mother lamented, "We have been blamed for his turning gay, but frankly, I think the children want this kind of life, and parents are handy people to abuse." The mother said she and her husband had written to their son, "We did not wish this on you. We live in fear of who you are with and how you will be disgraced or blackmailed. We know your old age will be lonely and bitter, and that secretly you feel dirty

Chapter 3. "Helen Help Us!"

and evil. So why do you take out your hate on the parents who love you?"[27]

Helen limited her answer to "perhaps you parents need counseling" to accept (though not approve) of their son's relationship and "you and your son will lose much of this bitterness."[28]

Five months later Helen did run a letter from another parent with a different perspective "as a counterbalance." The woman wrote, "I was not happy when I realized my son was homosexual because our society treats these persons with scorn and hostility." She added, "I realized that this was not a chosen way, but, instead, corresponded to some basic inner truth.... It is past time for us to realize that acceptance is more 'religious' than censure, that love is more important than any other thing, and if two people love one another, this is normal." The mother urged parents to "withdraw from their son's personal affairs" and watch and enjoy his life as a parent, not a co-participant in all of his relationships.[29]

One parent who wrote to Helen explained a rather unusual situation wherein she was fired from her job when her employer learned her daughter was a lesbian. She took exception to Helen's previous claim that "homosexuals are becoming more accepted" and asked that if losing your job because your child was gay was not prejudice, than what is? Helen had mercy on the writer and encouraged her to contact the local chapter of the Civil Liberties Union to see if her rights had been violated.[30]

Reactions to even what was perceived as gay conduct prompted one young man to write. He reported that he and his friends—all athletes—had decided to stop congratulating or greeting one another with any form of affection. "Young people are called fag, jolly, gay if they do any same-sex touching," he wrote. "Even girls have to be careful not to show much affection." He asked, "Why can't I hug a buddy and keep my reputation as a hetero?"[31]

Helen said she thought Americans were "getting better at touching, but it's a slow process, mainly because we're afraid the person we reach out to may back away." She added, "What with our Puritan stand-offishness and our fear of homosexual labels, we have a long way to go before same sexes greet each other with open arms. Meanwhile, a pat on the arm goes a long way toward saying, 'I like you.'"[32]

The increased number of letters about homosexuality prompted a reader to ask Helen to explain her use of the terms "latent homosexual" and "closet queen." The same writer asked curiously, "Would a male with breasts that seem to be getting bigger and female-type tend to be faggy?" Helen took the letter seriously and explained that a "latent homosexual" was someone who was actually gay, but did not actively seek gay relationships. "A 'closet queen' is a secret gay who only comes out with his homosexual friends," she explained. She also took issue with the use of the term "being faggy" and noted that some males naturally had larger breasts.[33]

The word "faggoty" came up in another letter from a reader who was concerned that a friend refused to see certain movies if she suspected the male actors were "known homosexuals" and particularly resented if gay actors played heterosexual roles. Helen seemed to have some fun with her answer, noting: "I say your lady friend has some pretty queer ideas."[34]

One woman had some fun with the idea of the perception of being gay—saying she read a story about one psychologist who suggested a theory that football was linked to homosexuality. The woman, who identified as a "football widow" because her husband watched so much football on TV, said the theory said football allowed men to grab and tackle each other, to hug and pat fannies, and was associated with words such as jock, score, huddle, end zone, pass and punt. "If my husband suspects he's watching a homosexual display, maybe I can get him unglued from the TV set on the weekends!" Helen seemed to enjoy the letter—replying that lots of folks come up with "theories, smearies."[35]

Another writer, who identified himself as a male nurse, expressed concern that people tended to assume he was gay. "This is a widespread stereotype that isn't true," he wrote. "When I say I'm a nurse, the eyebrows go up and I get avoided."[36]

Helen took pity on the man, saying, "People who stereotype by profession are as prejudice as those who reject by color. All male nurses, hairdressers and interior decorators aren't gay, just as all female truck drivers, machinists, and telephone linepersons aren't lesbians."[37]

A 1969 letter from a wife and mother asked for help with what to do about her husband who collected gay pornography and refused to have any sexual contact with her. The woman reported she had confronted her husband about his proclivities, "but he said it was none of my business and said it's because of me he has these things. He is furious and won't talk to a counselor." Helen's advice was succinct: Stop "drifting," talk to a professional, including her priest, about leaving the man and making him pay child support for their four children. "What with child support and perhaps a job, you can manage should you choose to leave him."[38]

Chapter 3. "Helen Help Us!"

Another wife wrote to Helen to declare her amusement at women who complained about losing their husbands to other men. "It's better than losing them to women!" she proclaimed, noting, "My husband and I have a pleasant arrangement. We were childhood pals and he and I shared all of our secrets, one of which was that he preferred males. Because of family, then later business, he could never come out of the closet. I was more interested in being in a career than being a sex object, but I needed a husband to avoid the spinster image."[39]

She ended, "We married with complete honesty. He's my 'adoring escort,' a handsome man who gives a somewhat plain woman status, and I'm his 'cover,' and he's very discreet. We're the best of friends, and known as the ideal couple." The writer assured Helen, "I'll wager many couples like us are living happy, peaceful lives. When you eliminate intense sexual emotions, you can truly be friends."[40]

Helen replied curiously, "Whatever turns you off," and then added, "I'm not sure how many married people could manage your sort of life, but if it works for you, I won't make judgments."[41]

In September 1976, two women who considered themselves married wrote to Helen about their desire to have children. "We lead exemplary lives, have good careers, plenty of money, and we're totally faithful to each other. But one thing is missing, we want a child." The women reported adoption agencies had reacted poorly to their requests to adopt a child and had even been turned away in their attempts at artificial insemination. Frustrated, the women asked, "When will our 'modern world' really accept us homosexuals? We could be better parents than half the man-woman couples we know, yet we can't adopt because we're still stigmatized."[42]

Helen tried some prognosticating about the future, and questioning the motives of the letter writer. She suggested that "your question might reach a sympathetic society in the year 2000, but right now I can't offer much hope.... Look, you have acceptance from friends, fine careers (which children would unbalance), a lifestyle you enjoy. Are you sure you're craving for a baby isn't an urge to prove gays can compete on all levels?"[43]

She added a dour note, "In today's world, you could bring down a lot of grief on a child who doesn't deserve it. Take what you have, and don't try to score a point by risking someone's happiness."[44]

As perhaps expected, weeks later another letter appeared taking Helen to task for her reply to the lesbian couple. The writer, a woman who identified herself as "a lesbian father," said gays should not have to wait until 2000 for the lives they deserve now. She reported that she and her partner had raised nine children together, five of whom had gone on to college, and all of which were heterosexual.

"The children do not lead unbalanced lives, nor have they unbalanced ours," she said. "Raising children in a homosexual relationship is not really any different than from raising them in the more traditional mother-father setting, except that very few gay marriages break up, a definite plus," the woman wrote. "Love is the most beautiful thing in the world, whether it's homosexual, interracial, heterosexual or what. Children from a marriage where there is love, reflect that love."[45]

Helen seemed interested—asking the reader to write again and provide more details—and suggested the woman had a life that would make an interesting book. She followed the lesbian woman's letter with another writer who shared, "It is as much a sin in God's eyes to commit homosexual acts as it is to commit first degree murder. So much for 'alternate lifestyles.' The Bible says sex is good only between husband and wife and all else is bad and sinful."[46]

Helen limited her reply to "I printed both of these letters; perhaps readers will tell me which one they think shows more compassion and love for mankind."[47]

A 1970 letter from a man introduced the phrase "I am a girl trapped in a man's body." The writer expressed worry about spending life alone and was clear he was not a homosexual. "I know there is now help for transsexuals, but where?" he asked. "I want an operation that will make me a woman."[48]

Helen recommended a January 1970 article in *Look* magazine about hospitals in the U.S. who had begun performing such "change-of-sex surgeries"—but only after extensive psychiatric and medical examinations. She noted the surgeries typically cost between $2,500 and $7,000 and offered the name of the Erickson Educational Foundation in Baton Rouge, Louisiana (operated by groundbreaking transsexual Reed Erickson), for more help.[49]

While "Helen Help Us!" broke ground for some of the earliest letters on sex change operations, gay adoption and marriage rights for homosexuals, there was no avoiding the seemingly uneven nature of Bottel's replies. One of the columnist's last letters on homosexuality was once again a discussion about whether a gay person could change their sexual orientation, a topic Bottel seemed willing to leave in play despite growing sentiment and opinion that such ideas were archaic.

At its peak, "Helen Help Us!" ran in about 200 newspapers across

Chapter 3. "Helen Help Us!"

the U.S. At the age of 72, Bottel ended her "Helen Help Us!" syndicated column and "self-syndicated" a column for Japan's largest newspaper, *Yomiuri Shimbun*, offering "western advice" for Japanese readers. She also authored books on aging, and wrote a column on aging for *Senior* magazine before her death in 1999 at the age of 88.

Chapter 4

"Ask Dr. Brothers"
—Dr. Joyce Brothers

Although distinguished from the more established advice columnists Ann Landers and Dear Abby by her professional credentials, it was in celebrity fame that Dr. Joyce Brothers easily outdistanced the Friedman twins, Eppie and Popo.

Earning her Ph.D. in psychology from Columbia University, Brothers laid claim to being the "founding mother of media psychology" based on her credentials in the advice business.[1] It was not psychology, however, that first earned her fame, but rather her encyclopedic knowledge of boxing that made her a TV game show star. She appeared on the hit primetime CBS game show *The $64,000 Question* in 1955 and '56 and quickly gained fame.

Since a producer at the show thought it would be interesting to have a woman demonstrate a keen knowledge of boxing—admittedly a male domain in 1950s America—Brothers put her doctoral studying skills to work. She told reporters she read every book she could find about boxing and that her outstanding memory skills served her well during a seven-week run on the show where she earned prizes.[2]

As the Associated Press reported in November 1956 about her success, "A blonde psychologist, Dr. Joyce Brothers of New York, won $8,000 in her boxing category by giving the ring names of four heavyweight champions after she was given their real names (of Rocky Marciano, Jersey Joe Walcott, Jack Sharkey and Tommy Burns)."[3]

A month later, Brothers had won it all with a United Press International photo moved across the nation showing her lifting up her check for $64,000 alongside boxing champs Gus Lesenvich, Bob Olin and Mickey Walker. The caption for the UPI photo described Brothers as "a comely blonde" and only the second person in the show's run to

Chapter 4. "Ask Dr. Brothers"

win the overall prize by answering a seven-part question regarding prizefighting.

Despite scandals that later ran shows such as *The $64,000 Question* off the air, Brothers escaped unscathed with no allegations of cheating raised against her. CBS Sports hired her to be the world's first-ever female color commentator for a boxing match in 1958, but her advice column grew from a television show she launched on a local New York station. Her program was so popular, she quickly was signed up to pen a column for *Good Housekeeping* magazine, and started making the first of hundreds of regular appearances on TV shows of all kinds. Brothers appeared 48 times alone on *The Merv Griffin Show* between 1962 and 1970, as well as 45 appearances as a celebrity panelist on a new game show, *Match Game*, from 1964 to 1969.

Psychologist Dr. Joyce Brothers, shown here in 1957, brought celebrity and expert clinical advice to her column. Dr. Brothers died in May 2013 at the age of 85 (Library of Congress Image LC-USZ62-117953).

Brothers' TV career ran the gamut from dozens of guest appearances as herself on shows as diverse as *The Daily Show, The Tonight Show, Charlie's Angels, Saturday Night Live, Mama's Family*, and even an animated version of herself on *The Simpsons*. She also made numerous film appearances, including *Oh God! Book II, The King of Comedy*, and *The Naked Gun: From the Files of Police Squad*.

Her readiness to conduct her craft via popular media made Brothers the object of criticism from many, most notably other psychologists and clinicians serving patients. It was criticism that went beyond that

Dear Abby, I'm Gay

leveled at other advice columnists because, unlike them, Brothers did have medical credentials for her practice. She responded to her critics during a speech in San Francisco once, defending against the commercialization of her practice, offering: "Even in situations like [appearing on] *Hollywood Squares* everything I say is valid psychologically. It's an opportunity to get little tips in."[4]

While Brothers readily appeared on TV and in films, she never accepted roles that made a parody of her commitment to doling out advice. In fact, the radio version of her program on New York station WMCA took a dramatic turn that made headlines in 1971. A woman caller to her show disclosed that she had consumed 15 sleeping pills and wanted to kill herself because of crippling and painful arthritis and a husband who tormented her.

Brothers spoke to the woman live on the air for 90 minutes, WMCA deciding to forgo 15 advertisements and two newscasts to extend Brothers' show long enough for the call to be traced. Eventually authorities found the woman in her New York home and were able to get her medical attention before she died. The story made national headlines as Brothers calmly tried to talk with the woman, assuring her, "I care. I care very much."[5]

The success of her broadcast media endeavors and the *Good Housekeeping* column easily led to a lucrative syndicated contract for Brothers to write a newspaper advice column that eventually appeared in more than 350 papers across the U.S. The column was most popular between the 1960s and 1980s, but dwindled as television began to take over more of her career and more of popular media.

Brothers' newspaper column, according to *New York Times* writer Margalit Fox, "was a bridge between advice columnists like Dear Abby and Ann Landers, who got their start in the 1950s, and the self-help advocates of the 1970s and afterward." As noted, she arrived upon "the American consciousness at a serendipitous time: the exact historical moment when Cold War anxiety, a great acceptance of talk therapy and the widespread ownership of televisions converged." Readers were willing to embrace Brothers, one reporter noted, because despite always "looking crisply dressed" she was "eminently approachable. In her pastel suits and pale blond pageboy, she offered gentle, non-threatening advice on sex, relationships, family and all manner of decent behavior."[6]

The issue of homosexuality was first raised in Brothers' newspaper column in 1966 by Brothers herself in answer to a question about why any woman would want to be a prostitute. Dr. Brothers cited a study

Chapter 4. "Ask Dr. Brothers"

by Harold Greenwald titled "The Call Girl: A Social and Psychoanalytic Study" that concluded women who turned to prostitution actually hated men—as many as 75 percent of them having had homosexual experiences. "Greenwald noted that large numbers of prostitutes are homosexual," Dr. Brothers wrote. "The call girl is definitely not happy in her work."[7]

Homosexuality came up again in the column with a 1967 letter from a reader who reported "the local florist in our town was arrested as a homosexual. The man he was arrested with was a long-time friend.... I don't see why these two men had to be humiliated like common criminals when they were not hurting anyone. With all this talk of civil rights, don't mature people have the right to choose their companions without interference?"[8]

Dr. Brothers responded that public opinion polls show that two out of three Americans "regard the homosexual with disgust and hatred. The majority favor legal punishment for homosexual acts even if performed in private."[9] She stopped far short of condemning such laws enforced against homosexuals, and in fact, seemed to offer at least partial endorsement for their existence.

"Psychologically, many men—especially in America where fathers are no longer the sole rulers of the home—feel uneasy about homosexuals," Dr. Brothers said. "[Homosexuals] are threatening to their manhood. Other men feel impatience for what they call such weak, sick characters."[10]

Taking a bold stand, Brothers said that no one had proven that sending homosexuals to jail "is a cure or a deterrent for homosexual behavior" and that the American penal system actually promoted sexual deviance behind bars. She added, however, that the Group for the Advancement of Psychiatry noted that arresting homosexuals "sometimes has the salutatory effect of enabling the individual to recognize the meaning and consequences of what he has done, and therefore, serves as a step toward recognizing and assuming responsibility of his own behavior."[11]

It was not clear if Brothers was advocating the threat of arrest (coupled with the work of a therapist) to help a homosexual to change, or resist their sexual feelings, or to avoid engaging in compromising behavior that might put them at risk of arrest? She simply stated, "The external control offered by the law may be of valuable aid to the therapist in motivating the individual into thinking about his difficulty."[12]

Another reader raised with Dr. Brothers their concerns about "a campaign to harass homosexuals" who met in a local park and reportedly "were a menace to women and children. But the homosexuals gathered late at night, when women and children weren't around, and as long as they didn't make any trouble, I can't understand why the men (in our community) were so upset."[13]

Dr. Brothers said generally public reaction to the male homosexual was "more severely regarded" than that to female homosexuals. "Certainly, no society could afford to encourage homosexuality as a desired form of sexuality for the continuing propagation of the species is necessary for its survival," she offered.[14]

"Our culture tends to have especially strong taboos against male homosexuality," she wrote. "Compared to men in other cultures, American men are unusually restrained in the amount of physical contact and intimacy that is regarded as normal between two males."[15]

Brothers shared that "the horror" that is felt when confronted with obvious homosexuality "can be considered a projection of our reaction to the realization of homosexual impulses within ourselves.... For some individuals, the fear of homosexual impulses in themselves is almost overwhelming. Aggressive and hostile acting out may result in an attempt to relieve some of the tensions arising from this fear, acts directed against homosexuals not being uncommon."[16]

She pointed out that men who seemed to take pleasure in ridiculing effeminate behavior in other men are actually engaging in a "defense against their own fears of homosexuality within themselves." The result, "homosexuals are often the victims of unwarranted attacks and discrimination. Society has the responsibility of determining where the line is to be drawn between protecting the rights of the homosexual and protecting children and adolescents from the few homosexuals who may be predatory."[17]

Violence associated with latent homosexuality was at the basis of a 1981 letter from an aunt who was shocked to learn her nephew had been arrested along with several other teens for beating a suspected homosexual. "My nephew says it wasn't 'unprovoked' because he feels the (homosexual men) don't have a right to be in the neighborhood," the aunt wrote. "What is wrong with my nephew?"[18]

Dr. Brothers said fear was at the center of how the boys had acted. "In most people, there is a certain latent homosexuality. It comes to the surface most frequently in prisons, in Army life, in girls and boys schools, any place where the sexes are segregated for long periods. Usually, people who become violently anti-homosexual are those who are

Chapter 4. "Ask Dr. Brothers"

terrified of their own secret inclinations. They strike out, either physically or verbally, in an attempt to destroy the enemy which really lies within them, but which they cannot face."[19]

Dr. Brothers took a rather provocative position in reply to a letter from a 30-year-old gay man who expressed a desire to "change his pattern" and pursue relationships with women. Several newspapers even ran the column under the headline, "Converting the Homo." In the letter the young man reported, "I feel I could leave the gay life with no regrets, but most of my friends tell me that is impossible and that I should concentrate on learning to be a happy homosexual, for there's no other way."[20]

Dr. Brothers replied, "Your friends are wrong and, in addition, they may have mixed motives in trying to persuade you to stay as you are. If they feel any guilt themselves, it may make them feel less guilty to think there is no choice and that they are in no way responsible for their present condition." She noted that homosexuals—like heterosexuals—"often try to relieve their guilts and anxieties by blaming all of their faults on their backgrounds, their parents and the problems of their early life. This can be a dangerous trap. One's family can become a scapegoat that provides an easy excuse for any behavior for which we don't want to assume responsibility."[21]

Brothers' response took a curious turn as she suggested gay men who wanted to change spend time with women, engage in regular eye contact with women, and even invite them out to dinner and other social events. She added that some research suggested homosexuals had lower levels of testosterone, the male sex hormone. "A qualified doctor could help you succeed on your new path," Dr. Brothers replied. "If you want to achieve satisfactory heterosexual relations, there is little doubt that you can."[22]

Parental responses to gay children were the subject of literally dozens of letters to Dr. Brothers from frightened or angry parents. Even how a child dressed and wore their hair could pose troubling questions. One mother wrote that she and her husband were at odds about how their 17-year-old son dressed—the mother describing him as "a fashion plate" while his father believed such attention or interest in his clothing suggested that he was a sissy. Dr. Brothers wrote that how adolescents dress was very important to their self-identity and that other teens often judge their compatriots based on how they dress, or what they possess.

"The general trend in male fashions today [in 1968] is toward more individualistic and colorful apparel, away from the standard dark suit, white shirt and tie that for many men is the definition of being well-dressed," Dr. Brothers noted. "Some people like to say that this trend toward brighter and more varied styled clothing for men is homosexual.... It is erroneous to suggest homosexuals dress in one particular style; many purposefully cultivate a rough, coarse, ultra-masculine appearance."[23]

Another parent wrote to Dr. Brothers asking what was the appropriate way to address the issue of the possibility of "a homosexual advance" upon her children, worried that her child may be subjected to such an incident. Brothers noted that "the unsuspecting and naïve child who is the subject of a homosexual advance either by a person of his own age or an adult may be shocked and frightened by the experience." She said many parents were reluctant to talk about such subjects with their children, but she suggested it should be discussed along with all issues of sexuality when children were age appropriate. She also cautioned that preadolescent and adolescent children sometimes engaged in homosexual experimentation, but that did not necessarily mean a child was a homosexual.

"Parents who are overly concerned about the possible homosexual seduction of their children tend to have erroneous ideas about the consequences of such an experience," she said. "For the child who has been raised to have a healthy identification of his sex, the attentions of a homosexual may be upsetting but need not be traumatic. The likelihood of coming into contact with a homosexually inclined individual is greater for boys than girls, but both should be given some idea how to handle the situation."[24]

One mother wrote to ask Dr. Brothers whether it was normal that her 15-year-old son "spends a good part of his allowance each week on muscle magazines." Brothers got right to the point noting that the question revealed concern that her son had some sort of "sexual disturbance by preferring males to females as sex objects" and declared that was not necessarily so. "There may be erotic overtones but there is also an element [of this activity] that is not strictly sexual," she wrote. "There is an impulse for self-appraisal and comparison, a measuring of the self against the appearance of others. There is also the pleasurable element of fantasy identification with the 'body beautiful.'"[25]

A mother's guilt about her son's disclosure of his homosexuality prompted another letter. The mother wrote, "I'm sick to learn my son is a homosexual! I feel so guilty as a mother, and I know what a tragic life is in store for him." The mother disclosed she learned her son's secret

Chapter 4. "Ask Dr. Brothers"

by rooting through his mail and finding a letter from an old boyfriend. "Now that I know this, it has changed our whole relationship and I find it impossible to trust anything he says," she added.[26]

Dr. Brothers tried to assure the mother that a homosexual child was not necessarily any less trustworthy than a heterosexual one, and there was no evidence that "he is less capable of controlling his impulses, sexual or otherwise, than any other individual." She asked the mom to consider that her son was feeling a great deal of guilt having to conceal this part of himself, and "because he feels he may have disappointed you." She urged the mother to trust her son and not to cut him off from her affection and support.[27]

To address the guilt the mother expressed, Dr. Brothers noted, "The old time-honored theory explaining the male homosexual as a product of a domineering mother and a detached or hostile father is now being disputed, partly because there are so many situations where this does not apply." She asked the mother, and her readers, to consider the views of Martin Hoffman, a clinical psychologist, who had studied homosexual behavior and concluded that "the most tragic aspect of the homosexual's life is the social stigma of being homosexual" and that "the sexual promiscuity that exists in the lives of so many male homosexuals may partly be due to social attitudes that prevent him from living with another man in dignity and openness."[28]

Not all of the parent's letters coming in were so serious—one parent writing that he worried his 17-year-old son might be homosexual because he had given up football to join an amateur rock band and had grown his hair shoulder length. Dr. Brothers suggested the boy was most likely "rebelling against your stereotyped view of what makes a man a man."[29]

A letter from a 22-year-old gay man asked Dr. Brothers to sign in on whether it was necessary or important for him to disclose his sexual orientation to his parents. Brothers replied, "I see no reason for parents and children to share sexual confidences of any kind. It can be extremely damaging to children when parents discuss their sexual problems with them, and it can also be damaging and painful when adult children discuss the intimacies of their sex life with their parents. Whatever has been done in the past cannot be wiped out by one discussion." Brothers urged the young man to ignore the advice of his friends about coming out and to respect his mother's privacy, and his own.[30]

Some parents were conflicted in their responses to their gay children. One mother wrote that she was inclined to accept and support her son even after he had disclosed his homosexuality. "His father was very upset and has threatened to disown him and cut him off from any inheritance," the mother wrote. "I will always love my son and I can't stand to see him suffer. I know he's hurt by his father's reaction. I also love my husband and I know he shares many of the same guilts that I feel."[31]

Brothers said, "While I sympathize with and understand your feeling of shock, it's important that if you can continue to love and accept this boy as he is, you have not lost him.... How you and your husband react to him now, however, will color your lives and determine whether you'll have a warm, friendly relationship with him in the future."[32]

A letter that may have raised eyebrows was printed in 1985 as Dr. Brothers responded to a letter from a family member concerned about "a raging homosexual"—"raging because he's so obvious about it. He imitates everything he can about women. He simpers, he wiggles when he walks, his wrists are so limp they look like nothing I've ever seen. Why does he have to flaunt it this way?" Brothers said that most gay men did not act that way, and that "raging" was an interesting choice of words since the young man "is in a kind of rage against himself and his way of life. He needs some psychiatric help, not necessarily to try to make him straight, but to try to help him adjust to himself."[33]

The number of letters coming in regarding homosexual-related topics prompted Brothers to run, for the first time, a column in November 1969 that took the form of a true/false quiz on whether her readers' views and knowledge about homosexuals was accurate. The column ran with the same statements annually for many years to follow. Brothers introduced the quiz by noting, "Homosexuality was once a topic that could only be discussed in whispers. Now the subject has emerged from the shadows, but there are still many misunderstandings about what the homosexual is and is not, and who is or isn't homosexual."[34]

The eight statements (and answers) she posed included assertions that studies show that most "normal" people do not have any tendencies toward homosexuality (false); overwork and mental fatigue are two great enemies of almost every homosexual and they tend to destroy his sex life (true); there is usually one single, major factor that leads to homosexuality (false); four percent of the country's males and two percent of the females are predominantly or exclusively homosexual according to Dr. Alfred Kinsey (true); if homosexuals could take some sort of "magic pill" to become heterosexual, they would do so (false); most male homosexuals can be recognized by their obvious peculiarities (false); the rate of neurosis is higher among homosexuals (false); and

Chapter 4. "Ask Dr. Brothers"

some psychiatrists feel that homosexuality may have little to do with sex proper (true).[35]

The letters Dr. Brothers received indicated her readers were operating under some rather unusual ideas—one man convinced that he could not make it as an interior designer since he was not gay and "all the fags" in his business were more talented than him. Another writer lamented the sense of victimhood that homosexuals seemed to embrace and was driven to start a movement to promote heterosexuality. Still another wrote his desire to cruise gay bars in search of anonymous sex was because of his wife's consistent cheating with other men. One woman also wrote concerned that her husband's intense interest in watching sports on TV was some indication that he was sexually attracted to other men, while another was worried that her adult brother's desire to have plastic surgery meant he was "a sexual deviate."[36]

How heterosexuals responded to gay people dominated many of the letters handled by Dr. Brothers, including one where the father of a "fag" called his son's employer and tried to get him fired for "perversion," and another where an employer openly stated he planned to fire an employee who recently came out to him. The employer noted he "blew his top" when he learned of the worker's sexual orientation, and was particularly incensed that "he says it is none of my concern" and "he seems proud of his sickness."[37]

"I've read enough about the gay community to know that this is very much my concern," the man said. "I intend to fire him and I don't think anyone can stop me." Dr. Brothers told the man that his views were wrong and that "if you're considering firing this young man only because of his sexual choice then you are certainly acting out of prejudice."[38]

Calling out the man's prejudice fit with the general trendline of Dr. Brothers' columns—perhaps best reflected in a February 1977 entry in which she responded to a reader who was disgusted that a religious leader had written a book that did not condemn homosexuals. "How could anyone who believes in God and the Bible do this when there's ample evidence that homosexuals are sexually and morally loose? They corrupt young boys, too, and I think society should take a stand against them," the writer expressed.[39]

Dr. Brothers took the reader to task noting that "there are many homosexuals who lead stable, productive, adjusted lives" and that "recent research shows no marked difference in the personal adjustment or level of self-evaluation between homosexuals and heterosexuals." Further, she noted sexual promiscuity and tendencies toward child molestation were no more common among gays than others. "Males," she noted, "generally tend to be more promiscuous than women."[40]

As further evidence of her viewpoints, Dr. Brothers devoted an entire June 1977 column to the issue of gay rights protections enacted by local laws, and most famously opposed by singer-actress Anita Bryant in Miami-Dade County, Florida. While not openly opposing Bryant's views that gays should not be allowed to teach in public schools, Brothers said psychiatrists were divided on the origins of homosexuality and whether it could be cured.

"Whatever the basis for becoming homosexual, the fact remains that they have—whether recognized or not—fitted into the patterns of society for a long time, many undoubtedly employed as teachers," Brothers wrote. "The irrational fears that have prevented homosexuals from enjoying the rights enjoyed by other citizens must somehow be allayed to permit an objective approach to the problem."[41]

By year's end, Brothers took a bolder stand during a public speaking engagement at Reno, Nevada, in October 1977. In her remarks she said any teacher accused of misconduct with a child should be removed, but added: "I feel very strongly that a homosexual teacher doesn't harm children. Child sexuality is formed at the age of 2 or 3. If a teacher is proselytizing in the schools, the person should be removed" but added, "there are no specific emotional problems associated with homosexuals. I'm very concerned about the removal of [the] rights of people."[42]

The issue of gays taking same-sex partners to high school proms also raised concern. "It depresses and frightens me to think a high school boy was allowed to take another boy to the senior prom," one letter writer wrote. "I think this liberal attitude toward homosexuality is going too far. After all, this has destroyed other civilizations and I have a feeling it may very well be the final blow to our own culture. If this kind of thing is allowed to exist, it will spread and youngsters will decide that if this is accepted, they, too, will join the parade of gays and get on the bandwagon."[43]

Brothers replied that "homosexuality is not a contagious disease" and that "young people are not going to be contaminated at a prom, or anywhere else." She also dismissed the idea that a nation would or could become exclusively homosexual. She added, after all, that "procreation is not the ultimate aim of proms, any more than it is of dinner parties. I can't honestly see anything wrong with allowing each student to invite a person of his or her own choice to such an occasion."[44]

Where homosexuals lived was a concern of one writer in 1981 who

Chapter 4. "Ask Dr. Brothers"

was frightened for the safety of her young boys after having learned that two new tenants on their block were open homosexuals. Despite describing the arrival of the two men as "a bomb dropped" on the neighborhood, the woman noted, "I have nothing against gays and if we didn't have children, I honestly don't think I'd mind too much. What really disturbs me, however, is that the children are all talking and I didn't want this issue to come up with my two boys.... What should we say to our sons?"[45]

Dr. Brothers said she believed children—especially teenagers—should be informed that homosexuality exists and that keeping silent on "anything forbidden or taboo is apt to take on special glamour." She repeated her statement that homosexuality was not contagious or a disease of any kind and reported that the American Psychiatric Association had recently dropped homosexuality from its list of mental illnesses.[46]

Not surprisingly, as Dr. Brothers' column entered into the 1980s, letters expressing concern about AIDS were more common. One of them came from an interesting angle, a wife who knew her husband often employed female prostitutes, and her worry that he could bring HIV home to her. Another wife wrote expressing concern about her bisexual husband and similar risks. A discussion of AIDS-related sexual activity followed, with Dr. Brothers suggesting the woman consider whether she wanted to have sexual relations with her husband under these circumstances.[47]

As Brothers advice column career came to a close, biographer Kathleen Collins wrote, "Joyce Brothers [was] to media psychology as Julia Child [was] to TV cooking programs—the principal popularizer and the most iconic and synonymous. Each brought her expertise into the mainstream, democratizing and demystifying. Brothers's pioneering role in television's entertainment-education continuum has been greatly underestimated, and she should be recognized as a standard bearer in American television culture who broke ground in numerous areas of the medium."[48]

Chapter 5

"The Worry Clinic"
—Dr. George Crane

Dr. George W. Crane once described himself as an "overeducated farmer" as he built an "advising" empire from his farm in rural northwest Indiana that produced one of the longest running advice columns ever, "The Worry Clinic."

Originally marketed as "Case Files of a Psychologist," it hit its peak in post-war America with millions of readers via more than 250 newspapers nationwide. Officially, Dr. Crane never retired from writing the column and was publishing articles and columns in one form or another up until his death in 1995 at the age of 94.

A fervent political conservative and devoted Republican (who once wrote speeches for the presidential campaigns of Calvin Coolidge and Senator Robert A. Taft), Crane was a psychologist and physician with degrees from Northwestern University. He rarely engaged in a personal practice of any kind, however, and quickly turned to newspapers and other media to reach his "patients" across the nation.

In addition to "The Worry Clinic" which debuted in 1936, Crane wrote a separate column called "Horse Sense" which offered topical quizzes for readers designed to help them solve problems and increase their use of logic and thinking. He also wrote several books and pamphlets, many of them in support of his syndicated newspaper column.

"The Worry Clinic" was offered six days a week and devoted two days of the week to issues of marriage and love, with the other days taking up issues of business, child care, personality development, and what Crane called "mental hygiene." Issues related to homosexuality were most often part of the love and marriage segment, but also were included in the "mental hygiene" portion of the column given Crane's absolute commitment to the idea that homosexuality was a form of mental disease or illness.

Chapter 5. "The Worry Clinic"

The Worry Clinic
By DR. GEORGE W. CRANE

Dr. George W. Crane, a psychologist and physician, offered one of the earliest newspaper advice columns known as "The Worry Clinic." Dr. Crane died in July 1995 at the age of 94 (courtesy *Elwood Call-Leader*—Newspapers.com).

Dr. Crane took special pleasure in the fact that he did not operate under a pen name—such as "the Jewish sisters" (as Dr. Crane referred to them) Ann Landers and Dear Abby. "I have often had readers exclaim that they thought the name 'Dr. Crane' was just a nom de plume or pen name," he said. "Probably most of the female 'advice' writers use pen names. But the medical columnists employ their own names, partly because in medical and psychiatric writing, the usual person prefers some scientific authority to back up the statements he reads."[1]

He assured his readers that no "ghost writer" was behind his column and that he had been born and raised in Chicago and drove to his Indiana home weekly to work on his other projects there. "When I mention our children or grandchildren herein, I do so because many of you readers have youngsters of the same ages and thus feel reassured to see that child problems are universal," he said.[2]

By 1968, Dr. Crane reported he still received more than 1,000 letters daily, but that he did not dictate personal replies to more than three percent of those and recommended requesting copies of his self-published "medico-psychological booklets" offered through his column. He said of the three percent of letters he reviewed, about 150 of them earned a personal reply sent to the writer via the U.S. Mail. "I personally type all of these columns, using two fingers on each hand, which I learned from the touch [typing] system in high school," he reported.[3]

Dear Abby, I'm Gay

By the time of his death in 1995, Crane was little remembered by anyone under the age of 40, but was well known to generations of readers, as evidenced by *Chicago Tribune* columnist Bob Greene's take on Crane's life and death. Greene made note that if the goal of Crane's column was to relieve or reduce worry and stress, it didn't quite work out that way. Greene joked that Crane's column served the purpose of "making people worry. You could wake up eager, bright-eyed, happy, raring to face the sunny new day, and by the time you read "The Worry Clinic" you felt like crawling back underneath the covers and locking all the doors."[4]

Greene cast Dr. Crane as one of "the most influential journalists of his time" given that his columns "showed a perceptiveness about the press that was so acute everyone missed it.... The effect of Dr. Crane's "Worry Clinic" was to give his readers something new to worry about every day. Yes, he attempted to offer solutions to the worries he wrote about, but what he did was introduce additional worries into the lives of even his most formerly cheery readers."[5]

The Chicago-based Hopkins Syndicate marketed Crane's column (and later radio program) in *Billboard* and other national publications as a "noted psychologist" who could gin up significant reader (and radio response). Hopkins gloated that Crane's radio program, a daily 15-minute program called "Psychology in Action," served "a powerful good will" for radio listeners, and would be a big hit for any commercial sponsors. WGN Radio in Chicago claimed, for example, that listeners of Dr. Crane's show generated more than 2,000 requests for show transcripts (sold at 10 cents apiece).[6]

"This swift rise in popularity in radio began 10 years ago when Dr. Crane pioneered the idea of a daily newspaper feature on applied psychology," the Hopkins Syndicate claimed. "It clicked from the start. Presently, popularity polls consistently list him among the three top favorites of all American columnists—first among women."[7]

Both Dr. Crane's radio program, which was far outlived by his newspaper column, could be grim—not just on content—but on presentation as well. Accompanied by his stern and taciturn photograph (with

Opposite, bottom, left: Two affectionate prison inmates accompanied one letter to Dr. Crane's "Worry Clinic" as he discussed his concerns about single-gender institutions such as jails, prisons and schools in "promoting homosexuality" (courtesy *Elwood Call-Leader*—Newspapers.com). *Bottom, right:* A case study about struggles a young man had in wanting to date girls prompted this drawing accompanying "The Worry Clinic" (courtesy *Ogden Standard-Examiner*—Newspapers.com).

Chapter 5. "The Worry Clinic"

Left: "The Worry Clinic" often featured line drawings that depicted the "case file" being discussed by Dr. Crane. Here an effeminate man is depicted writing a love letter to "Dearest Bob." *Right:* One of the dangers Dr. Crane warned parents and young girls about via "The Worry Clinic" were unwanted school-girl crushes (both courtesy *Elwood Call-Leader—* Newspapers.com).

Dear Abby, I'm Gay

Left: "A pansy man" depicted in one "Worry Clinic" letter to Dr. Crane from parents worried about their homosexual son. *Right:* A letter from a young man Dr. Crane termed "a mamma's boy" featured this drawing (both courtesy *Ogden Standard-Examiner*—Newspapers.com).

a mustache that made him resemble a cross between movie villain Peter Laurie and Presidential hopeful Thomas Dewey), Crane's column was also often presented with an animated line drawing the loosely resembled the content of the "case file" presented each day. For some reason, the "case files" were numbered (apparently to give them some authenticity?) and a patient's name, often just a first name and last initial, and an official "diagnoses" from the doctor.

It was never entirely clear whether the "case files" presented were actual patients Dr. Crane had encountered, and in the era in which they were presented, there was little or no concern—apparently—about disclosing confidential patient information.

At times, Crane would indicate a letter as having come from a reader, but more times than not there was an element of "creative fiction" that seemed to be at play in his queries. This latter point may have been by design—Dr. Crane was not objective in terms of political, social or religious issues and carried his conservative ideology with him at all times. Further, in the era in which he operated, a doctor (even one who never had a regular professional practice) was not to be questioned. To further buttress his bona fides in this area, the earliest columns offered

Chapter 5. "The Worry Clinic"

by Crane were always quick to note Crane held both an M.D. and Ph.D. from Northwestern University.

Although he was a doctor, his positions related to homosexuality did not bring out the compassion in him as he frequently offered unsympathetic replies. His very first foray into discussing homosexuality came early in the newspaper column's life—a December 1936 "case file" of a patient described as "Carney"—an athletic 23-year-old man with a college degree. Carney asked for Dr. Crane's help with the fact that he was in love a woman 15 years his senior who was not interested in leaving her professional position, and becoming his wife. As a final "kicker" in the case, Carney discloses that he had a strained relationship with his mother and, "until I fell in love with this girl, I had associated with men, and have been homosexually inclined. But I have been weaned away from my attraction to the male sex by this girl, and I am eager to marry."[8]

Dr. Crane's "Worry Clinic" often warned parents about keeping their daughters (and sons) from spending too much time with friends of their own gender. In one column he mistakenly once promoted co-ed interactions with the term "bisexuals" (courtesy *Ogden Standard-Examiner*—Newspapers.com).

Dr. Crane wasted little time in diagnosing Carney as a classic case of a "mamma's boy" who maintains an unnatural affection and connection to his mother. In case Carney missed that message in words, the illustration with the column included a young man with a sign tied around his neck that read "Carney denies he is a mamma's boy."[9]

"Because of his basic love for mother, however, he refuses to love another woman of nearer his own age, so he often compromises by becoming unusually attached to those of his own sex," Dr. Crane explained. "We call such individuals homosexuals."[10]

Crane said Carney's big athletic figure and masculine interests notwithstanding, Carney was a homosexual and was interested in an "abnormal love." Dr. Crane added, "Because of his peculiar mother attachment and homosexual trend during college, this [older] girl may represent such a nice fusion of just those attributes which he needs, that she may be the very solution to several of his problems."[11] Dr. Crane took his advice no further, and instead asked readers to think about what they would advise this young man.

In April 1937, Dr. Crane offered the combined case of "Alden" and "Irene," two twenty-somethings who lived in Chicago. Alden wrote in to complain that Irene would not get serious about getting married and that "she is too fond of her own sex. She has a girlfriend whom she idolizes. They prefer each other's company to that of men. Irene is such a wonderful girl that I hate to see her chained to a homosexual life."[12]

Dr. Crane quickly shifted into declaring the case as part of a larger, more dangerous trend. "There are thousands of girls just like Irene," he wrote. "And probably an equal number of men. The problem is becoming even more acute in this modern age where economic conditions prevent early marriage, and where divorce takes one parent out of the home."[13]

The good doctor offered the first of a long series of assertions that he would sustain over the four decades of his column that "homosexuality is a normal reaction in childhood." He posited that adult homosexuals were essentially psychologically maladapted adults who failed to journey properly through the phases of childhood and adolescent development.[14]

"It is very difficult to change an adult homosexual into a normal man or woman," Dr. Crane said. "It is possible, and I have personally counseled many who have made the transition, but they must be determined individuals. Most of them don't want to change. And it is very difficult to alter the habits of a person who refuses to cooperate, who is content as he is."[15]

In the case at hand, Dr. Crane said his further research indicated that Irene had "attended" the birth of a younger sibling when she was nine years old—and it was a difficult delivery. As a result, "Irene vowed never to have anything to do with men.... We must remember that childhood experiences are often so emotionally powerful as to defy later adult logic."[16]

Chapter 5. "The Worry Clinic"

Dr. Crane seemed pleased to report that via his counseling of Irene, she gained an understanding of her lack of development and "was resolute enough to start dating Alden. Eventually he had a stronger appeal to her than did her [female] roommate."[17]

Later, Dr. Crane offered the case of a 20-year-old college man named "Donald" and the development of his sexual affair with a 40-year-old man. Interestingly, Dr. Crane said the case was presented to him by the dean of the college where the young man attended after love letters between the two men were intercepted and confiscated. One of the letters, written by Donald while home on vacation away from Bob, openly expressed the affection the men shared. As Dr. Crane put it, "The older man has showered gifts upon the boy. They fondle and kiss each other as would a normal young man and his girlfriend."[18]

After the letter, Dr. Crane acknowledged to his readers: "Some of you readers will react with nausea to such saccharine protestations of love and devotion by one grown man for another.... The attachment is called homosexuality. It is duplicated widely, for in the army and navy, in prisons and men's as well as women's colleges, in rural as well as large cities, we have hundreds of thousands of such victims of this immaturity."[19]

He repeated his earlier claims about arrested development of some people as being the cause for such feelings—and that homosexuality was "a normal stage" of childhood development. Likely perceiving the fear the homosexual love letter had planted in the parents reading his column, Dr. Crane advised that 95 percent of adolescents move on to a normal attraction to the opposite sex, but "to avoid this unfortunate result, we should not isolate our children during puberty from members of the opposite sex. It is dangerous to permit young people to live exclusively with their own sex during this formative period in their emotional development."[20]

Prevention of homosexuality was the best cure, the doctor said, acknowledging that changing the affection homosexuals felt for one another was difficult—but not hopeless. In case any of Dr. Crane's words made it clear that Bob and Donald were worthy of scorn—even nausea inducing—the column was accompanied by a crude drawing of a suited young man with pursed lips and a limp wrist holding a pen over a letter addressed to "Dearest Bob" and surrounded by heart-shaped fairies with wings.

Featuring a drawing of a young woman leering at another—under the caption "Beware of Schoolgirl Crushes"—Dr. Crane next presented a letter from a distraught father in May 1938 about his 27-year-old daughter identified as "Vera." The drawing and content of the column was the first in a long line of cases Dr. Crane presented that portrayed homosexuals as predatory individuals who would pervert "normal" affection between friends into "nauseating" interactions.

The father wrote, "Vera is too fond of a girlfriend with whom she shares a small apartment. This girl was her roommate at college. The two had a crush on one another, which during their campus days, I thought was innocent enough. Now they are as devoted as man and wife. They hug and kiss like two newlyweds. Their behavior is so sentimental and mushy as to be nauseating."[21]

Dr. Crane declared that Vera and her girlfriend confirmed his point that individuals who are not developed emotionally stop at a "gang" or "homosexual level" that is normally reserved for children or adolescents. He affirmed that "crushes" between girls were common, but should be redirected toward members of the opposite sex. "If circumstances, or prudish maternal dominance, or isolation in a girl's school, prevent the girls having access to a boyfriend, then she may find herself abnormally attached to a member of her own sex," Dr. Crane wrote.[22]

There was little attempt at compassion or understanding for Vera (or her girlfriend) as Dr. Crane added, "Most people view such a situation [of homosexual affection] in the same light as leprosy, and they can hardly bring themselves to name the dreaded words, adult homosexuality." Jokingly, Dr. Crane quoted a young woman who worked in his office as once only able to refer to a homosexual as, "Oh God, one of those things!"[23]

Offering little specific help to the father concerned about his daughter, Dr. Crane recommended readers avoid placing their children in situations where they were almost exclusively around members of their own gender. "Homosexuals are in love with each other, and they don't want to change, but they are indulging in juvenile behavior and would be far happier if they would grow up, emotionally," he concluded.[24]

Dr. Crane was quick to warn parents about dangers in almost every corner of life—even in something as simple as an appropriate salutation for a letter. One case he highlighted noted that boys would feel like "a sissy" if they signed a letter "Your beloved son."

"In America today, we see little evidence of food starved youngsters," he wrote. "But even in the best of homes we can find children who are being stunted in their emotional development by overly fond parents who monopolize their youngsters, and refuse to let them lead

Chapter 5. "The Worry Clinic"

normal lives." In case the point was missed, Dr. Crane placed most of the blame on women: "Widows and divorced parents are especially prone to molly-coddle children."[25]

The tradition of exchanging Valentine's greetings between classmates became the focus of several columns offered by Crane. A local school board member expressed concern that boys and girls should not be exchanging such messages, but Dr. Crane deemed it an innocent practice. "As a matter of fact, it is psychologically wise to teach children that they should look to the opposite sex for their emotional attachments later in life," he wrote.[26]

He warned of "the big psychological danger" that boys will become too attached to their own sex, or that girls will develop "dangerous" crushes on other girls. "Homosexuality is all too common nowadays," he asserted.[27]

Citing the case of a former patient known as "Phyllis" who had attended only girls' schools and developed crushes on female classmates, "You can guess the result. She is now 32 years of age, teaches school and her 'girlfriend' is the gym teacher in the same large school. Neither girl has ever had an interest in men. They are homosexuals."[28]

A 1938 letter came from the son of a professor, a young man named "Hugo," who confessed romantic feelings and attachments to boys. Hugo's letter seemed to draw more compassion from Dr. Crane that normal. Hugo reported a sad reality that his affections were often taken advantage of: "My boyfriend usually bleeds me for all the money he can get, and after he has affronted me for months, I finally get the point and look elsewhere for another pal."[29]

Dr. Crane said Hugo "is a good example of a man who is an adult in years, but a child in his emotional age" and added, perhaps surprisingly to some readers, "There is no disgrace, nor adequate reason for society's looking down on him with horror as if he were a leper. It simply means that his environment did not predispose him to normal emotional development."[30]

However understanding Dr. Crane's words may have seemed, they were certainly undercut by an accompanying line drawing of two obese jail inmates dressed in striped uniforms, both affecting effeminate poses and batting large eyebrows under the caption: "Hi pal!" The drawing not only drew on the stereotype of homosexuals as effeminate sissies, but also introduced them as potential criminals.

Once again, Dr. Crane argued against boarding schools for boys and girls as potentially dangerous to a child's development where they can "miss the wholesome influences which build heterosexual attitudes." He also revisited his frequent claim that "it is never too late for an adult homosexual to grow up emotionally, but it requires more perseverance than most of them will spend."[31] In another letter, Dr. Crane also warned about female "homosexual teachers" who are prudish and dislike boys and men and as a result, often grant them low grades on assessment tests as an act of revenge against them.[32]

In a May 1941 letter, Dr. Crane took up the case of a 21-year-old man identified as "Ronald W." who had suffered an abusive childhood in a home led by a father eventually committed to a mental asylum. "I have shunned girls, for I felt I could never marry and go through such an ordeal as my parents did," he wrote. "All of this conspired to make me feel unwanted. Girls were taboo, so I drifted into contacts with men of vulgar tendencies. Now I am revolting against the miserable state in which I find myself, but I feel there is no hope. Do you think I can win this fight, Dr. Crane?"[33]

The letter—suggesting that a person could simply "drift" into a homosexual lifestyle must have been frightening for many to read. Perhaps even more frightening was Dr. Crane's suggestion that the father was driven to insanity by "a frigid wife." He quickly blamed Ronald's "present difficulty" and homosexuality to his early home environment.[34]

"When suffering and pain, or anguish and fear, are so intimately linked with marriage in the minds of developing children, the latter are often driven away from the thought of marriage to a member of the opposite sex," Dr. Crane explained. "Denied a legitimate outlet in a happy life, he may seek a devious homosexual outlet."[35]

Although in past cases Dr. Crane seemed to emphasize how difficult it was for a man like Ronald to change, in this case he breezily offered: "Ronald must turn his thoughts to the opposite sex and go through the motions of dates and dances until enough pleasure becomes attached to womanhood to offset his childhood's unpleasant conditioning toward marriage." He added it would take work, "but anybody who rules his life by his brain, he can remake his entire personality and even alter his tastes and emotional attitudes."[36]

A 21-year-old musician identified as "Reginald" may have put Dr. Crane's ideas to the test. He was unwilling and disinterested in giving up his homosexual relations, despite his family's concerns. Dr. Crane noted, "A great difficulty arises in trying to change a homosexual into a normal emotional adult. He or she doesn't want to change! He is ardently

Chapter 5. "The Worry Clinic"

attached to his own sex, and naturally has no desire to break up what he regards as his own true love affair." The comments reflect that Dr. Crane never entertained the legitimacy or sincerity of feelings of love or affection between two people of the same sex—which emphasizes that many of the letters about "changing" homosexuals would come from their family members—and not from homosexual men or women themselves.[37]

Crane offered a dismal outlook—"Homosexuality can be converted into heterosexuality if the *victim* is willing to rule his life by his brains instead of by his emotions. If he realizes that homosexuality is an *inferior stage of emotional development*, and that love is only a mass of emotional habits which can be made, broken and then remade more wisely, the patient may then force himself into a more mature pattern of life" (emphasis added).[38]

A 1942 letter came from a commercial artist in Chicago identified as "Webb," and Dr. Crane used his fear of being touched to warn parents about the danger of older homosexuals "initiating" young people into their deviance. Again, Dr. Crane suggested a predatory risk of homosexuals, but also used the occasion to advertise the availability of a new pamphlet he had written, titled "Sex Problems of Young People," available for 10 cents a copy, plus postage. He urged readers to "give it to other young people who are unduly self-conscious or terrified about lightning and sudden death, venereal diseases and insanity, or who are afflicted with nightmares."[39]

In January 1943, Dr. Crane prefaced his column with a remark that seemed to indicate editors at some newspapers had previously edited the case records presented. He wrote: "You readers are fortunate in having a scientific editor who is far more liberal than average. The average newspaper would censor this case record even in this enlightened age. But such hiding of facts and fear of truth actually increase the condition [of homosexuality] in this case study." The case in question, 19-year-old "Robert W." was from a father who had discovered he is homosexual. "We have learned the truth, and mother is prostrated with grief and shame." As expected, the father wanted to know what he could do to change his son.[40]

Dr. Crane opened his reply by proclaiming that changing the boy's sexual orientation was entirely possible and added, "By means of this column and the mail service, I have helped many homosexuals of both sexes alter their personalities until they were normal again." With no way to confirm Dr. Crane's claims (and likely no one interested in challenging it), the idea of changing one's sexual orientation remained an active prospect promoted by Crane.[41]

The environment for homosexuals was not positive, Dr. Crane seemed to understand. "Millions of Americans look on homosexuality as something worse than leprosy," he wrote. "They are afraid to mention the word. Many American newspapers react with similar prudishness. But homosexuality is simply a scientific term to describe one type of love attachment."[42]

Crane's follow-up remarks represent a very early challenge to existing attitudes among editors—and society as a whole—about the entire consideration of homosexuals. While hardly supportive or affirming of homosexuals, Crane at least believed the matter needed to be openly discussed. At times Crane seemed to try and praise (or guilt) editors into keeping his column, noting at the start of a case study about sodomy: "Be grateful to your newspaper for helping combat delinquency and divorce via factual medical and psychological data."[43]

Trying to at least prepare readers—and newspaper editors—for the content of the case studies, Crane opened a December 1943 letter by advising: "This topic has been rather taboo in America in past years, although it needs to be fully discussed so that parents can take adequate measures to protect their children against the dangers."[44]

The case involved "Carolyn P."—a 19-year-old college sophomore who family members feared was being recruited into becoming a lesbian. The family reported Carolyn was sometimes prevented from visiting with her family, and the other woman would often make many phone calls and check-up repeatedly on her whereabouts when away from their shared apartment. Her family was "at wit's end" and wanted to help her break free of a homosexual life.

Crane was blunt: "This problem of homosexuality has been ignored by the public in past generations, but ignoring the danger doesn't prevent it or help solve the problems of those who ask for aid. Yesterday, I dictated letters to probably 35 or 40 homosexuals, for my mail this week seems to be loaded with such queries as the one from Carolyn's family." Crane was convinced "we need to face facts and analyze this *homosexual condition* of America" (emphasis added).[45]

In a bit of a turn for Dr. Crane (who seemed to heretofore grant no credibility or legitimacy to intimate feelings felt by homosexuals), he acknowledged Carolyn and her girlfriend "actually love each other just as ardently as boy and girl sweethearts" because "the potential capacity or instinct for love is inherited." That said, he made clear he viewed such

Chapter 5. "The Worry Clinic"

relationships as "unwise, unsound and destined for unhappiness."[46] On more than one occasion, Dr. Crane made it clear that in his worldview, "the usual sex taboos are adultery, homosexuality, auto erotic practices, sodomy, and purposive abortion."[47]

A day later, in responding to a case involving another 19-year-old woman, this time "Mary G.," words such as "fairy" and "pansy" were used as "synonyms" for the term homosexual. He added, "Homosexuals are not born that way. They could all be transformed into heterosexuals if the motivation and willpower were adequate."[48]

In February 1944, two years before the draft was ended for World War II, Crane offered the case file of "Larry R.," a 32-year-old man dismissed from the Army for homosexual conduct. Larry told Dr. Crane he was suicidal—"How can I ever face my family? I have a younger brother who is now a captain in the air corps. He always looked up to me and thought I was swell."[49]

As expected, Larry worried that his civilian life would be ruined as well once word got out that his military discharge was tied to homosexuality. He confessed that prior to going to war, "I vowed to break the habit and have prayed. My clergyman has helped me, but ever so often, I succumb to temptation."[50]

Dr. Crane reported that "literally hundreds" of men like Larry had consulted with him during the period of the war. "Recently, I spent two full days at the request of a Chicago clergyman trying to get a naval officer transferred to a new field as a means of giving him a second chance, but his superiors wouldn't give him that chance," Dr. Crane reported (apparently with no concern about the specifics of the case stated violating anyone's privacy).[51] In a later column, he would assert, "Thousands of high-ranking officers in the military service, as well as enlisted men, have been washed out of the service for homosexuality."[52]

Crane took issue with Larry's claim that he was "born that way" and stated unequivocally: "Nobody is born with a love for anybody. We all have the instinct or potential capacity for love, but whether we shall focus on our own sex, is purely a matter of training." He dispensed with Larry's concern and did not address the issues the man raised about his post-military civilian life being impacted by the military discharge.[53]

Less than a year later, in May 1945 as the war was coming to a close, Crane ran another case emanating from the father of a 23-year-old Navy midshipman (identified as "Morris") dismissed on a charge of homosexuality. "We are so mortified about the matter," the young man's father reported. "To think, here I am a prominent business executive and I find

Dear Abby, I'm Gay

my son dismissed from the Navy for such degeneracy! It's unthinkable, Dr. Crane! The boy must be losing his mind." To add insult to injury, the man's father added: "I've told him to stay away from home and try to launch his life anew in some other city."[54]

Dr. Crane stated again that the boy was not born that way, but developed such feelings as a result of environment and arrested development. He introduced a new idea, as well, suggesting that homosexual adults tend to form "gangs" and "clubs" of fellow members, "using mysticism and ritual, to the point of signing their names in blood. Adults fixated at this 'gang' level are then called homosexuals, or fairies, pansies, etc., as is the case of Morris." Again, the "advice" or counsel ended with claims that he could be converted to being heterosexual, but it was unlikely. Beyond that, Dr. Crane seemed to have no desire or interest in offering further help (at least via the newspaper column).[55]

By 1946, it appears Dr. Crane's column began running previously published letters again. Some of the details of the letters were changed, but were essentially the same as the first time. It is unclear if editors knew the columns were being recycled, or whether Crane was involved in the recycling. Because newspapers often would trim columns for space, or hold them for days when more space was available, seeing a column run for a second time was not particularly unusual.

In November 1951, Dr. Crane took a swing at discussing the merits of contemporary women's fashion, highlighting the case of "Annette" who was concerned about "bizarre and harsh" fashion trends such as red nail polish, unnatural hair dyes, lacquered or brittle looking curls, and "mannish, unnatural costumes."[56]

Dr. Crane's first advice was that women needed to smile more—that a smiling woman was almost always more pleasing and attractive than "a sour puss with a glum expression on her face." He noted, "A radiant smile, plus only a clean gingham apron can transform the average woman into a very charming personality." He further argued for skirt lengths that were "well below the knee" help make a woman look taller and slimmer. "Fat girls should avoid flowered fabrics, belts, square-necked frocks, tight strands of beads and rings," he recommended. "Avoid horizontal lines and cultivate the vertical dimension. Excessively thin girls, however, should do the very opposite."[57]

Other advice included, "Hide your defects and the male imagination may rate you more attractive than you really are," Dr. Crane said. "Accentuate your femininity! Avoid masculinizing fads and fashions, such as puffed shoulders, slacks and brittle looking fabrics. Don't adopt

Chapter 5. "The Worry Clinic"

ultra-short haircuts, either those that make you look like anemic boys and no real male gets a thrill out of kissing or fondling a 'half-man.'"[58]

As might be expected, Dr. Crane drew a line between what he considered "troublesome" female fashion design and male homosexuals. He further suggested that "girls are probably driving men into homosexuality by the boyish haircuts, cigarettes and liquor, vulgar language and slacks. If a man wants to fall in love with a man, he'd prefer the real McCoy instead of the female imitation."[59]

A case study involving Tom, a mid–20s man discharged from the military for homosexuality, allowed Dr. Crane to opine on his views regarding the proper behavior for developing boys and girls. He noted, "Girls thus should doll up and use rouge, lipstick and nail polish to become more appealing to boys" and "boys [should] wash behind their ears, slap oil on their hair to make it stay in place, and generally try to attract the attention of teenage girl classmates."[60] Dr. Crane would run many such letters over the years, including a February 1964 letter from a mother distraught that her 23-year-old son "Albert" had been discharged from the navy for engaging in homosexual conduct. Albert's mother was particularly incensed that her son had moved to San Francisco and was living an openly gay life and living with two other gay men. While suggesting this mother not too harshly judge her son, Dr. Crane nonetheless pronounced him "retarded emotionally" and someone who possessed a "psychopathic personality who would show no remorse or any sincere concern for their own mothers."[61]

Another desperate mother wrote to Dr. Crane after her son wrote home to report he was being discharged from the navy along with four other men for homosexuality—and confessed that he had, in fact, been sexually involved with other men. "He was very penitent and begged us to do something to help him," mom wrote. "His father consulted a psychiatrist at once, for we didn't know what to do. This doctor suggested there is very little likelihood of a cure, so he recommended that our son lose himself in a large city."[62]

Dr. Crane was incensed by the idea that her son "lose himself" in the city among a community of other homosexuals, but noted "thousands of young men (and women) are being washed out of the military service for this same reason." Crane was convinced not all hope was lost—although he knew it would require a determined young man willing to change. He said he often advised patients, "Act the way you ought to be, and soon you'll be the way you act."[63]

Homosexuals were a major portion of American society—Dr. Crane

Dear Abby, I'm Gay

estimating as many as 10 million men and women were gay—or 10 percent of the total population. Crane's estimate matches those promoted by Dr. Alfred Kinsey in his earlier studies, but agreement between Crane and Kinsey was otherwise absent.

In a 1952 answer to parents worried about their emerging lesbian daughter, Dr. Crane declared: "This newspaper column justifies its existence, if it did no more than to warn you parents of the hazards of homosexuality. It is estimated that millions of Americans are either full-fledged or potential homosexuals. They are often brilliant 'A' students and may come from the best families."[64]

In April 1955, Dr. Crane devoted most of his column to the first-person account of "Jerry F."—a 29-year-old man who was orphaned as a boy. Detailing his life of struggles, Jerry noted, "The biggest problem in my youth was the fact that some older men initiated me into self sex practices and homosexuality." Jerry said he worried he was headed for a mental institution, but had received help via Dr. Crane's booklet, "Sex Problems of Young People."[65]

"I learned that a homosexual can change if he will exert enough willpower," Jerry wrote. "You said that homosexuality is simply an immature or juvenile stage in emotional development, so I vowed I'd grow up." Jerry reported he had forced himself to begin to like giving goodnight kisses to women he would date, and when he felt like straying, he would re-read Dr. Crane's booklet. "Besides, I realized I had become somewhat sissy during my homosexual period, so I had to watch my mannerisms, my gestures and even the way I talked and walked."[66]

The excruciating details continued, "I kept on dating different girls and resolutely ignored all homosexual tendencies and temptation, which was very hard, for misdirected passion is just as strong and blinding as the normal type of love. I took your advice and avoided girls in taverns, and instead I selected nice, religious girls and if ever one started to drink, I'd drop her like a hot potato."[67]

Although "Jerry's" letter sounded like it was actually written by someone promoting the value of Dr. Crane's booklet—it continued on with the "good news" that Jerry had successfully married "a nice girl" and become a father. The couple also used Dr. Crane's "famous 'Tests for Sweethearts' and I fell completely in love with her. I find that heterosexual life is far superior to my former homosexual way of living."[68]

Not coincidentally, the column ran during the period in which Crane and a group of fellow psychologists and ministers were launching one of the nation's first "computer" dating services—known as the

Chapter 5. "The Worry Clinic"

Scientific Marriage Foundation. Dr. Crane boasted that Jerry's letter "shows the tremendous value of the daily newspaper in helping change human lives constructively."[69]

A March 1958 column took up the "threat" homosexuals posed to children under the age of 18 related to child sexual molest. Dr. Crane made no distinction between homosexuals and child molesters—for the purposes of his column, the two terms were synonymous.

Crane used the case study of "Don," an 18-year-old college freshman, who was squired by an older English professor who took him to dinner and invited him to his home—all as a front for engaging in a homosexual relationship. The young man exclaimed, "It never dawned on me that the professor might be one of those fellows they call homosexuals!"[70]

Dr. Crane quoted a police chief from Saginaw, Michigan, and the superintendent of a Catholic school to issue "a special warning to all parents about the dangers of homosexuals" and "thus forewarning a child, for even men of college age such as Don in today's case, may not be aware of the clinical signs of sexual offenders."[71]

The "safety" tips to avoid homosexual molest included warning children to never get into an automobile with a stranger; never take candy or money from a stranger; don't go into a stranger's home or workshop or room; never let anyone "fuss with your clothing"; and never leave the school, playground or theatre with a stranger.

Crane warned that sex offenders could be found in both rural and urban communities, and that young boys "should be skeptical of men who shower affection on them or when women gush and kiss their own sex in romantic fashion, beware, for this is often a part of the build-up that the homosexual launches to win his or her victim."[72]

"Homosexuality is far more prevalent than parents dream of," Crane wrote. "Fortunately, modern newspapers are educating the public via this column to a lot of sexual dangers that used to be ignored.... So warn your children against illicit sexual advances both from the opposite sex as well as from their own sex."[73]

A two-part case study offered in 1964 openly suggested that "Albert" had become a homosexual only as a result of childhood sexual molestation by adult male men. "I was only 10 years old when an older boy initiated me into homosexual practices," Dr. Crane quoted Albert as telling him during counseling. "I tried to break away, but he was older and stronger so he forced me to submit until he graduated from high school. Meanwhile, he had told a couple of his friends about our relationship, and so they threatened to tell my parents unless I submitted to them. So I found myself involved in a ring of homosexuals that the habit became so strong that I couldn't break free."[74]

"Gangs of homosexuals" existed in the mind of Dr. Crane, convinced that gangs of them were forming formal allegiances in order to recruit other young people into homosexuality. It was a key component of not only his attempt to explain homosexuality, but also to continue to marginalize it as a mental or psychological defect that needed the help of doctors like him.

By 1965, Dr. Crane was not only on board with "applied psychology" to answer such concerns, but also was now advocating the controversial work of British researchers Dr. M.P. Feldman and M.J. MacCulloch who had begun experimenting with a form of "aversion therapy" to "cure" homosexuals. Dr. Crane referred to their work as "ingenious" by flashing pictures of attractive males on a screen—"The homosexual was provided with a switch by which to remove the photo of such sexual temptation. If the victim does not remove the picture within eight seconds, then he suffers an electrical shock, which links pain with his pleasurable contemplation of the enticing male. And he keeps on receiving the electrical shock 'til he does push the button and thus remove the picture from view."

In Dr. Crane's view, "sooner or later he thus learns to remove the picture before the eight-second time limit and the photo of the attractive male thus becomes altered into a signal that a painful experience will follow, making viewing of an attractive male an unpleasant experience."

Not surprisingly, after electric shocks are applied and the dreaded attractive male image is removed, Dr. Crane was pleased to report it was replaced in the British experiments by the photograph of an attractive female. "This is the standard method by which we train and retrain rats or guinea pigs ... but we have also discovered that a combination of pain for the wrong plus pleasure for the right choice, will still speed up his learning," Crane noted. He declared the troublesome experiments "cleverly arranged" and in line with the laws of conditioned reflex.[75]

The predatory nature of homosexuals was a common theme as Crane's column evolved—a September 1965 column entirely devoted to the account of a man who was trying to help his attractive young secretary turn from her lesbian lifestyle. The boss (who was taking a rather inordinate amount of interest in his employee's personal life) reported that another more masculine woman (employed as a high school physical education teacher) was the aggressor in the relationship. The PE

Chapter 5. "The Worry Clinic"

teacher "was so intensely jealous that she wouldn't let this girl even dine with her boss without spying" and added "the masculine dame follows her everywhere, even worse than a jealous suitor," scaring anyway any chance for a "normal" relationship with a man. Dr. Crane's only comment was "Most homosexuals usually encounter an older aggressor who initiates them early on" and the answer to "warn your children of such dangers" could be found by writing for a copy of Crane's booklet, "Sex Problems of Young People."[76]

A case study examining the onset of venereal diseases among sexually active heterosexual teenagers also quickly veered off into links to homosexuality. While acknowledging that teen venereal disease among girls and boys was too common (as high as 100,000 U.S. cases in 1964), Crane asserted "homosexuals are now one of the most common spreaders of such ailments" because "homosexuals admit of having six or eight different sexual contacts in a single day, and thus spread venereal disease widely. Remember, too, that homosexuals are of both sexes!"[77]

Other provocative topics would follow, including a June 1967 column in which Dr. Crane reported back on a seminar he led of more than 1,000 "church-going women" who asked many questions about marriage and sex. One question came from a woman concerned about her husband's unusual sexual demands, and she wanted to know more about what sodomy was. Crane made the quick biblical connection to sodomy and anal intercourse and reported—likely to a shocked audience—that "this is far more prevalent than many fastidious Americans even dream of" and added that "teenagers should be warned of all such sexual pitfalls before they leave junior high school."[78]

Crane said interest in anal intercourse (which he identified as "anal eroticism") represented an arrested understanding of physical anatomy and "it is usually restricted to homosexual relationships by two males. But I have brought this hush-hush subject out into the open so you can help educate your teenagers properly."[79]

There was a Dr. Crane booklet for seemingly every problem presented—a wife who had discovered her husband's homosexual past was told to request a copy of his "Sex Problems in Marriage" booklet.[80] Three years later, Dr. Crane had written a new booklet for wives titled, "How to Prevent Platonic Marriage" in which he took up proper roles for husbands and wives in relationships, and again denounced what he viewed as the increasing number of effeminate or homosexual men—"boldly publicizing the fact they are homosexual and even trying to marry other such half-females!"[81]

Dear Abby, I'm Gay

Cross-dressers were occasionally the subject of a "case file" offered by Dr. Crane, but most often the good doctor deemed the participants in that activity as not likely homosexual, but rather heterosexual males who suffered addiction (similar to alcoholism or gambling). A 1963 letter from the adopted parents of 19-year-old "Tom" was an exception, with his parents declaring that he not only enjoyed cross-dressing, but was a homosexual, and that he wanted to be a female. "He has women's lingerie in his dresser drawers and even some false hair so he can dress up as a girl," his mother reported. "Tom now realizes we know his secret, so he argues and tells us lies about his whereabouts.... Is there any medicine that would work short of castration?"[82]

Dr. Crane said "Tom" was a transvestite which he defined as "a male who adopts girlish clothing, as well as rouge and lipstick." He added, for good measure, "Women nowadays have made it a habit to imitate the attire of the male sex as well." Although the parents did not ask, Dr. Crane was quick to note that their son having been adopted was not a factor in his homosexuality, because it was a developed state, not a born attribute.[83]

He concluded by breaking the news that "drugs and medicines have little effect on homosexuals. Even such an extreme method as castration was little influence, too, for homosexuality is largely a mental habit. Cutting off the hands of pianist will not change the latter's interest in piano music."[84]

The nature of women's apparel and dress seemed to make its way into Crane's column on a regular basis, as evidenced in many letters where he would chide women for their clothing choices or even tobacco use. Even a December 1963 letter from a man who was concerned that he and his wife were too opposite to be successfully married drew such analysis. "Many a husband has reported to me that he has become platonic with reference to his wife because of her boyish haircut, her smoking, swilling down highballs, using profanity or telling risqué stories, and her adoption of other male traits," Dr. Crane wrote. "Many husbands tell me when they wake up and see their wife lying on the pillow beside them she looks like a teenage boy. Some husbands even report a vague homosexual revulsion."[85]

Dr. Crane turned his appeal directly to women—having long ago cast aside the original question about how opposite personality types attract. He noted: "If you girls wish more vividly to understand this reaction, would you feel very romantic about a male who dressed in feminine lingerie, used women's rouge and lipstick, and minced along on

Chapter 5. "The Worry Clinic"

high heels? Obviously, you would not! Then why do you girls act like sheep and meekly follow the silly fashions and fads that reduce your own feminine charm?"[86] The cause of these "foolish female fads" in women's fashion and hair styling, Dr. Crane noted, was "devised by homosexuals" who sought to "defeminize women."[87]

He concluded his remarks by recommending appropriate use of perfume, having any sort of "physical blemish" corrected by a doctor, have "surplus hair" removed via electric needle, consider "plastic and dental surgeries" for needed "medical miracles," and, of course, "a jolly personality can offset most of your minor defects!"[88]

A 1969 letter from "Grace," a 38-year-old wife concerned about finding her husband's porn stash of "nudie" magazines prompted Dr. Crane to take the woman to task about maintaining her appearance in order to "keep her husband." He advised about wearing revealing nighties, avoiding cigarettes, and even body odor and bad breath as key to getting her husband to abandon his interest in pornography. He also recommended she send for his "medical booklet" titled "How to Lose 10 Pounds in 10 Days" for 20 cents. "As you lose your excess blubber, your seductive appeal will zoom," he assured.[89]

Another writer in the same era, 28-year-old Lola wrote to get Dr. Crane's view on the appropriateness of mini-skirts popular with women at the time. He affirmed he believed such apparel was contributing to the rising divorce rate, noting that men didn't visit areas where prostitutes could be found in mini-skirts because they were looking for wives. "Obviously, I am speaking frankly, for most of you teenage women use no more gumption than silly sheep who also stampede, even to their own doom," he asserted.[90]

Crane equated current fashion trends with a biblical story involving a goat known as a "Judas goat" who led sheep astray to their doom. "You coeds have been following similar but two-legged Judas goats called fashion designers," he wrote. "Many of the latter 'goats' are homosexuals, anyway, who vent their spite at the female sex by making you appear ridiculous or by leading you to your social doom!"[91]

Always a very religious man, Crane's devout Methodist views were often interspersed in the advice given to readers, including quotes from scriptures. Even in matters of emotional and psychological "maturity," Crane used the example of Jesus as the model: "Christ's going to Calvary is the top example of the highest level of emotional maturity."[92]

In October 1967, after reading a national news wire story about Glide Memorial United Methodist Church in San Francisco and its

Dear Abby, I'm Gay

ministry and outreach to gay and lesbian members, Dr. Crane had something to say. The Glide church was being used, Crane asserted, by "ultra liberals" who had welcomed "a notorious organization called the Vanguards, comprised of male prostitutes, to use the church as its dance hall. It also made office space available to the Vanguards, and even let them employ (the church) as its base of operations." Crane said he was familiar with homosexuals—which apparently in his worldview were synonymous with prostitutes—"but we attempt to help them" not pander to them.[93]

For the record, Vanguards was a short-lived gay rights organization founded in San Francisco in 1965 to address the needs of gay and lesbian youth tossed from their parents' homes to the streets. It did not promote prostitution, but rather sought to offer a safe gathering place for gay youth left on their own. The organization folded in 1967.

Crane occasionally shared with readers speeches he would give to regional or national meetings of various Christian organizations. In October 1973, Crane wrote about speaking to a meeting of pastors from across the Midwest on the topic of "Marriage Counseling" and shared that the topic of "the increased prevalence of homosexuality" was raised often—including the apparent concern that "some married men later turn to homosexuality" despite being married to women. "One basic homosexual secret needs wider exposure," Crane wrote. "It deals with the lower erotic verve of many men, due either to the effects of cigarettes or possibly the ingested female sex hormones fed to cattle and poultry to tenderize such meat."[94]

Beyond the rather specious claims that homosexuality or female hormones in meat could be the "cause" of homosexuality, Dr. Crane clearly was placing the responsibility—or blame—for male homosexuality on the part of heterosexual women. He said the same causes were in play with married men who frequented prostitutes on the side.

It was not only Dr. Crane's views on homosexuality that appeared to be out of step with the growing gay liberation movement, but he clashed with women's liberation as well. In 1971 and 1972 he ran several columns attacking the push for women's rights—and as expected—linked the movement to predatory homosexual behavior by lesbian women seeking to recruit other females. A July 1973 column specifically warned young women that they not only had to be cautious of the sexual advances of men, but also against "lesbian coeds who try to fondle their roommates and thus develop homosexual relationships."[95]

In a surreal column, Dr. Crane detailed at length techniques

Chapter 5. "The Worry Clinic"

homosexuals (including lesbians) use to recruit teenagers. "The public often thinks of the male homosexual as being slender and effeminate," he wrote. "While that applies to many of them, there are big burly male homos who are over 6 feet tall and weighing 200 pounds. Similarly, female lesbians (homos) are not always the large masculine type of women."[96]

He warned, "Sometimes a very frail looking girl may be the aggressor in launching her roommate into a lesbian relationship. Like the older male who tries to molest children, such an aggressor may start by making gifts to her intended victim. She may offer her roommate some of her clothing or cosmetic lotions and perfumes."[97]

As if he had not described the "grooming process" in enough detail, Dr. Crane continued, many lesbians "like to touch their victim's hair, either by stroking it or by offering to comb it or arrange a new hairdo." Even platonic kisses on the cheek are suspect: "Instead, a cheery little peck on the cheek for the lesbian becomes more frequent and she wants to kiss her roommate more often and with greater fervor. She even prolongs the kiss in the erotic manner ... trying to inflame her girlfriends' passion."[98]

The detailed description went on and on: Lesbians often sought roommates "to occupy a double bed with them so that during sleep they can place their arm around their companion's shoulder. Next, she begins to stroke her roommate's skin and fondle her breasts. If the intended victim pushes the lesbian's hands away, she can always act as if she had been asleep when the sexual prelude began."[99]

He also cautioned that "female homos" were often fond of plying their "victims" with alcohol—such as wine—to engage "a shortcut to their speedier conquest of the innocent girl, and the liquor becomes a convenient 'smoke screen' for more aggressive erotic fondling."[100]

Adding in some political and espionage intrigue, Dr. Crane said, "Homosexuals also use the standard Russian technique of infiltration by advancing two steps; then maybe backing up one step, after which the process is repeated. Once the lesbian has completed the conquest of her female partner, the latter begins to feel bewitched by the lesbian's erotic charisma. For whoever initiates an innocent victim into a complete sexual climax thereafter holds almost a magical power!"[101]

Hilariously, Dr. Crane used the term "bisexuality" repeatedly in a December 1972 column in which he argued for allowing boys and girls to join together in one scouting organization, rather than separate Boys and Girl Scout clubs. "Scouting, which formerly focused on the pre-teen groups, thus is to be commended for now taking advantage of the greater motivating value of bisexual scouting," he wrote, without understanding how his words might be received by all readers.[102]

There were other signs that Dr. Crane's reign as a pre-eminent advice columnist were coming to an end as public sentiment and social morays began to pass him by. In another December 1972 column, Crane openly criticized a competitor, Ann Landers, for her "obsession with homosexuality" and her opposition to "computerized dating organizations" (the latter of which Dr. Crane operated from his Indiana office).

Dr. Crane's words could fall hard on homosexuals—men or women—and on many others he discussed in his columns. He offered little hope or encouragement over the many decades of his work to LGBTQ people and their loved ones. However, he did muster a measure of compassion in July 1983 when issues of personal sexual conduct hit close to home. That year one of his two sons serving in the U.S. House of Representatives from Illinois faced scrutiny for his admitted sexual affair with a 17-year-old female intern.

Rep. Daniel B. Crane, a Republican who represented a conservative southern Illinois district, admitted he had "succumbed to temptation" (again, placing the blame on others) by engaging in sex with a 17-year-old girl. He and U.S. Representative Gerry Studds, a Massachusetts Democrat, were both implicated in the scandal involving House "pages" (or interns). Studds admitted he had engaged in a sexual affair with a 17-year-old male page, and came out as openly gay. The House Ethics Committee recommended a reprimand for both Crane and Studds, but no criminal charges were brought. Crane ran for re-election in 1984, but lost his seat and returned to the practice of dentistry. (Studds, meanwhile, was re-elected every year until 1996 from his more liberal Massachusetts district.)

Dr. Crane was sought out for comment on his son's fall from grace, and "The Worry Clinic" practitioner was in a joking mood about the entire matter. He attempted to deflect attention from his son and onto U.S. Senator Edward Kennedy (known for his personal lapses) suggesting that his son would more "appreciate Teddy Kennedy now." He told a reporter that at least half of the members of Congress engage in sexual relations outside of marriage, and added, "Washington and New York are the Sodom and Gomorrah of today" a"it seems alcohol and sex can't be controlled in Washington."[103]

CHAPTER 6

"Mary Haworth's Mail"
—Mary Haworth

"Mary Haworth's Mail" ran as a regular feature of *The Washington Post* from the mid–1930s to the early 1970s. Started as *The Business of Living*, the column was renamed "Mary Haworth's Mail" and eventually ran in more than two dozen other newspapers across the United States via the King Features Syndicate.

Known for her smart, educated responses to the problems presented, Haworth fastidiously echoed the powerful influence Sigmund Freud held over most of twentieth century American culture and society. Haworth, via Freudian psychiatrists she contacted, promoted the great Austrian neurologist's ideas that formed the basis of psychoanalysis in the era of her column.

Haworth's devotion to the truth and solemnity of psychiatry could win her both praise, and criticism, but mostly won her readers. She openly abdicated any perceived role she might have claimed to be the sage others sought for advice and counsel, and instead promoted herself as a "vessel" or vehicle through which such help could flow.

Redbook magazine declared, "Each community should have its own Mary Haworth," as it noted her "wise counsel" was carried in U.S. newspapers reaching more than 20 million readers. "Her letters come from all parts of the world," a reporter noted. "Homespun human counsel. Biblical references and the prescriptions of modern psychiatry, all form the pattern of counsel given daily by Haworth."[1]

It was high praise for the former *Washington Post* "newsroom gal" who started her career in 1933. Asked to write an advice column for *Post* readers, it quickly became so popular that King Features Syndicate picked up the column for nationwide distribution in 1944. Still living in a world where what a woman looked like was a key descriptor (as opposed to what she knew or had accomplished), a 1953 profile 20 years into her career noted Haworth was "tiny and fragile," the mother of two daughters who dressed "simply but smartly in tailored clothes, usually topped by a perky hat."[2]

Haworth told reporters that every word of her column was her own, and that she engaged a specific hierarchy before answering the problems presented to her: her own "homespun philosophy," the Bible, or psychiatry. Haworth said she enjoyed the "high regard" of psychiatrists for "her important contributions toward educating Americans that mental illness is not a social disgrace, but a disease requiring proper diagnosis and treatment."[3]

Like many of her counterparts in the advice business, Haworth used a pen name for her column. Her real name: Mary Elizabeth Reardon Young. She was granted the column in an era when the publisher of *The Washington Post* "accorded women a free hand in managing the 'women's department' of the newspaper." Along with the Mary Haworth column, *The Post* also offered a daily column of "female satire" titled "The Gentler Sex." Haworth's take on the problems of readers was an instant hit. Among her earliest fans was physicist J. Robert Oppenheimer—"the

A 1945 *Minneapolis Tribune* advertisement for the "Mary Haworth's Mail" advice column (courtesy Star Tribune Media Co.—Newspapers.com).

Chapter 6. "Mary Haworth's Mail"

father of the atomic bomb"—who viewed Haworth as different from other advice columnist for her commitment to providing "high-class advice."[4]

One of Haworth's most important backers was Frank McLearn, a managing editor for King Features Syndicate. While Haworth's column gave advice, McLearn claimed it "revolutionized" the genre. "Mary Haworth anticipated the modern interest in psychiatry, she developed a new angle," McLearn said. "She does very good thinking herself, but she backs up every opinion with sound advice from physicians, clergymen, priests. It shocks readers a little but makes them really face up to their problems."[5]

"The truth is," Haworth told a reporter, "I find thinking an arduous task, especially when combined with judging, deciding and thereafter writing out one's conclusions in lucid, readable prose. In this respect I am no different than other thinkers."[6]

Haworth had another unusual practice—when she received a letter from a reader who needed help, but the letter was not selected for publication for some reason—she would still write back to the person. She felt particularly obligated to do so, she said, when a professional psychiatrist was offering the reader advice she thought could help change their lives or situation. By 1953, however, Haworth's columns came with a short disclaimer at the end that read, "Mary Haworth counsels through her column, not by mail or personal interview." This likely reflected the growing popularity of her column and the resulting increase in the volume of requests for help.[7]

In one public presentation, Haworth told her audience she longed to know "if you really do help your anxious correspondents; whether you've seen any of the people who write you; and whether they ever report back on the advice you give." As an advice columnist, she said, "you want to know how [readers] like your work; and whether you practice what you preach, and believe what you say. For myself, the blanket answer to these questions is yes."[8]

Her "practice what you preach" remark reflected Haworth's sensitivity that her marriage (like that of other advice columnists) had not survived and ended in divorce.

Historians who researched "the rise" of *The Washington Post* noted Haworth's column was symbiotically linked to the newspaper's success—"Mary Haworth's Mail" becoming the most read feature in *The Post* for many years. As one review of her work noted, "Instead of writing drool on such questions as, 'Shall I neck on my first date?,' Miss Haworth writes conscientiously, but with an astringent Irish wit, as a combination human-relations counselor and psychiatrist."[9]

Viewed through a contemporary lens, Haworth's advice could be controversial, but surely reflects the era in which it was written. One example is found in *The Annapolis Log*, the most popular column in the Naval Academy's newspaper, with her frank advice in 1944 to a U.S. Navy wife who was lukewarm on the idea of becoming a mother. The young wife expressed angst that she would be pregnant for nine months (or more) alone while her husband served overseas in World War II. Calling the woman out as "hare-brained," Haworth said her immediate reaction to the woman's reluctance to be a mother was "a blend of nausea and dismay." Haworth told the young wife to work to "overcome your own selfishness" and "have the baby, by all means, no matter what the inconveniences."[10]

It was rare for Haworth to print letters of criticism from readers, but the very first known reference to "homosexuality" in her column came in July and August 1944 as a female reader asked for help in dealing with her husband, whom she described as "an imminent alcoholic." Among the possible causes for the increasing drunkenness, Haworth said, could be "latent homosexuality" concealed deep within the man's ego.[11]

"Psychiatric jargon" was front and center in July 1945 when Haworth took on the concerns of a 50-year-old widow who was considering marrying again—this time to a man, also in his 50s, who had never married. The man had, until recently, been the sole supporter of his mother and sister and was prone to "cross and unresponsive spells" in the relationship. Mary wasted no time consulting psychiatrists who attributed the man's moodiness—bordering on hostility—to either "hardening of the arteries" or, more likely, a "mother fixation" that meant he was unconsciously drawn to "an emotional drift towards homosexuality." Mary concluded, "In light of the specialist's speculations, it seems safe to say you would be changing for the worse and not for the better" by marrying the man.[12]

A year later, Haworth took on the troubles of a 40-something man who, in the midst of an apparent mid-life crisis, was craving a "harem" or multiple female sexual partners, all to the predictable dismay of his wife. Admitting that he had often cheated on his spouse before, and had sought (and not received) his wife's blessing to open their relationship to outside sexual entanglements, the man declared, "I am convinced that sex is the strongest force in the world; and there is no stronger bonds of

Chapter 6. "Mary Haworth's Mail"

tie in marriage than sexual desire equally matched and subsiding at an equal rate as the years go by."

Mary Haworth was having none of it. "A specialist with whom I discussed your story says bluntly that you are not nearly the man you think you are." Citing the man's obvious immaturity, insecurity, instability and "general under-development of personality," she noted sex was mistakenly viewed as being at the center of the issue. Haworth's psychiatric experts noted the man's problem was not sex or his glands, but his personality. "The man's conviction of insatiable potency undoubtedly refers to a desperate unconscious drive to conceal even from himself great anxieties he feels in relation to women," Haworth's unnamed expert said. "Maybe he is hostile to women. Maybe unsure of himself. Maybe latently homosexual." As expected, the prescribed treatment was intense psychotherapy.[13]

Another writer, an immigrant mother of two teenage sons, reported her struggle with the increasingly American lifestyle of her sons, including their desire to stay out at night with their friends. Haworth commiserated with the worried mother, but added an interesting dash of fear: concern that the boys were locked in an "inward struggle for self-possession" as they worked to break free of their traditional family. "Young men in revolt of mother-bossing often lead to alcoholism, homosexuality, or other forms of waywardness." This December 1946 column is the first where Haworth openly placed homosexuality on a scale of "waywardness" (along with alcoholism) and in an answer that seemed to rely more on her own instinct (rather than that of a consulting psychiatrist), she urged mom to butt out of her son's lives, and seek counseling for everyone.[14]

Haworth's advice in this instance did not sit well with all readers, with a January 1947 reader response taking her to task specifically for suggesting the teenage boys were susceptible to homosexuality by staying out late at night. As one writer (identified only as "P.P.") chastising Haworth noted, teenage boys staying out late at night were *not* seeking the intimacy of other men, but rather chasing females. Saying Haworth's take was "phooey," the letter writer said, "More likely than not they are out with somebody's spoiled and wayward daughter!" Haworth took a direct blow from the writer who noted, "It seems that you are so befuddled by psychiatric lore that you can't see the forest for the trees. I can't make up my mind whether to send this kick to you or to your editor, but I'll bet he's thinking just as I am."[15]

Haworth fired back, defending her reliance upon psychiatry

Dear Abby, I'm Gay

as the basis for her answers. She cited statistics on the level of mental disorder in the U.S. (including noting that 1.7 million draftees for World War II were rejected from service because of mental and personality disorders). She also noted 40 percent of medical discharges from the military were due to some mental or emotional disorder. "Is that enough to show which way the wind blows?" Haworth asked in retort.[16]

As World War II drew to a close, Haworth took more and more letters from veterans and their loved ones attempting to adjust to life after military service. One 20-year-old wife complained her previously "normal" husband came back from military service a troubled alcoholic who refused to work full-time, and instead relied upon her earnings. Haworth immediately suspected a "mama's boy" and that "front-line war experience would play havoc with a personality already so damaged." Haworth warned his "twisted" emotions could devolve into an "incipiently homosexual pattern."[17]

Haworth and her Freudian experts seemed to spot—or suspect—homosexuality at almost every turn. A 1952 letter from a single woman trying to break off a sexual affair with a married man brought Haworth's warning, "He feels incapable of authentic matehood and may shrink from psychiatric insight, lest he come upon homosexual worries in his unconscious mind."[18]

A letter later the same year from the wife of a philandering husband brought a similar reply, with Haworth unveiling what she and her experts termed was a "Casanova complex" in which a seemingly heterosexual man seeks to override his truly homosexual desires by becoming a sexual meanderer. His inner fear of being homosexual, Haworth noted, may be "driving him to Casanova extremes as if to disprove the suspicion that lurks in his mind."[19] The same "Casanova theory" was back in yet another reply, this one to a woman whose fiancé had lied to her about his sexual promiscuity—Haworth suggesting his peccadillos were a result of "fighting a homosexual bias and seeking safety—or superman camouflage—in the role of 'ladies man.'"[20]

A March 1953 letter sufficiently beat around the bush at the real issue—a married woman writing that her husband was, among other things, a fraud, a sinner, an evil or crazy man, and "a perverse, atheistic [man] strongly attracted to Communism and attitudes that spell death to the soul of his profession."

Haworth got right to the point: "Indirectly you are saying, among other things, that your husband is homosexual, which I gather [is] a

Chapter 6. "Mary Haworth's Mail"

horrendous tendency from society's view." Mary said the man sounded as if he were "generally demoralized, helplessly lost in a maze of error."

"Ambivalent sexuality, leaning towards homosexuality, usually has roots in badly distorted filial feelings—that is, in resentful maladjustment to one's parent of the same sex," Haworth wrote. She quickly cast the man along with other "anti–God, anti-democracy individuals" who shared common traits with homosexuals, leaving little doubt that a homosexual man was at the bottom of society's barrel in 1953. In the end, Haworth urged the woman to break free—particularly for the sake of her children—and leave her husband to seek needed psychiatric care on his own.[21]

The barrier broken where Haworth openly discussed homosexuality outside of the realm of possible mental or psychological causes for certain disorders and problems, another letter writer later in 1953 asked for help for her daughter. Noting that a fellow student in a theatre company had confessed to her he was homosexual, she had subsequently "fallen" for another boy who also disclosed a "fixation" with another boy. As a result, the young woman was suicidal, and she and her mother worried about why homosexuals were drawn to her. The young woman's mother admitted the homosexual men needed psychiatric help "to overcome their deviate tendency" but wondered if her daughter needed help as well?[22]

Haworth's reply further degraded gays—noting that the girls "ill-starred affinity for derelict types may reflect an ingrained unconscious feeling she has of being intrinsically inferior to healthy average persons her age." Mary said it appeared the young woman "relaxes only towards obviously reject-material—i.e., individuals who shrink from the robust interchange of self-confident heterosexual living."[23]

Other problems came in—a young woman whose college professor was cruel and demeaning to her in front of other classmates, or a wife whose husband pinched and teased his step-daughter relentlessly—all concluding that the men were likely suffering from "latent homosexuality." Haworth noted that among bachelors and divorced men lurked "latent homosexuals who are obscurely spiteful toward dependent feminine women."[24]

It wasn't until 1957 that Haworth finally printed a letter actually from a person who was struggling with homosexual feelings. Headline writers for Haworth's column had a field day, the version carried in *The Tampa Morning Tribune* being representative: "Discovery That Son Is Deviate Stuns Parents, Who Ask for Help." The parents in question had intercepted letters their teenage son had written to another boy openly expressing romantic feelings.

Pushing their son to participate in more athletic activities and to avoid "any feminine pursuits at all," the parents noted (aptly), "Like most parents, we don't understand this sexual maladjustment and don't know how to cope." They closed their letter asking for suggestions on books they could read to "become more enlightened."[25]

Mary Haworth told the beleaguered parents, "So far as I know, there isn't much reliable literature available keyed to a non-specialist understanding of the complex subject of homosexuality, its causes and chances of cure." Perhaps not considering her previous replies as in any way derogatory toward homosexuals, Haworth offered an almost sympathetic rift that noted: "The mists of ignorance, prudery and misconception with which [homosexuality] has been surrounded are beginning to lift a little; and a time may be fast approaching when healing light will begin to break in upon this demoralized mix-up of the human personality."[26]

Quoting Dr. Edmund Bergler (an Austrian-born psychoanalyst who believed homosexuality could be overcome) and author of a 1956 book *Homosexuality: Disease or Way of Life?* Haworth noted that Bergler believed some people deviated from "normal development" and mistakenly viewed themselves as a "third sex" along with all of its resulting "shame and megalomaniac conceit." Haworth viewed Bergler's book was one of "hope for the deviate who really wants to get straightened out."[27]

Haworth noted Bergler's challenge to Dr. Alfred Kinsey's previously published ideas about the commonness of homosexuality and faulted Kinsey with introducing a "dangerous element of complacency to the homosexual's sick confusion." She quoted Bergler's claim that "the homosexual's real enemy is not his perversion, but his ignorance of the possibility that he can be helped, plus his psychic masochism, which leads him to shun treatment."[28]

Perhaps the "hope" Haworth said she found in Bergler's concepts came from his claim that "homosexuals may have been tragic in the past, before therapeutic psychotherapy methods were worked out, but today the only tragedy is ignorance, and sometimes, lack of funds for treatment." Unwittingly, Bergler (with Haworth's help) was introducing a problematic issue that would vex gays for many decades to come—that homosexuals were not people to be understood, or even to be pitied, but people who were actually to blame for their own lack of "normal" adult development and who needed to change.[29]

Chapter 6. "Mary Haworth's Mail"

In May, June and July of 1957, Haworth may have shocked her readers considerably, running three strangely similar letters from young, college-age men struggling to adapt. One letter came from a 20-year-old man who described himself as "exceptionally good-looking with an IQ just short of genius and a marked talent in music and art." The second letter came from a 21-year-old college senior about to be commissioned as a respected military officer. The last came from another 21-year-old who said he was "considered one of the most brilliant students ever enrolled at this university."[30]

Each young man expressed dismay at their exchanges with females, the first two men describing fear or disinterest in intimacy with women. In quick succession, Haworth suggested the men were battling feelings of homosexuality (with the third "brilliant student" writer openly admitting he harbored gay feelings but wanted to proceed with plans to marry a young woman). The more open 21-year-old said he contemplated suicide and added, "I want to be a member of the 'first sex,' not the third. But I am not strong enough to do all this without help.... I have hit the wall and it seems there is no place for me to go except down to the kind of life I most detest—bringing shame to my family and friends."[31]

The letters are painfully difficult to read half a century later because of the fear and pain emanating from them. Each of the young men viewed any idea of being homosexual as patently loathsome, and openly questioned their manhood and "weakness" to conform to society's expected norm. Haworth seemed to understand the pain, telling one of the men that "you are far from being a mistake of nature" and noting "you obviously have a good mind with a direct apprehension of the truth of things." She offered, "I think you can have a man's life by clear-headed effort."[32]

Haworth quickly focused on each of the men's descriptions of their mothers as being dominant or ever-present in their lives (and the seemingly requisite absent or indifferent father). Haworth covered familiar territory about how a scenario such as this "primed" the young men for "defensive dreams of distraction toward homosexuality." She opined, however, "this direction is not an irreversible trend."[33]

Urging, as expected, psychoanalysis for each of the young men, Haworth also drew in issues of spirituality by adding, "Strength to save yourself comes from God when you persistently ask for it" and recommending "going for all the help you can get from psychiatry, religion and right associates."[34]

Keeping the "right associates" was at the center of an April 1959

Dear Abby, I'm Gay

letter to Mary from a mother of a 19-year-old boy concerned about her son's plans following high school graduation. The mother reported her son had abandoned plans to join the military, and broken off an engagement with a young woman, in lieu of traveling "to a western coastal city" with two other young men, "one of them an unmarried music teacher."[35]

If the reference to "an unmarried music teacher" wasn't "code" enough for Haworth, the writer noted, "I regret to add that his late hours and evasive answers [about his activities] cause me to feel, inevitably, that a tendency toward homosexuality is developing. I hope I am wrong, but how can we, as parents, help our son to stay on the right track?"[36]

Mary Haworth seemed perplexed on how to answer—starting with "It seems very late in the date to try to rescue a high school graduate from the wrong track of homosexuality, if and after he has begun to follow seasoned leadership over that road." (The "seasoned leadership" Haworth referenced no doubt referred to the aforementioned "unmarried music teacher.") She suggested the "safeguard against such misadventure" (such as homosexuality) needed to begin in the boy's infancy with a mature mother and father who understood their roles (including a father "who wears the pants in the family").[37]

Since the pattern was set for her son's "probable drift into dangerous company, my advice is to get first-hand guidance from a family service agency, or psychiatric counselor.... You need to sort out your foggy intuitions in candid discourse with an understanding specialist. Then you will begin to develop an awareness of how to cope in pulling him back from poison, if possible."[38]

In August 1960, Haworth again took a chance by printing a letter from a 20-year-old young man who confessed to being "headed for homosexuality" although he had yet to act on his "daydreams." The young man seemed defiant about seeking any more help from a counselor or minister, having tried both before. Haworth was adamant that the young man "stop the nonsense of trying to manage your case, and trying to present you are in normal or adequate social health" and get outside help.[39]

As the letter indicated, there was a small, yet growing movement among homosexuals as the 1960s opened that suggested trying to find acceptance or happiness with one's sexuality, rather than the angst and pain of trying to change. Known as the "homophile movement," the earliest gay rights activists began forming organizations as early as the 1950s in the U.S. (and elsewhere in the world), and began suggesting a new way for homosexuals to think about themselves—one that stepped

Chapter 6. "Mary Haworth's Mail"

from the shadows of shame and into the light of legitimacy as a human being.

The evidence of such feelings showed up in Haworth's column in September 1962 as the mother of a 33-year-old gay man wrote in distress about the openness with which her son was acting. She reported her son "frankly stated he just isn't interested in women" and refuses to talk to a psychiatrist. "He is nice looking, a wonderful personality, highly intelligent and has a good job," the mother reported, "but this one aspect of his life disturbs me." To end her letter, the writer disclosed she had left her husband because "he had many of the mannerisms my son displays" and she "verified my feeling that (my ex-husband) was homosexual."[40]

Mary Haworth quickly addressed worries that her son's "condition" was based on heredity and said "presumed authorities" she talked with "guardedly confirmed that one may inherit certain predispositions" from a parent. "But the predisposition need not prevail," Mary said. She also outlined her previously stated positions that "parents who produce deviate sons" often could be traced to families with "a dominant mom and the weakling dad who dances to her tune." In the end, however, given that the young man was a 33-year-old adult, Mary urged the mother to focus less on trying to "change him" and more on "achieving emotional maturity in your own right."[41]

The letters kept coming in—but Haworth's evolution seemed to slow. Descriptive words such as "sickness" and "problem" remained a mainstay in her replies, such as in one written to a reader in 1963 wanting to know how to recognize a homosexual. The reader also posed the soon-to-be-ubiquitous question: are homosexuals born that way or made that way? While the notion of homosexual liberation may have been making initial progress in some quarters, Mary Haworth had a ways to go. "Homosexuality is *a moral sickness* of sorts that has its roots in the unconscious mind and emotions.... I believe it is not so much an inborn bias as it is a by-product of psychological mishandling, probably," she wrote (emphasis added).[42]

Haworth seemed less certain about how to recognize a gay or lesbian person: "Intuition tells you, I think, in the subtler cases. And others, of course, advertise their *problem* in their looks, dress and behavior" (emphasis added).[43]

Recognizing a homosexual was at the base of a sorrowful letter from a young wife who said she had come to believe her husband was a homosexual. The woman referred to her husband as a good father to their two children and a good provider—and as someone who denied he was homosexual after she had confronted him with her suspicions.

Despite the reader saying she did not want to consult a physician or a minister, Haworth said that was her best option. "What kind of solution do you expect from this column?" Haworth asked pointedly. "Are you clinging unconsciously to a childish notion that a magic remedy for the trouble may be found.... That this column, for example, may 'say the word' that will make everything turn out all right? Don't you see the contradiction of asking for advice and, in the same breath, drawing the line against taking logical steps to help yourself, and maybe, also your husband?"[44]

Haworth referred to her husband as suffering from "a moral aberration" and "psychological deformity" and having a personality "not in good working order" and "out of conformity to nature's design and intent." She ended her rather tough-talk with suggesting the young woman had purposefully selected a partner that was "as immature as yourself" and pushed for professional help.[45]

The interruption homosexuality seemed to be to marriages continued with a noteworthy letter in September 1963 from a man who admitted he had proposed marriage to the daughter of a prominent citizen—"the merger of the town's two leading families"—and had done so to meet parental expectations. In the interim, however, he continued a sexual tryst with the son of a prominent politician, and was ending his engagement in order to live with his male lover.

"We are now together again, and we both have jobs and I've never been happier in my life," the writer listed only as "G.S." proclaimed. The letter surely was one of the earliest portrayals of a gay relationship between two men as resembling marital solitude.[46]

"I have accepted myself for what I am and like it that way," G.S. wrote. "Why can't more people show us more tolerance? The majority of [homosexuals] are not as perverted as many would seem to think."[47]

While Mary Haworth was willing to "break the rules" and allow a gay man to describe his relationship in positive terms, her response quickly took things back to more familiar territory. "May I assure you that you are speaking from the shadows of ignorance and from a childish sort of weakness of character, as you try to assuage your valid personal guilt and trying to pass the buck to Dame Nature," she wrote in reply. "You are not speaking from a reservoir of wisdom, enlightenment and responsible knowledge on the subject of human nature."[48]

In a sad ending, Haworth acknowledged an adult man can decide

Chapter 6. "Mary Haworth's Mail"

for himself how he wants to live his life but suggested his life choices were wrong. "Why don't you apply the brakes, reverse your course, and start the steep climb back towards the stars?" she asked.[49]

It didn't take long for a reader to take issue with Haworth's reply—less than a month later a reader wrote in offering criticism of her "advice" to the homosexual man who seemed to be moving toward acceptance of himself. Comparing homosexuality to other "mental disorders" such as schizophrenia, nervous breakdowns or suicide, the writer appealed for more compassion. Operating from a "disease perspective" about homosexuality, the writer asked: "Who chooses the diseases with which one shall be afflicted?" The writer further urged Haworth to "use your column to educate the public and this man's family to the problem of homosexuality as a sickness" and point him toward "sympathetic understanding" that could offer him hope.[50]

Interestingly, the writer was not suggesting compassion on the basis of understanding or even acceptance, but rather as a means of helping the young man change. With such compassion and understanding from his family, the writer noted, "he may be such strengthened to reverse his course when he finds family, church and medical specialists helpfully disposed."[51]

Haworth seemed in agreement and remained steadfastly convinced of the "sickness" the young man was suffering: "It is the homosexual's responsibility to save himself, essentially, by taking the right road, early or late. As he makes the right choice in that respect, it becomes possible for reinforcements to come to his rescue on all sides."[52]

The letters appealing for "compassion" and "understanding" were interspersed, however, with letters that openly suggested, for example, one married man had lost interest in sex with his wife (following her pregnancy) for malevolent reasons. Haworth suggested the husband was a homosexual pushing him toward "powerful undercurrents of hostility to the female sex" and that he likely was seeking "to have revenge on the sex [women] he hates, for reasons deeply hidden in his formative history."[53]

The mother of two sons—both teenagers who had announced they were homosexual—was greeted with a similarly clinical response, including a detailed description from Haworth about the role dominant mothers and absent fathers seem to play in creating homosexuality in their sons. Haworth posited that homosexuality was akin to alcoholism or narcotics addiction that could be overcome with "psychiatric assistance and the help of God's grace [combined] with the patient's willingness to work for moral ascendancy over aberrant inclination."[54]

It wasn't until 1968 when Mary Haworth began to show some openness about the realities of homosexuality. She quoted Dutch psychiatrist Dr. C.J. Trimbos who offered, "Homosexuality cannot necessarily be overcome by psychiatric treatment, but this does not mean psychiatrists cannot often do a great deal to help" and offered that religious or moral leaders could also be of help to homosexuals.[55]

The use of Trimbos' ideas was a radical change for Haworth, who heretofore had followed psychiatric doctrine that said homosexuality was a sickness to be treated in a clinical fashion—with the ultimate goal to create a heterosexual.

Later in 1968, Haworth also gave column space to a British medical journal's suggestion that a Vitamin-B deficiency may be a factor in determining homosexuality. The same column included reports from Protestant and Catholic leaders indicating that people of faith had mistakenly created "a climate of social aversion to homosexual persons" and new advocation for "contact with homosexuals based on human respect rather than condescending pity."[56]

She expanded upon Dr. Trimbos' view of homosexuality when responding to a young man who wrote worried about how to deal with the reality of his sexual orientation. Haworth quoted Trimbos as saying, "No one has ever made himself a homosexual"—offering perhaps an early tip to the "nature" versus "nurture" argument that seemed to have illustrated her views for many years. Trimbos offered: "We can begin to talk about guilt, or rather responsibility, only in connection with what the person does as a result of his sexual feelings and inclinations. The feelings, the inclinations, are not bad, or good as such. At most they are simply a natural impulse as invitation to human action."[57]

One of her last columns regarding homosexuality came in April 1972 from a young man who had just learned an older male he once admired was gay, and was proud of it. The young man was worried about being a "Judas" for wanting to break off the friendship—but Mary Haworth, by this time, seemed to have adopted a "live and let live" attitude. She advised, "Your friend is older and mature for his age, and he definitely doesn't need your quaking fellowship, and probably is accustomed to losing out with various tentative friends, when his homosexual commitment comes to light."[58]

Before she retired her column for good, Mary Haworth told a *Post* reporter that she took particular pleasure in hearing back from writers

Chapter 6. "Mary Haworth's Mail"

who had resolved their once desperate issues. "I found a growing sense of satisfaction in the work," she said, "largely because of the kindly attitude of the readers toward the things I try to do. I do believe absolutely everything I say; and as for 'practicing what I preach,' I think it's easier for all of us to see what's to be done than it is to do it. I try to do as I say, as best I can."[59]

Chapter 7

"Dear Meg"
—Margaret Whitcomb

During her life, Margaret Whitcomb rubbed elbows with some of America's highest society members, splitting her life between New York City, Beverly Hills and Palm Springs, California. Early in her life, she lived in Paris and eventually returned to the U.S. where she served a stint as a media advisor and writer for President Richard M. Nixon, and a writer for *Life* magazine. In Europe, she actively promoted the European Republican Committee for Americans living abroad but supporting GOP candidates back home.

Her European contacts proved valuable as she convinced British media impresario Rupert Murdoch in 1973 to include an advice column in his growing cadre of American newspapers, including *The San Antonio Express-News*, *The New York Post*, and *The Star*, a weekly celebrity tabloid publication. Whitcomb's "Dear Meg" column in *The Star* proved so popular, it was one of the first features offered by Murdoch via his new newspaper syndicate. Her column highlighted her friendly personality so much, in 1975 she started a late-night talk show on WNBC Radio in New York City and made regular appearances on *The Regis Philbin Show* on WNBC-TV. Before she retired, she edited *50 Plus*, one of the first national magazines for senior citizens.

When talking about her column in 1982, Whitcomb said, "I don't have all the answers to all the problems, but perhaps I can help people make decisions that will better their lot." She believed each letter written to "Dear Meg" presented a challenge and wrote the column, "Mostly because people want a third opinion, usually in the case of domestic problems. You know, sometimes people get so involved in problems, they can't see the forest for the trees, they don't know what to do, and an outside opinion can clear the way."[1]

She also acknowledged that some people wrote to her "just because

Chapter 7. "Dear Meg"

they're lonely" and said a full 50 percent of the letters she received were from adolescents. "I understand what it's like to be misunderstood," she said. "I was a problem child even though I was raised by a loving family. By the time I was 19, I was married and divorced, a college dropout, zigzagging around, spending my alimony."[2]

An early "Dear Meg" letter about homosexuality came from a 15-year-old girl who said she felt great pressure to "make her parents proud" since her siblings had experienced many problems. She was troubled, however, by the fact that she had "fallen in love" with a 31-year-old lesbian woman. The writer said she was confused—having dated boys before—but now was worried she was, in fact, gay.

Meg answered gently, "Homosexual feelings are extremely common in adolescence and over a quarter of all teenagers will have at least one homosexual experience. Such attractions are not necessarily unhealthy or abnormal—nor do they mean you are gay."[3]

Another teenager wrote asking for Meg's help with an older male friend who often referred to him as "fag" and "gay"—although the writer said he was straight. Meg kept it simple: "People who resort to name-calling and stereotypes are revealing a deep-seated sense of inferiority." Regarding the name-calling bully? Meg offered, "I'd be willing to bet he has some questions about his own sexual identity and thinks the more he blows his horn about his prowess with women, the more likely they are to get out of his way. I'd do the same, if I were you."[4]

Meg also affirmed a letter from a gay man who urged other parents to keep their explanations of homosexual relationships simple—sans sexual details. The letter was in response to a parent who was worried that their 8-year-old child was asking questions about homosexuals. "Kids aren't born prejudiced, they have to be taught," the letter from "Been There" indicated. "Nor do they have a lot of anxieties about homosexuality; they only care about being 'bad' or different.'" Meg said she agreed—"Your views make a lot of sense."[5]

As was seemingly the case with every advice columnist, married couples dealing with cross dressing (particularly a husband's desire to wear women's undergarments) wrote to Meg either stating their opinion or seeking help. One letter demanded Meg make it clear that a man who enjoyed such activities was not necessarily gay, and another claimed that such activity was simply adding sensuousness to a relationship.[6]

Meg took a libertarian approach, offering: "Whatever turns you both on, honey. You are not alone, and there are many understanding wives who are okay with this."[7]

Dear Abby, I'm Gay

An alternate or unusual relationship also prompted another letter, this one from a 30-something woman who secretly held romantic feelings for her gay male best friend. She reported spending weekends with the gay man and his lover, and was considering his request that they get married and she serve as the mother to his child. In the days before gay marriage was legal, it was an arrangement that perhaps more than one couple considered. The reader asked, "Should I marry him and give him a child?"[8]

Meg was not shy in her reply: "What on earth for? What's in it for you? You will never be number one in this man's life—which is what marriage is all about—and he will never be there for you sexually. The fact that you are even considering a favor of such magnitude suggests you may have hang-ups of your own about marriage. I would not bring a baby into the union you describe."[9]

"Dear Meg" columns published in June and July 1985 included letters from two different women struggling with the same issue—their husbands were slowly returning to their former homosexual lifestyles. Both women reported they knew of the homosexual past of their mates, but now several years into marriage, their mates appeared to be "slipping back into old habits." Meg suggested the men were "reverting to his natural sexual preference—despite what probably was a real struggle to make a success of marriage and fatherhood." She recommended both women contact Straight Partners, a support group for men or women married to gay people.[10]

Family structure was at the center of a letter from the mother of a 35-year-old lesbian woman who was shocked to learn her daughter was planning to adopt a child (not a baby). "My husband and I are terribly concerned about this. Can she legally adopt a child? What effect will her homosexuality have on the youngster? Won't life be awfully hard on a little boy or girl whose mother is gay? Our daughter is a good person, but we feel she is making a mistake."[11]

Meg made note that several surveys of children raised by homosexual parents had concluded that a parent's "sexual preference has little or no influence on a child's sexual identity." Meg said, "I think homosexuals should have the same right to adopt as straights have. There are thousands of children waiting for adoption, and, in my view, it is unfair to deny them the right to a caring, nurturing home solely because of a parent's sexual proclivity."[12]

One closeted gay man wrote to Meg in the midst of the 1980s AIDS crisis frustrated that he did not want to appear effeminate as the other

Chapter 7. "Dear Meg"

gay men he met, and feared greatly the scorn of others due to AIDS. He wondered where he could find someone like himself? Meg seemed perplexed by the letter and said she talked to her gay friends who told her "there's no 'secret' way homosexuals recognize each other. Where do you go to meet them? The same places heterosexuals go."[13] A similar letter years later asked how gay people knew who other gays were—and Meg introduced her readers to the term "gaydar"—noting, "You've heard of radar, well gay people call it gaydar."[14]

Another young man asked for Meg's help on how to stop a false rumor that he was gay. Meg replied in colorful terms: "A rumor, once spread, is as hard to unspread as butter. Your best bet is to bite the bullet and go straight to the source and stop the story." She added, "Unfair prejudice against homosexuality is one of the few forms of bigotry still socially acceptable in the U.S. today and cheap shots that a person is a 'faggot' or gay are especially prevalent among teens."[15]

A 1984 letter from a gay teen prompted a series of follow-up letters to "Dear Meg." The original letter explained how the young man's mother had made it clear that she would rather he would be dead than be homosexual. While Meg reported later that letters in support of the young man ran 5-to-1 in his favor, surprisingly some parents did write in quoting scripture in support of the idea that it would be better for their gay child to be dead.

Meg said she sided with an Alabama mother who wrote, "I'd rather have my wonderful boy any shape, color, religion or sexual preference—alive than dead." She pleaded with the original letter writer to "please don't deprive the world of you because of your mother's momentary (I hope) insensitivity."[16]

An unusual letter from a gay reader came from an elderly gay man who had just lost his mate of 40 years. "I fear being alone more than most men my age because I am different," the man wrote. "People joke about 'aging gays' and regard them as quaint and eccentric or garrulous or silly.... We have a bigger fear of growing old alone because we have no families to look after us, as you probably know, and it is virtually impossible to find a new partner because youth and beauty are such a big part of the homosexual world."[17]

Whitcomb thanked the letter writer for "bringing up a subject that has been neglected far too long" and provided her an opportunity to promote Senior Action in Gay Environment (SAGE), a group of trained volunteers including social workers, doctors, lawyers and others who serve the needs of elderly homosexuals, particularly in the age of AIDS.

Dear Abby, I'm Gay

"A typical problem the senior gay encounters is when a partner becomes seriously ill and he (or she) is not permitted to visit because he's not 'family.' A SAGE volunteer will approach the hospital or nursing home and explain the nature of the problem."[18]

AIDS was on the mind of the sister of a gay man who reported her brother appeared frozen in fear by the impending crisis. "What can we say to reassure him?" Meg suggested the man speak to his doctor and keep up to date on the latest information about AIDS and avoid a sexually promiscuous lifestyle.[19]

Another AIDS-related letter came from a gay man who was in an "open relationship" and that his partner had engaged in outside sex with others. "Now we fear the worst because he is always tired and feeling poorly," the gay man wrote. "[My partner] won't ask the doctor about the possibility of AIDS for fear of being isolated from his friends and others." Meg urged quick action—"Persuade your companion to see his physician now. His privacy will be protected by the ethics of doctor-patient confidentiality," and also urged the men to contact the Gay Men's Health Crisis for help in dealing with AIDS in their relationship.[20]

In November 1985, Meg devoted an entire column to a morose and sad letter from "an AIDS victim" who said he was a 28-year-old Ivy League–educated engineer who had contracted HIV. "Dear Meg, This is the most important letter I will ever write. I pray you will print it," is how the letter began.[21]

The young man noted he did not think he was at risk of contracting AIDS because he was not sexually active in the years he believed AIDS was at risk. "My message to all gays and bisexual men is this: Celibacy is the only way this terrible disease can be controlled. If you want to live, give up the gay life, at least until a vaccine against AIDS is developed."[22]

Continuing, he noted, "There is no way of knowing who is 'safe' and who isn't. People will lie to you, or they may pass along the disease unknowingly. Don't invite a death sentence.... Better to be a healthy hermit than a dying man."[23]

The letter concluded, "It is too late for me, but if my plea saves one life it would be worth it. I hope you can print just part of my message, Meg." Meg agreed she would, noting that "your words of wisdom should hit home with every thinking person, straight or gay. I thank you from the bottom of my heart for taking the time and effort to write. God bless you. You are in my prayers."[24]

Perhaps as expected, follow-up letters came from those who did not agree with all aspects of the letter from the man dying from AIDS.

Chapter 7. "Dear Meg"

One wrote, "I think it is unrealistic to expect people to remain celibate. Gay men should inform themselves about the safe-sex campaign by calling a gay or AIDS hotline in their community. I agree that promiscuity is unwise, but I think few are called to celibacy, whether they're homosexual or heterosexual."[25]

AIDS had the power to change many things, Meg told her readers. A 1988 letter from a man who drove a taxi—and spotted his brother-in-law going into a gay bar—prompted an unusual reply. The man wanted to know if he should tell his sister of what he had discovered, or stay out of it? Meg, surprisingly, said, "Before the AIDS epidemic, I'd have advised you to stay out of the situation. But male homosexuals, especially those who have multiple gay sex partners, are a high-risk group. The gay bar scene doesn't sound promising. Today, I believe most wives want to be told if their husbands are gay and bar-hopping—if they don't already know."[26]

Chapter 8

"Ask Beth"
—Elizabeth Winship

When 90-year-old Elizabeth Winship died in her sleep in a quiet retirement home in Minnesota on October 23, 2011, she was, for some, just another elderly woman at the end of her life. For others, however, she was recognized and remembered as a woman who revolutionized newspaper advice columns in general, and helped advance knowledge and teenage understanding of sexuality.

As writer Diane Anderson-Minshall wrote for the national gay publication *The Advocate*, "When she died, more than a few LGBT fans shed a tear. That's because from 1963 to 1998, Winship's "Ask Beth" was one of the few people offering real advice to teens—and that meant a lot of queer and questioning kids."[1]

Never known as "Beth" by her family and friends—instead called Liebe—her "Ask Beth" column originated with *The Boston Globe* and eventually was offered to more than 70 newspapers across the United States by *The Los Angeles Times* Syndicate. Newspapers in rural or more conservative areas of the nation quickly took a pass on running "Ask Beth," but her influence and reach remained large.

Boston Globe reporter Joseph P. Kahn reported in 1998, as Winship prepared to turn over the reigns of the "Ask Beth" column to her daughter Peg after 35 years, that her column was responsible for breaking a major barrier in the *Globe*'s newsroom.

"Long ago I got a letter from a young man concerned about penis size," Winship explained. "An editor at *The Globe* told me they couldn't print that." The word "penis" violated the standards of the newspaper (and many others, likely) and she was stuck.[2]

Winship consulted with her husband, Tom Winship, the powerful executive editor of *The Boston Globe*, who recommended that she "stick the letter in a drawer for a few months and try again." Taking the advice,

Chapter 8. "Ask Beth"

Winship submitted the column again a few months later "and it sailed right through without a problem."[3]

Not coincidentally, such "risqué" language for an American newspaper was likely more acceptable because it came from "Ask Beth," a column always carried with a genial, friendly photograph of Winship. Her open smile and friendly way attracted many people to ask her questions they would never ask their own mother—but people who still wanted a mom's perspective. Winship, the mother of four children, even authored a book in 1972 titled, *Ask Beth; You Can't Ask Your Mother.*

Kahn noted in his profile of Winship that "Beth's longevity and influence is at once broadly societal and specifically maternal." He suggested her column overcame much of "what we find in the mainstream media these days [which] adds little to our sexual knowledge, and a whole lot to our prurient national interest. A column like Beth's, aimed particularly at teenagers, keeps sharing on the subject [of sexuality] because it knows the correct notes and how to play them."[4]

Winship herself said she witnessed a rather revolutionary change in the attitudes and concerns of young people over the tenure of the column, noting that while early letters from young women asked whether they should "make out" with a boyfriend on a first or second date, advanced to later letters asking whether they should have sex with the boyfriend after one or two dates. Other "new" issues that made their way into her column included sexual harassment and bullying suffered by teenagers, and violence in schools. Consistent issues from the start from teens addressed inter-racial dating, homosexuality, incest, and abortion.

"My guess is that teenagers today can articulate more," Winship said in 1998. "But I'm not sure they mature any faster." Although "Ask Beth" was not originally planned as an exclusively teenage advice column, the volume of letters from teens made the transition easy. "It soon turned into a teenage advice column when I realized how difficult it was for teenagers to get answers to their many questions and problems," she said. "As soon as I started answering their questions honestly, young people started asking more serious questions."[5]

In noting the maturation of her readers, Winship also acknowledged she had grown as a result of the column. She acknowledged in 1998 that at times some of her past advice may have been misguided. "I never even knew what anorexia was," Winship said in 1998. "When girls wrote in concerned about their weight, I was telling them to look into diets. There was a lot of stuff I would not do now."[6]

Dear Abby, I'm Gay

A 1976 Gay Rights March during the Democratic National Convention in New York City reflects the growing gay liberation movement (Library of Congress Image LC-U9-32917-36).

The two topics that drew the most responses, however, were contraception/abortion and homosexuality. In the early days Beth recommended psychiatric care and counseling for gay teens who wrote to her. "Times have changed," Winship said. "I had several close gay friends early on in my career, and so I was getting good advice [from them] too."[7]

Two letters to the editor printed by *The Boston Globe* on the same day in May 1985 reflected the difference of opinion about the topics and advice Winship offered up. One reader from South Hamilton, Massachusetts, wrote that Winship's column offered a "prevailing attitude that homosexuality should be considered acceptable behavior and that our society is at fault for its lack of tolerance." The writer noted that while "unjust persecution of gays" does occur, "I cannot condone homosexual behavior," and added, "What distresses me about Beth's comments is her statement that 'gays' orientation is not their choice' because this implies that homosexual behavior is inevitable.... I disagree."[8]

Another letter, from a reader in Quincy, Massachusetts, praised "Ask Beth" for being a help "at a time when prejudice and hatred are being taught as virtues" and that Winship offered appropriate "understanding and mercy" via her column. "Thank you, Beth. Of late, the print media

Chapter 8. "Ask Beth"

have offered little space for homosexuals to tell how they suffer from prejudice, scorn and hatred."[9]

The very first mention of a gay topic in "Ask Beth" appears to be a September 1972 letter from someone calling themselves "Naïve" wanting to know what the Gay Liberation Front was. Beth offered a succinct reply with no elaboration: "It is an organization which was formed to fight the laws and social customs which discriminate against homosexuals and bisexuals."[10]

In January 1974, "Ask Beth" offered its first full letter about homosexuality from a reader asking, "What makes people homosexual anyway? Is it like a disease?" Beth noted that "the exact cause of homosexuality isn't really known" and outlined that there were two major schools of thought—nature versus nurture. She dispensed with the "cause" discussion rather quickly and went to "the fact that you ask [about homosexuality] reveals another question. Why does our society consider homosexuality a mental disorder?" She noted in history, homosexual love was once "considered as acceptable as heterosexual love."[11]

"Today, many people are working strenuously to rid this country of its prejudice against homosexuals," Beth wrote. "Therapists are more apt to ask patients if their sexuality is giving them satisfaction, rather than inquiring what type of sex life they have." Regardless, she said she was convinced that "most people would elect heterosexuality if given a choice, but I realize I may be quite wrong."[12]

She concluded by declaring, "There is no doubt, however, that it is not a disease and that it is not contagious, either. If you are ambiguous about your sexuality, you could be seduced. But even a passing homosexual experience can't turn you into a homosexual against your will."[13]

"Ask Beth"'s open discussion of homosexuality—devoid of any judgmental or scornful language—seemed to prompt more letters. By March 1974, letters directly from gay youth were included in the column. The first letter came from a 14-year-old boy who expressed fear that "I have homosexual tendencies" and wondered whether the Gay Liberation Front chapter in his community could help him.[14]

Beth replied, "At 14, you haven't got your adult male personality all together yet. How could you? You are just maturing physically and you haven't had any sexual experience.... So it is not a bit unusual for you to feel some vagueness about your sexual identity." She agreed it is easier to talk about sex with his friends than with his parents, but added his sexual thoughts at this time of his life "are by no means indicative that your future sexual direction will be homosexual. Some boys do indeed wind up preferring homosexuality. Most don't."[15]

She added, "Avoid the Gay Liberation Front, because while they are very supportive to anyone who is committed to homosexuality, they present a one-sided model to those who are not. You want heterosexual role models at this stage." Perhaps not convinced the young man was, in fact, gay, Beth added: "Soon you are going to get up the courage to ask a girl out. I'm confident this will put your fears to rest."[16]

A year later, a 16-year-old boy wrote in to report that he had begun to "face the fact that I am probably a homosexual. I tried telling myself that it was just a stage of life … but I know that I am just pretending. I need to talk to somebody, but who?" The young man ruled out talking to his parents or friends—"they would never understand."[17]

Beth's response reflected a compassion many other columnists seemed to miss—and seemed to speak beyond the letter writer and to the greater audience of readers. "Kids who are having problems about their sexual identity must be among the loneliest people on earth. Where can you go for help? Our society places such a terrible stigma on homosexuality that it is no surprise you don't dare go to your parents." She noted most parents—and other adults—have little experience "with this problem" and end up calling their kids "sick, or worse. Few of those who can accept the situation would know how to deal with it constructively."[18]

Winship wrote about what she knew—as the mother of four teenagers. "No teenager would dare confide this in friends, either," she shared. "Most kids in our high schools today won't accept anything that is very different, and sexual difference or 'deviation,' would bring down such fierce contempt and ridicule it would be unbearable."[19]

While noting gay bars provided an "accepting atmosphere" for gays to meet one another, teens such as the young man writing to her who was under the legal age to enter a bar were at a loss for safe places. The "Ask Beth" column then made history as the first-ever to advocate for a teen gay youth program, such as existing "Gay Hotlines" operated in major cities, and Project Lambda, a community-based and federally funded program for teenagers 12 to 17 who identified as homosexual. "Staff [there] work with kids on all problems, whether it be with school or with the law. They also assist kids in their relationships with family and friends, give career counseling, and recommend therapy if needed," Beth reported.[20]

Project Lambda received one-year of funds approved by the Boston

Chapter 8. "Ask Beth"

City Council in 1975–76, but funding was withdrawn after objections were raised. In 1977, the organization reformed itself as the Committee for Gay Youth.[21]

Winship's suggestion to seek advice and counsel from Project Lambda produced a letter of protest in August 1975 purportedly from a young person who had sought their help and complained, "They simply encouraged me to 'come out' and there were strong suggestions that drugs would get me over my 'inhibitions.' This is not what teenagers need in my opinion."[22]

While not being specific, Winship did go in reverse on her advice to seek out Project Lambda. She said she had consulted with two psychiatrists who work with homosexual clients, and even visited the Project Lambda meetinghouse herself. "However, since printing the column, I have received several letters from persons who, like you, complain strenuously about the kind of counseling they got at Project Lambda. I wrote to the director of the project asking for an explanation, but got no reply. Therefore, I feel I must withdraw my recommendation." Winship said the entire episode was "unfortunate" as "we badly need good counseling for young people who are having difficulties in connection with their sexuality."[23]

The continued need for resources for gay youth was mirrored in a February 1976 letter from a writer describing himself as "a 16-year-old, blond, blue-eyed male" who reluctantly dated girls in order to hide his true feelings for other guys. His biggest problem, however, was a female friend who had learned his secret and gave him fear that "she will spread it all over the high school soon. Homosexuals don't go over in my school. I desperately need advice."[24]

Beth pointed the reader to the Gay Hotline in his community and said, "You should get immense relief if you discuss your problems with someone who understands, and knows how to cope with the loneliness and ostracism homosexuals feel in most parts of our society."[25]

One young female reader wrote in to try and understand what it meant to be bisexual, especially given that she held sexual feelings for both boys and girls. "What is the difference between being open and affectionate with those you like and being a bisexual?" Beth was direct: "The difference is whether you are expressing sexual arousal or fondness. Not all physical affection is sexual." She noted, "Gay liberation has made people much more conscious of homosexuality. This produces tolerance, aid and comfort for those in real trouble, which is good. It also creates some groundless fears in young people, which will cause a few problems until we start teaching people to understand human sexuality better."[26]

Another young woman wanted to know if her love of the color purple meant that she was gay. The reader noted that other students in her school had declared that the color purple was gay. "Your schoolmates are bananas," Beth replied, adding: "Color preference is not linked to sexual preference" (using "preference" rather than "orientation").[27]

The silly question about wearing purple prompted Beth to offer once again, "Many teenagers today are anxious about being gay. This is mainly due, I think, to the liberation movement bringing the topic to everyone's attention. What is needed is sensible sex education at home and in school to give kids honest and realistic information about the subject."[28]

Winship's progressive views about sex education and acceptance of homosexuality contrasted dramatically with other advice columnists of earlier eras—such as Dr. George Crane. Homosexuality "is probably not a developmental phase" Beth wrote to a 17-year-old gay young man. "Most people who are going to be homosexual feel pretty sure that this is their sexual direction fairly early in adolescence. They are not confused by their sexual identity, but are very anxious and concerned about what life as a homosexual is like."[29]

A similar theme was offered in reply to a 14-year-old boy who wrote he believed he was gay and was seeking "to be cured." He reported schoolmates regularly referred to him as "a faggot and a queen. I'm losing a lot of friends." First, Beth assured him that it was not necessary to adopt a "label" for himself this early in life, but that homosexuality is not a disease, and therapy does not reverse it. "You don't need to be talked out of or into anything," Beth wrote, "but rather helped to make up your own mind."[30]

Later, a 15-year-old boy wrote in to describe an ongoing sexual relationship he was having with a 25-year-old gay man. Beth declared that "there is some danger in being seduced by an older and persuasive person, especially if it is someone you admire" but took no further issue with the fact that an adult was engaging a sexual relationship with a teenager.[31]

Winship took a similarly judgmental-free perspective to a letter from a young woman who was concerned that her volleyball coach stood around in the girl's locker-room to ensure that every player took a shower. "Is there cause for alarm?" the girl asked. Beth noted that the coach was already rumored to be a lesbian, but that "kids are quick to

Chapter 8. "Ask Beth"

label someone gay, but in reality it is very difficult to know if someone is homosexual or not unless the person tells you.... Even if your coach is a lesbian, you are not in danger" and cited a Kinsey Institute study that "disclosed that homosexuals are less likely than heterosexuals to make aggressive attacks on others. Females practically never do." She added, "If you prefer the coach not watch you showering, ask her to stop. But don't jump to conclusions about her motives."[32]

Two years later, however, a letter from a 12-year-old boy who said a 17-year-old male babysitter had initiated sexual contact with him brought a stern reply from Beth. The boy said his babysitter told him he was gay, "and I was curious and he did some funny things with me. He was gentle and said it was harmless" but he wondered if he should tell his parents.[33]

"You must tell your parents, and you musn't have this boy for a sitter anymore," she wrote. "While one such experience won't turn you into a homosexual, it isn't wholesome to be seduced in any fashion. If you were a girl of 12, and a 17-year-old played with you sexually, I would certainly advise you to tell your parents, to protect you and others from future molestation. Therefore, this sitter ought to be treated the same way."[34]

That said, Winship said, "I hope your parents have the compassion for the isolation and confusion that a gay teenager faces, which probably contributed to this boy's loss of control. I have concerns for him, as well as for you, because of the continuing public outcry against homosexuals."[35]

A letter published nearly a decade later, however, from a 16-year-old high school boy indicated he was having a long-term sexual relationship with his wrestling coach, and worried that it was at risk of coming to an end since his family was planning to move to another community. "I love my coach very much and want to live with him, but it would destroy my parents if they found out I'm gay. What should I do?"

Winship tread carefully regarding the issue of a high school coach or teacher engaged in a relationship with a minor, and replied firmly: "Being involved with a teacher who is older and more mature puts emotional pressures on any student and would be terribly destructive if you were discovered. He is taking advantage of a minor, and breaking the law as well as the professional code of conduct for teachers. A teacher should never seduce a student of either sex. He should be stopped before he pursues other students. Painful as it is, it's lucky that you are moving. It's most unwise for either of you to continue a relationship of this kind."[36]

Dear Abby, I'm Gay

While many letters came from gay teens themselves, one letter came from a young woman who had discovered by accident that her brother was gay. "I always thought he was 'a great brother,' but then one day one of his friends let slip that he was gay," she wrote. "My brother told me that he wouldn't change. This is too much for me to carry around. I can't tell my parents. He says if I love him, it shouldn't bother me and I do love him, but it does bother me."[37]

Beth noted that the young woman's discovery "was a terrible shock, of course" and noted, "You have undoubtedly been taught that homosexuals are evil, immoral and criminal. The Judeo-Christian ethic considered homosexuality a cardinal sin, so we adopted this idea into our social values and laws. But it is not true in other places, nor has it been in earlier times."[38]

She tried to reassure the reader, "Your brother is the same person he always was—kind, generous, loving," and she advised that it was not her job to disclose this matter to her parents. "It is to be hoped that he will himself do so one day," but in the meantime, the young woman should learn all she can about homosexuality "so that you can accept him as he is" and recommended Wardell Pomeroy's book *Boys and Sex*.[39]

Another sibling, this time a 12-year-old brother of an older brother who had come out, wrote to express concern that this could mean he also would be gay when he was older. "For many years people have told me I'm very much like my brother, does this mean I am going to be gay also?" Beth reassured, "The chances are very, very slim. Resembling your brother has no bearing on your sexual direction."[40]

Another young woman wrote to Beth about discovering one of her best male friends from high school had "decided" to become gay now that he was in college. "What would make a guy suddenly turn gay like that? Should I go on being friends with him?" Beth disabused the reader quickly that "people don't suddenly turn gay" and that her friend had trusted her to reveal his true sexual identity to her.[41]

"There is no reason to stop being friends on this account," Beth assured. "Homosexuality is not contagious. Whether your reputation is threatened depends on the prejudice of your college and your friends. You must decide on the basis of how strongly you feel about your friend."[42]

Later in 1977, a 14-year-old girl who had come out to her parents as a lesbian was asking for help in getting her parents to accept her. Beth acknowledged, "Most parents hope their children will be heterosexual," and said that many adolescents experiment sexually. "Therefore, there is

Chapter 8. "Ask Beth"

some justification for your mother's hope that you may just be passing through a phase of development, and that if you meet a boy you like very much, your feeling towards the opposite sex may change. This does happen. Sometimes it does not."[43]

Beth told the young woman that "a parent cannot change the sexual behavior of a child by their attitude" toward their child and that "denial, anger, criticism or rejection further destroy confidence at the very time an adolescent needs support the most." Reflecting her own value system as a parent, Beth wrote, "Parents can be helped to realize that this is still their beloved child" and "they can learn to understand some of the alienation and emotional problems a young homosexual feels. They can help their child strive for a happy and fulfilling maturity regardless of her, or his, sexual direction."[44]

Parental consideration of a gay son was at the center of a December 1978 letter about the difficulty of accepting their son. "Homosexuality is still considered such a stigma in our society that parents finding a child is gay feel tremendous fear and grief," Beth wrote. "The subject was barely even talked about until recently, so it's no wonder your parents don't know how to cope. They see it as a sign they have failed. They believe you could change if you wanted to, whereas the truth is that homosexuality and heterosexuality are determined very early in life, and not subject to much change in either direction."[45]

Another letter from a heterosexual posed an interesting corundum—a young man was dating a girl who had told him she was actually a lesbian but needed to keep dating him as a form of cover for her family and friends. Rather than being insulted by being used, "Chuck" wrote asking how he might convince his "girlfriend" to become straight instead.

Beth suggested that he could not change her sexual orientation, but could convince her "through your loyalty and attention" that he was a loving friend. "But if she is truly a lesbian, you cannot convince her she's not" and that "your understanding can help in this case ... by not withdrawing your friendship, but don't expect her to be your girlfriend."[46]

Letters such as this often prompted Beth to suggest various books that could help—such as *A Family Matter* by Charles Silverstein or *A Way of Love, a Way of Life* by France Hanckel and John Cunningham. Clearly, Winship wanted to offer help—some of the letters received could be heartbreaking, from teens contemplating suicide, or living on the streets having lost their homes after revealing their sexual orientation.

Dear Abby, I'm Gay

A letter in March 1983 came from just one such youth—who lamented that it did not seem hopeful he could become heterosexual and added, "I would rather take my life than live the rest of my life as a gay." The letter—signed "Miserable and Desperate"—obviously troubled Winship. She said she did not want to give false hope that a person could change their sexual orientation, but that psychotherapy would seem to be in order to help him learn to deal better with his reality. "Even if you are not able to become a straight person, with understanding therapy you could learn to accept being gay, and lead a rich and fulfilling life."[47]

The decision on whether to "come out" was at the center of many, many letters in "Ask Beth." In reply to one teen asking whether he should tell his parents, Beth replied: "It's an extremely delicate question. Many parents can accept their son's homosexuality, but only after a very difficult period of adjustment. Some suspect, but prefer not to know. Others find it just impossible to cope with. Parents tend to believe it's their fault and feel awfully guilty about what they consider their child's 'mental illness.' Homosexuality is not a sickness, and nobody is to blame. Parents also worry about what friends and family will think about their child's future happiness."[48]

One parent offered a hopeful letter in October 1982 when discussing how she had dealt with a 20-year-old daughter who had come out as a lesbian. "It just about killed us ... [but] after months of heartache, we discovered PLFAG [Parents and Friends of Lesbians And Gays] who came to our rescue with support. Now we have accepted our lovely daughter and will give her all the love just as we ever did."[49]

The mother wrote to Beth that her initial fears were how family, neighbors and church members would react to her gay daughter, "but PFLAG is helping us deal with this too." She said her letter was written to perhaps help other parents facing a similar situation. Winship was, as expected, supportive, noting, "Learning that one's child is homosexual is a big shock" and praised PFLAG for the help they were providing across the country.[50]

Between 1979 and 1988, Winship's home newspaper, *The Boston Globe*, would run a full-page version of "Ask Beth" in its Sunday editions devoted to singular topics—including homosexuality. In introducing the feature, offered under a title of "Help for Homosexuals," Winship wrote: "It is difficult to have a friend whose sexual orientation is different from yours, especially if he's a male. Affectionate demonstrations between women are permitted in our society, but our men, unlike those in other countries, seldom hug or kiss each other.... The idea persists

Chapter 8. "Ask Beth"

that homosexuals are avid to seduce other males. It's false, but it adds another element of anxiety to straight-gay friendships."[51]

The Globe repeated the feature on August 24, 1980, under the title "Being Young and Gay." For that installment of four letters, Beth wrote, "More and more help for gay youth with problems is now available. Psychiatrists used to fear that homophile help centers would try to solve their problems toward the gay way of life. However, reliable gay organizations bend over backward not to be advocates or 'recruit' anyone. True homosexuality is not a 'stage,' and calling it one does more harm than good. It is not a choice but a condition, not something one can be talked out of."[52]

For the December 1981 installment of a full-page of letters about homosexuality (titled "At the Crossroads of Adulthood"), Winship introduced the letters by noting: "In adolescence, kids are examining what it means to be a man or a woman, and almost all worry at some time or other about their sexual direction. Because society still holds some exaggerated fears about homosexuals, kids acquire unrealistic ideas. Some believe they can 'catch' homosexuality, or that their manners and dress may make them 'turn gay.' Others believe that gays are to be feared and therefore scorned, despised and ridiculed." Beth took a different view advocating for "more understanding or tolerance" for homosexuals by teens—and their parents.[53]

Under the title "Sexual Preference: A Natural Selection," Winship offered another full page of letters devoted to questions about homosexuality in September 1982. She took on the "causes" and any ideas about "cures" for homosexuals in her introductory remarks: "Psychiatry now recognizes that homosexuality is not a disease, nor is it something that people choose. Occasionally a person who has not previously been attracted to members of the opposite sex may change after psychotherapy or analysis, [but] this usually means that the person was not truly gay but had developed a fear or dislike of the opposite sex."[54]

In 1988, the full page of letters about homosexuality took up the risk facing teens about AIDS and provided Winship an opportunity to promote her ideas that the best defense against becoming infected was information. "Adolescents often experiment with drugs and sex; education about how to avoid AIDS is the only protection teenagers have [and] school-based clinics are essential."[55]

The advice "Ask Beth" would give to readers about seeking counsel from gay organizations or support groups was occasionally taken to task by readers. One critic was offended by Beth's advice to a 15-year-old girl

Dear Abby, I'm Gay

suggesting that she may be a lesbian. "How dare you put that idea into a young girl's head? Think of the life you may have condemned her to by such flip and thoughtless advice!!" Continuing, the angry reader identified only as "Horrified in Highland" noted: "You and Ann Landers pride yourselves on being so liberal, but always giving statistics, never a firm moral opinion, steering our young people in the very directions you pretend to discourage."[56]

Beth clarified that the writer had misread her response and emphasized that the young woman may be developing physically or was just not interested in boys. "You can't 'turn' someone into a homosexual, even by insisting they are.... Never mentioning homosexuality dooms hundreds of thousands of kids to suffer in silence, for many kids ARE worried about it. Some will be gay, others not, but not talking about the issue helps neither."[57]

A straight woman who identified herself as a "former homosexual" in her teen years criticized Winship's take that psychoanalysis could not help a homosexual to become heterosexual. The writer reported she experimented "passionately" with lesbian relationships as a teenager, but with the help of a psychotherapist she had changed her ways. "Beth, you do a disservice implying that sexual direction cannot be altered by psychoanalysis." Beth was not convinced, declaring: "I know of no evidence that anyone who was truly homosexual or heterosexual and wanting to change, has been able to alter their sexual direction through therapy. They may change their behavior, but not their true orientation."[58]

Another reader wrote, "I am bothered by the advice you gave," the writer wrote. "Why did you not suggest [the gay youth] go to a professional counselor, or his priest or rabbi? I feel you are just tossing him to the devil when you advocate that he get help from people who are already committed to homosexuality."[59]

Beth replied, "I have been discussing the problem of adolescent sexuality with professional counselors, both gay and straight, over a period of many years.... I have concluded that a teenager having some uncertainty about sexual direction should talk to a straight counselor. However, those who are quite sure they are gay, but very concerned about how to cope with this, should seek help from the gay community. It is easier for gay teenagers to consult people who share their concerns and experience of social abuse."[60]

The "social abuse" of gay people was clearly on display via a troubling July 1981 letter from a boy who reported his high school wrestling coach refused to let him try out for the team because of persistent

Chapter 8. "Ask Beth"

rumors in the school that the boy was gay. "All of the other guys told him I am gay, though I don't think I am. I think he was dead wrong to do this," the boy wrote.[61]

Beth urged the boy to have another conversation with the coach to make sure that the reason he was not accepted for the team are what he thinks they are. "Possibly he was trying to protect you from being harassed by other boys on the team," but cautioned, "Preventing you from wrestling could make others even more convinced that you are homosexual."[62]

The obvious discrimination—based on rumor—against the boy did not go unnoticed by Winship. She said, "Most teachers are sympathetic to students' thoughts and desires," but that if talking to the coach did not work, "you can always talk to higher authorities. I am certain no coach has the right to keep a student off any team for this reason."[63]

Cross-dressing was an occasional issue raised as well—an October 1982 letter being typical—a 15-year-old boy who confessed he enjoys putting on women's underwear and other clothing when he was alone. The boy wondered whether this fetish made him a homosexual, despite the fact that he had a steady girlfriend. Beth advised, "It is not uncommon for people, especially males, to enjoy cross dressing: all men who do so are not homosexual. No one knows for sure what makes a person a transvestite, or gay." Winship said it was encouraging that the boy's mother was aware of his activity and had not prevented it or shamed it for him but cautioned that "it may be asking too much for her to condone it. She probably worries that if the neighbors discovered you, they would be very disapproving."[64]

The first letter Beth handled regarding a transgender issue came in June 1980 from a 20-year-old man who was "longing to be a female" and that "a female is in me trying to emerge." The young man had heard of a surgery that could make him female but needed advice.[65]

Beth said "psychiatrists do not know why some men feel they really are women in a male body, and vice versa" and clarified that "transsexuals are not homosexuals" but that local gay support services may be of help. "And be sure you get long, thorough counseling before you seriously consider the gender-change surgery," Beth wrote. "It is a drastic step and the results are still very controversial."[66]

As the 1980s opened and the reality of the AIDS pandemic sweeping the globe became real to many Americans, it is not surprising that "Ask Beth" began to receive letters about the risk or danger of HIV and AIDS. The first letter on the topic came in May 1983 from a teenage girl who was confused about AIDS and had heard "it was a new kind of tampon, but I hear kids talking about AIDS like it's some kind of disease. Should I be worried?"[67]

Beth explained that AIDS stood for Acquired Immune Deficiency Syndrome first identified in 1981 and causes the human immune system to fail, leaving individuals susceptible to a variety of diseases. She confirmed AIDS was sexually transmitted and spread via intravenous injections. At the time the letter appeared, Winship reported 881 cases of AIDS had been reported in the U.S., and that 40 percent of those infected individuals had died. She also noted 75 percent of the victims of AIDS "were male homosexuals who have had multiple sex partners."[68]

Beth advised, "What we must all realize is that exposure to ALL sexually transmitted disease is greatly increased through having sex with many different people. To reduce risk of uncurable diseases like herpes, and AIDS, which is so deadly, do not be casual about sex. Know your partner. Do not be promiscuous. Condoms and foam are the best prophylaxis."[69]

In later columns, Beth revisited the issue of AIDS and clarified that the Human Immunodeficiency Virus (HIV) caused AIDS and was now likely impacting one to two million Americans. Beth clarified that it was still unclear if everyone with HIV would develop AIDS. As was her normal practice, she listed community-based and government resources available to help in educating about HIV and AIDS.[70]

AIDS seemed to prompt a lot of unusual fears, including those expressed by the mother of a young man set to serve as a summer camp counselor. She was worried for her son as one of his fellow camp counselors was gay. "That man will be there again this summer and I'm worried about AIDS. Is it a risk? Suppose they share the same tent?" Beth clarified that "AIDS is not spread by casual contact" and that the virus causing it did not survive well in open air. She cut to the bottom line by noting, "If your real concern is about your son's sexual direction, talk to a counselor and see how you and he might learn to communicate about it."[71]

Another reader took Beth to task for suggesting that AIDS was spread primarily through homosexual sex. "You should make sure heterosexual couples know they have the same risk. Don't add to the myth that AIDS is God's punishment against homosexuals. People who believe this feel justified in wreaking violence on innocent people." Beth apologized for "giving the impression" that only homosexuals were at risk and noted that in Africa AIDS was most common in heterosexual

Chapter 8. "Ask Beth"

women. She emphasized, however, that "AIDS does not require multiple exposures" and added that intravenous drug users remained at risk. "The risk of contracting AIDS is still very slight if you stay away from needles and practice safe sex. Don't be promiscuous. Always use a condom. Many women now carry them."[72]

Another reader openly accused Beth of being partially responsible for the AIDS-related death of a young man. The reader accused Beth of sharing false information about the incubation period for HIV. "You wrote that AIDS takes eight or more years to develop after exposure. This is the falsest statement I have ever seen printed about AIDS." The writer noted, "A friend of mine died within three years of having been exposed.... Patrick would be alive now if your information were true." Beth defended her answer noting she said it could take "up to eight years or more to develop AIDS," but then said, "I regret this error very much, especially if it gave anyone false expectations."[73]

In 1998, Winship handed off the "Ask Beth" column to her daughter Peg (who had a background in counseling and had assisted in answering letters to the column since 1993). At the time, *The Boston Globe* acknowledged that only about 30 newspapers were carrying the "Ask Beth" column, down from its high of more than 70 more than a decade earlier. Peg Winship noted that at one time her mother's column had been "a voice crying in the wilderness of sexual ignorance" but noted that many other resources were now available to teens, especially since the arrival of the Internet. Peg Winship continued the column until it finally closed in 2007.

Chapter 9

"Tell Me About It"
—Carolyn Hax

Both of the most famous advice columnists of *The Washington Post* came to the job not out of any expertise in counseling, psychology or social work—but instead out of earning their stripes as a newsroom journalist.

The Post's first advice columnist, Mary Elizabeth Young (who wrote under the nom de plume "Mary Haworth"), worked her way into the position from "the women's pages" between the 1930s and the early 1970s, a similar path followed decades later by the contemporary version of the column—"Tell Me About It" by Carolyn Hax. *The Post's* bio on Hax notes that she started the column after five years as a copy editor and news editor in their Style section.[1]

"The column exists because I walked up to an editor one day and suggested we start an advice column," Hax explained. "At the time, in spring 1997, I had worked in newspapers for seven-plus years and at *The Post* nearly five, so I was not new to the media. But I don't have any advanced degrees in journalism or in head-shrinking of any kind.... The column was intended from the start to be the kind of advice you'd get from a friend if that friend were relatively stable and brutally honest and had possibly gotten up on the wrong side of the bed that year."[2]

As the column premiered, it was marketed as "especially popular with the under-30 crowd" and in its first few months had "generated gobs of letters and emails from readers craving advice." *The Post* promised that Hax's "witty prose is entertaining and provides sage, yet hip advice for teens, twenty-somethings, and anyone seeking a healthy relationship." Each of the columns was accompanied by drawings by noted cartoonist Nick Galifianakis, Hax's now ex-husband.[3]

Hax readily noted she possessed no specific experience to offer advice, other than a B.A. in history and literature from Harvard Univer-

Chapter 9. "Tell Me About It"

sity. She is the author of a 2001 memoir, *Tell Me About It: Lying, Sulking, Getting Fat and 56 Other Things Not to Do While Looking for Love.*

Hax's divorce from Galifianakis in 2002 after eight years of marriage, and subsequent remarriage months later to a long-term friend, made headlines as she announced she was pregnant with twin sons via her relationship with Ken Ackerman. She and Ackerman married in November 2002.

She announced her divorce to readers in November 2001 sharing that she and Galifianakis were splitting up "only as married people, though, and amicably" and said that as the "parents" of the column, they would remain "irreplaceable friends [and] we're still humming along, in some ways better than others. Except for being sad as well. I'm not going to get into the details, but I will say I've known this was coming."[4]

The "bombshell" of her divorce and subsequent pregnancy by her lifelong friend Ackerman caused more than a few readers to question Hax's frequent caveat: "Know and respect yourself before you get into a serious relationship." She addressed the concerns directly in her "Live Online" segment with one reader commenting facetiously that she was "just the sort of example I'm proud to see in an advice columnist. [Are you] planning on getting strung out on prescription drugs, maxing out your credit cards or filing for bankruptcy any time soon?" Another commented, "Always thought you were a hypocrite—thanks for the validation."[5]

She attempted to explain that Ackerman had been a good friend to her in the months leading up to and after her divorce from her husband, and that the pregnancy was planned (although the marriage was not). "We had merrily launched a life together when it began to creep up on both of us that we owed it to the kids to get legal" and get married.[6]

She added, "I agree, to a degree, I have certainly done some things myself for which I have scolded others, and worse. I'm hardly a saint. What I don't do is defend these awful things I did." She seemed ready to shut down the discussion of her personal life by noting, "I made a decision the day I launched this column that I wouldn't answer specific accusations of wrongdoing, because that's a no-win proposition. I look bad no matter what I say. So, all I will say is that I have no ethical hangover from Kenny [Ackerman]."[7]

Regardless of the headline-making changes in her personal life, the column went on. Hax told readers she intended to continue to draw heavily from personal experience, "particularly my mistakes, particularly the mistakes that lit up the sky and can still make me wince more

Dear Abby, I'm Gay

than a decade after the fact." She acknowledged that her responses to her readers often carried a pointed, even "unusual tone," but confirmed "I'm afraid the 'unusual tone' is all mine. *The Post* gives me enormous freedom to rant as I please, and I've never asked my editors why because I'm afraid if they start thinking about it, they will change their minds."[8]

In reviewing her column, reporter Mary Shustack of *The Journal News* in White Plains, New York, wrote that "Hax is known for being quick to point out when somebody's making a fool of themselves—or being taken for a fool. She's free with her words" and possesses "a self-described 'potty mouth' and has to keep in mind that her column appears in family newspapers" and offer advice that aligns "with elements of what is acceptable in contemporary culture."[9]

"While no Ann Landers or Dear Abby ... Hax does come across age-old themes," Shustack concluded.[10]

She is well-suited to the task, said *Washington Post* Assistant Managing Editor Mary Hadar, who hired her. "We were looking for an alternative to the kind of preachy columns that were out there speaking to young adults. Carolyn provided a young voice. The idea is she speaks to young readers in terms they can relate to."[11]

The column eventually grew to be syndicated to more than 200 newspapers nationwide and added a regular live "call in" segment on *The Washington Post's* web site hosted by Hax. Portions of that broadcast are later shared with readers of her print column as well.

Early letters to Hax reflected the original intent of the column to appeal to the "under 30" crowd, including a letter from a gay man who decided to rent an apartment with a straight man—one who seemed happy to tease him sexually, while remaining unavailable. "I was prepared to accept him as just a friend.... But then he started behaving in a very seductive manner toward me. I weakened and told him I loved him. Quick as a flash he said, 'I'm flattered, but I told you I was straight.'"[12]

Hax wondered whether the "straight man" fell into a category in between gay and straight—perhaps "graight." The roommate could be bisexual, but she advised the gay man that having spent two years in close quarters with the straight man, a romantic breakthrough was not likely. She accused the "straight" man of being a tease. "It's the classic tease: flirt with someone you know wants you, and watch him/her go mad while your ego inflates." She recommended moving on and finding someone who would respect you.[13]

Another gay man sought Hax's advice about how to overcome his fear of disclosing his sexual orientation to his traditional Asian family.

Chapter 9. "Tell Me About It"

"They have been pressuring me to get married for quite some time, which is in keeping with the norms of our society," the writer noted. "In my cultural milieu, people marry not because they want to, but because it is considered the fulfillment of one's social duty."

Hax said she found parental pressure to be "under glass at the Irritant Hall of Fame" for all people, gay or straight. She went on to chastise the reader for delaying any longer and encouraged the reader to "be their son." She then asked and answered her own rhetorical question about what he had gained from four years of waffling? "Four years closer to not having parents. Four years and no closer to the truth. It's not the pressure you fear, but the disappointment," she said. "Parental disappointment [is] the most crushing kind. They want a straight married son, and you ain't it ... nothing you do will change it. It's over, done with, out of your hands. You're gay. It's liberating, knowing what you can and can't change."[14]

While such a letter invited a more lengthy, thoughtful response, others would get rather short-shrift treatment. A February 1999 letter writer asked, "I'm gay, but some of my 'closest' friends don't know. Do you think I should share this information with them?" Hax kept it quick: "Yup. They can't be 'close' if you're keeping a secret like that. Good luck."[15]

Not all gay people writing to Carolyn Hax were particularly conflicted. One 15-year-old girl wrote saying she believed she was lesbian or bisexual because she felt no emotional connection to boys. "With girls, I'm attracted both mentally and physically," and despite her struggle, she felt her progressive parents would accept her regardless. "Do you know of anyone whom I could get in touch with to help me figure this out?"[16]

Hax replied, "You're 15—you're *supposed* to be emotionally flummoxed by guys," and she said she would benefit from exploring the issue further by contacting support agencies, such as the Trevor Project or a local LGBT Youth Talkline. "Just don't feel as if you have to declare yourself as anything right now," Hax wrote. "You are who you are regardless of society, of parents, of friends, of hotlines.... Labels have a way of creeping in to your self-image and choking off everything else.... Now ask yourself questions, give yourself time, and see where the whole thing lands."[17]

A high school senior about to leave for college asked for Carolyn's advice about how "open" he should be about his sexuality once he arrived on campus. "I don't want to create more problems for myself than I have to," he wrote, "but I am afraid if I am too open then guys will think I'm after them, or I will be ostracized before anyone gets to know me." Hax suggested the young man be true to himself, but also seek out a myriad of campus support organizations where he would be welcomed as a gay man and to ignore homophobic antagonists: "Remember, a homophobe by definition spends more time thinking about men having sex than a man who has sex with men does. These are threatened, insecure people."[18]

A Utah youth wrote to explain an unusual situation where his older brother had come out to the family, only to be "kicked out of the family" by his religiously conservative mother. Interestingly, the gay son refused to abide by the "banishment" and instead regularly attended family events and visited with his siblings. "When mom tells him to leave, he just smiles and tells her that he loves her, and then ignores her," the younger brother reported. "He has told her repeatedly that 'revoking family membership' isn't within her powers. He told her to revoke the law of gravity while she was at it."[19]

Hax seemed amused and impressed with the tactic the gay man was taking in dealing with his homophobic mother. "Your brother is an impressive human being," she wrote. "He's being true to himself, firm but loving with your mom, attentive to his siblings, crystalline in his imagery—be still my writer's heart—all without being punitive toward the mother who rejects him for who he is. Wow." She suggested the younger brother step out of the battle and "balance what you believe against what you need and feel."[20]

The homophobia of family members was at the center of a letter from a gay man who said his parents seemed to blame his gay friends for his homosexuality. Hax replied, "Isn't it interesting that the people who are most freaked out by homosexuality ... are the ones who seem to believe you can catch homosexuality by brushing up against it in the supermarket?" She encouraged the young man to quiz his parents about whether *they* could be recruited into being gay. "Then sit back and enjoy the are-you-out-of-your-mind? chorus."[21]

She gently advised the young man that his feelings were his feelings, and although he has caused others pain, he should not be "so sorry that you'll let [your parents] foist all their doubts and frustrations on a convenient third party." She added, "Chances are, it took time and an open mind [which you may well have gleaned from your parents] for you to embrace this part of yourself. So don't expect them just to accept you overnight."[22]

Parental reaction to a gay child—or at least a perceived one—could

Chapter 9. "Tell Me About It"

prompt emotional cries for help to Hax. In March 2000, a mother wrote reporting she was convinced her eight-year-old son was gay. "He has been acting more and more effeminate" and has increasing problems with his stepfather and stepbrother admonishing him to "stop acting like a homo and start acting like a man." The heart-broken mother wrote, "If he is gay, how can I protect him from the world?"[23]

Hax quickly dispensed with the idea that any parent could protect their child from the world. "All you can do is love your child, and by loving them, encourage them to like and accept themselves. That's where their strength comes from to deal with the raging jerks of the world."[24]

The "outside world," however, was not the only problem—with Hax referring to the woman's husband as a "troglodyte" who would dare to use a word like "homo" around a child. She reminded the mother, "You brought the ignorant thug into the house, so take responsibility and give him some crash diversity training." She was firm: "I don't care which way a kid leans, calling names is unacceptable. Slurs are unacceptable. Fear and hatred and bigotry are unacceptable."[25]

Hax concluded that if the harassment continued, the woman needed to "stand up to your husband quickly and publicly" and said her son "needs to see he isn't the problem, your husband is."[26]

The "openness" of gay family members—and their emerging families that included children—seemed to cause increasing tension among some readers. One mother wrote distressed that her son and daughter-in-law had announced they would no longer attend family events that included her lesbian daughter and her family (including children). The mother asked, "Do you think that children are able to understand this? Will seeing their auntie with a woman wrongly influence them?"[27]

Hax shared that "homophobia takes many forms" and believed it was unfair that other members of the family would have to "pretend" to be something they were not around children. "It's good to explain to children that not all families are the same," she replied. "While there isn't any special age to introduce family differences, it's good to use children's life experiences as learning opportunities ... [and thus] explain differences to children and expand their experience and understanding of individual differences."[28]

Reflecting the new complexity of family compositions, Hax also tried to help a young woman whose serious boyfriend appeared embarrassed and overly angry about his now openly gay father. "I really don't know what to say when I feel his father's behavior has been reasonable," such as inviting his partner to dinner.

Hax encouraged the young woman to ask her boyfriend the next time he gets angry, "Any chance you're really angry about something else? Because it doesn't strike me as egregious for your father to bring his partner to dinner."[29]

Disbanded marriages because one partner "discovers" or at least begins to embrace their true sexual orientation produced letters from both husbands and wives. A July 2010 letter from one woman described a difficult situation in which although she and her husband had divorced agreeably so he could pursue a gay relationship now that their children were grown and gone from the house, he wanted to remain in the closet. His now ex-wife wrote to Hax about the closet she had been unwillingly placed into.

"I feel like my past marriage was a lie for so long, I never want to lie to others again," she wrote. "I need the support of my friends. His family is very hurt and confused and ready to blame me." Under pressure from his family, she finally broke and told his loved ones that her ex was gay and that caused the marriage to end.[30]

Carolyn Hax was sympathetic, advising the woman that she had done her part, helped raise her children, and even when the marriage was dissolving, "worked hard to keep the divorce amicable.... But enough is enough." She defended the woman against any accusations that she had "outed" him as any sort of payback and that "this is about securing needed support and removing the weight of secrecy."[31]

Another woman wrote detailing that she was now 50 years old and been divorced for 10 years after she had "put two kids through college." She had recently had "become involved" with a woman and reported, "I suppose I'm gay now." While family and friends had been supportive, she worried intensely about how her older and more conservative colleagues would react.[32]

Hax replied that she didn't owe any personal revelations to her colleagues and that she presumably was living an overall honest life. "Don't hold back out of shame," she said, "but don't act out of consideration for those who don't give a rat's backside what colleagues do in bed, regardless of orientation." She also zeroed in on the writer's use of the word "suppose" to describe her sexual orientation. "Before you do anything, know where you stand on it all. It's not enough to 'suppose.'"[33]

The decision of a married man to "come out" as transgender after a decade of marriage prompted an August 2016 letter to "Tell Me About

Chapter 9. "Tell Me About It"

It" asking for help. Reporting that her husband now considered himself a lesbian woman, the letter writer expressed feelings of betrayal, confusion and being "weirded out."[34]

"Should I 'fake it until I make it,' or let myself flinch when she tries to hug me dressed as a woman, or something in between," the woman asked? Getting divorced, the woman reported, was out of the question because of their two small children.[35]

Hax suggested the woman contact the Straight Spouse Network for help to talk through her shock and focus on how to be a seamless co-parent. "Going it alone makes no sense," Hax added, and suggested, asking for a reprieve from hugs or other affection for now. "She has had a lifetime to process this; you've had days. You can say that kindly, too.... You can be both thoughtful and real."[36]

As part of Hax's online discussion of the problem, another woman shared that she felt tremendous resentment toward her transgender spouse and was being criticized for not just accepting that only the outside appearance had changed. Another listener noted that the situation reveals that "gender means something" and that "it is not exclusively a matter of internal or external expression. It is both."[37]

Heterosexual friends of married friends and family members often seemed interested in inserting themselves into the sexual orientations of others. One woman wrote concerned that although she had confronted a colleague about her concerns that her husband was gay, the woman was doing nothing to end her marriage, and refused to talk about the subject any further. The writer asked for Carolyn's help in getting the woman "out of denial."

Hax was clearly irritated with the suggested intrusion—she directed that the woman should "never, not gently, not roughly, not with discreet tactical brilliance, not ever" approach the subject with her friend again. "If there was such a thing as boundary school, I'd sentence you to it. Because, oh my wow, this is none of your business!"[38]

She noted that "I'll venture you just really want your friend to be happy," Hax wrote, "but if your idea of helping her to be happy includes a first step of having to persuade her she's unhappy, then that's your flashing red railroad-crossing barrier, your Do Not Disturb hangtag, your singing telegram reminding you to butt the heck out."[39]

A self-described "professional hag" wrote to ask whether the amount of time she spent with gay men was keeping her from meeting an appropriate mate? "I feel very comfortable with gay men, they treat me with more respect; it's like getting the best of both worlds," she

Dear Abby, I'm Gay

wrote. She said straight men seemed repelled from her because "they're scared of all the queers surrounding me" and noted the obvious, "you don't meet too many straight guys in gay bars." She asked: "Do you think I have some sort of 'male issue?'"[40]

Some of the pointed nature of Hax's tone was on display in her response as she noted she hesitated to answer "any question that appears too stupid to justify the newsprint" and suggested her problem with meeting a mate was not just about location. "I suggest you have 'cool issues' that drive you toward a reliable source of attention," she wrote. "What better way to stand out than to be the beloved outsider, the mascot? Everyone knows mascots are cute. And fun! And totally extraneous!"[41]

She advised, "No matter how fun it is to swing with the boys, no matter how strong your friendship, they're getting their real intimacy elsewhere.... You're not their kind of guy [and] your 'professional hag' role makes you more gimmick than person." She suggested the young woman grow up and stop relying on an old crutch—her gay male friends—that was allowing her to escape "the twin burdens of human complexity and rejection. (It's not me, it's the queers!)"[42]

Hax also answered a letter from a gay man who worked as an elementary school teacher. "I do not believe in discussing my personal life with the children, something the rest of the staff seems to do constantly," he wrote. "Because of this, the children are now asking me straight out if I'm gay. These kids are all under 13. How do I explain to them that I am gay, or should I wait until someone brings it up?"[43]

Replying that "I am not normally pro-closet and I can't believe I am about to endorse yours," Hax rejected the idea of breaking the rule of not discussing his personal life with young students. "You're clearly tired of dodging, so make the next dodge stick. Teach them. Explain that their feelings are private until they choose to share them in class—and that the same is true about you." She cautioned, however, that the young teacher make sure his supervisor was aware of the situation, and "prepare for a parent or 12 to protest" and it was important to have support in place first.[44]

Slights and mistreatment of gay people surfaced in a variety of letters to "Tell Me About It," including one from a family distressed that everyone in the family was invited to stay at a relative's home—except a gay son and his partner. Another gay man wrote reporting that although he had readily agreed to be a groomsman in a friend's wedding, he was the only groomsmen not invited to the rehearsal dinner the night before the wedding.

Chapter 9. "Tell Me About It"

"I thought it a bit odd that there was no rehearsal dinner ... [and] I didn't think much of it. Soon afterward, the bride's parents emailed a link to snapshots of the weekend. Several of them were clearly of a rehearsal dinner, with everyone in the wedding party and their significant others), except me."[45]

Confirming that the invitation was not lost in the mail, the gay man reported no one asked him why he was missing from the dinner party. "I suspect the groom's parents (who belong to a conservative religious denomination), deliberately excluded me because I am gay. I am very hurt, not only by the action itself, but by the apparent tacit approval of my friends. Should I say something?"[46]

Hax offered a pointed reply declaring the incident "the social equivalent of a hate crime" and encouraged the young man to speak up. "When friends do something you perceive as offensive, you're not just the spokesman for your own feelings anymore, but also for the group you feel was diminished by the action in question." She encouraged him to act to "abet future offensive behavior" by his friends.[47]

Although Hax regularly took questions related to LGBT topics, she was also clear to distinguish between when the letter was a gay-related topic and when it was not. One gay man wrote to disclose that his partner had been insulted by "ignorant" remarks made by a grandmother-in-law and was pushing his partner to "tell off" his grandmother for her uninformed questions and remarks about gay life. Hax wrote, "This wants to be a question about homosexuality and conservatism and family, but it's not. It's a question about respect between two people in a relationship, and about maturity."[48]

She noted that the gay man reported his grandmother had been generally accepting and likely meant no harm. "When your boyfriend 'railed' at you to 'tell off' your grandma, the real target wasn't grandma herself," Hax said. "The target was your carefully-considered decision to accept her as she is. Your boyfriend is trashing your judgment."[49]

To settle the matter, Hax suggested to carefully consider again whether his position about grandma was correct and if so, explain it to the boyfriend and "own" the decision. "How he responds to that—to you, your judgment and self-possession—and how you respond to him will tell you what you need to know."[50]

Asked about her life as an advice columnist in 1999, Hax shared, "I've been telling people what to do in my advice column, 'Tell Me About It' for two years and two weeks and people have responded, 'Who the hell are you?'"

Dear Abby, I'm Gay

She deemed it a "fair question" and noted that a quick look at her qualifications to be an advice columnist were scant. She admitted her readers were right when they noted "it takes gall to advise strangers."[51]

"Some people out there hate the column, and really, really hate me, and probably hate my dog," she said. "I have a special name for these critics, though: 'Readers.'"[52]

Chapter 10

"Dear Prudence"
—Herb Stein, Margo Howard, Emily Yoffe and Mallory Ortberg/Daniel Lavery

The "Dear Prudence" column, started by *Slate* magazine in December 1997, began with a bit of a mystery as to who *was* "Prudence." Eventually syndicated to more than 200 newspapers (and later expanded to popular live, online chats), the column was offered under the promise that if offered "advice on manners and morals."

The author of "Dear Prudence" was eventually revealed to be noted economist Herbert Stein (father of actor Ben Stein). Stein, who served as Chair of the Council of Economic Advisers in both the Nixon and Ford administrations, was just the first of several "Prudence" proprietors in the life of the column. As *The Boston Globe* noted, Stein lasted only five months in this rather unfamiliar role of advice columnist and "returned to his more accustomed forum, delivering windy macroeconomic pronunciamentos on *The Wall Street Journal's* op-ed page."[1]

In March 1998, "Dear Prudence" was taken over by Margo Howard (wife of actor Ken Howard) and daughter of Esther "Eppie" Lederer (Ann Landers). Howard left in 2006 to start her own online column "Dear Margo" which ran until 2013. "Prudence" apparently had not paid Howard what she thought her words were worth—as she launched her new Yahoo-based column she lamented that *Slate* magazine had paid her "like an honorarium" for her work.[2]

Respected journalist Emily Yoffe took over column in 2006 after having penned *Slate*'s "Human Guinea Pig" column. Yoffe said she brought "my life experiences, many great, some rotten, to the task of answering [readers'] dilemmas."[3] Yoffe remained at the reigns of the column for nine years until 2015 when she announced she was moving on. At the time she told a reporter she had noted some "reoccurring themes" among the letters sent to Prudence: "Mothers-in-law, husbands addicted to porn, impossible officemates, [and] crazy brides."[4]

Without a doubt the most controversial aspect of the "Dear Prudence" column ever came in February 2012 when Yoffe decided to run a letter from a young man who disclosed that he was part of a long-term incestual relationship with his twin brother. Seemingly overnight, the term "twincest" was introduced to millions of readers.

The letter writer explained that sexual contact between him and his twin brother started when they both were adolescents and one of the boys "came out" as gay and was the subject of unrelenting ridicule and bullying. "My brother was the only one I could turn to for support," the man wrote. "We gradually started experimenting sexually with each other. After a couple of years, we realized we had fallen in love. Of course we felt guilty and ashamed, and we didn't dare tell anyone what we were doing."[5]

Most readers did not know the very first "Dear Prudence" author was actually noted economist Dr. Herb Stein, once an economic adviser to presidents Richard Nixon and Gerald Ford. He's shown here in a 1971 faculty photograph from the University of Virginia. Stein, the father of comedic actor Ben Stein, died in September 1999 at the age of 83 (courtesy University of Virginia Digital Production Group).

The two brothers had sought counseling—hoped that they were just "going through a phase"—and went off to college apart from one another. "But we never fell out of love with each other, so after graduation we moved in together and have been living discretely as a monogamous couple ever since."[6]

The two men consulted a criminal attorney to determine whether they could be charged with violating state incest laws. "The sexual aspect of our relationship faded away many years ago," the letter indicated. "We're physically intimate, but it's limited to kissing and cuddling for the most part.... We're at peace and very happy."[7]

From therapy the brothers had been told that "this phenomenon

Chapter 10. "Dear Prudence"

is actually not uncommon among gay males" and had extended their relationship to living together and generally were not seeking long-term relationships with others. Dealing with family and friends was proving difficult, however, and they remained closeted about their relationship "for fear [others] would find our relationship shocking and disgusting."[8]

Prudie expressed surprise at the letter, but said, "I'm going to take you at your word that you two are happy." She suggested they continue to remain discrete about their relationship, but "split the difference in your approach to family and friends" and that making a blanket announcement to them "will give everyone the vapors."[9]

"Ultimately, your choice is your business, but a limited version of the truth should back everyone off," she wrote. "When people ask when you're each going to go out there and find a nice young man, tell them that ... you both have realized that living together is what works for you."[10]

Upon Yoffe's departure, Mallory Ortberg took over the "Dear Prudence" column. Ortberg, daughter of well-known television evangelist John Ortberg, came to the column from her own feminist-based website, The Toast. In February 2018, Ortberg, who identifies as "queer," announced she was participating in gender and sexual identity therapy and planned to transition. "I've spent a lot of time thinking through this and going to support groups," Ortberg explained. "I started medical transition after an initial 'trial period'.... I've been dealing with realizing that the feelings [about gender] I had before were not the whole story."[11]

Ortberg eventually transitioned and came to be known as Daniel M. Lavery and continued writing the "Dear Prudence" column. In its current iteration, Lavery hosts live online chats with readers and experts with transcripts of those published online later by *Slate*.

One through-line that has remained a "Dear Prudence" mainstay is the closing salutation first introduced by Stein who ended each response on an interesting note—such as, "Prudence, modestly," or "Prudence, ruefully," or even, "Prudence, inexactly."

Stein's influence, however, did not include any letters from readers regarding LGBTQ issues, with no such letters on that topic appearing until a year into Howard's control of the column. A February 1999 letter appeared from a woman concerned her new boyfriend might be gay. The reader wrote detailing that her new boyfriend possessed "nearly all the characteristics of most gay men that I know."[12]

Margo Howard—in her role as "Prudence"—wrote, "your gentleman

Dear Abby, I'm Gay

friend could be straight or gay, but he is definitely effeminate. He could be highly repressed, he could want to use you as cover, he could be in denial about being one of nature's bachelors ... or he could genuinely want to build a relationship with you." She urged against confronting the man about the issue and instead suggested she focus on whether a friendship sans sexual contact was enough. "Your task now is to decide if you wish to have him stay in your life as any of the following: a bisexual partner, a platonic friend, or a straight though swishy companion." She signed the letter, "Prudie, empirically."[13]

Another woman wrote in two years later with a different twist on the story—the fact that her openly gay male friend seemed to want to spend all of his time with straight women, and as a result, attracted unrequited crushes from the women. The writer confessed that she herself even found herself "enamored" of him.

Prudence urged the young woman to find a new friend. "This man is playing an odd game" announcing that he's gay, bemoaning the fact that he doesn't have a boyfriend, all the while engaging in heterosexual flirtations. "He's either a narcissistic tease, enjoys causing conjecture, or very confused." She noted the Australians would say, "He doesn't know if he's Arthur or Martha."[14]

Having broken the "gay barrier" in the column, a September 1999 letter came from a gay man slated to be the best man in a straight friend's wedding. The gay man, who noted that not everyone was "fully aware of my 'persuasion,'" was concerned that he would fail at hosting an appropriate stag party (traditionally organized by the best man). Of particular concern was whether only the groom's straight friends or his gay friends should be invited.[15]

Replying as "Prudie, festively," Howard said she did not know exactly what goes on at stag parties and suggested the gay man find a straight man to play co-host. "That way you'll come up with an evening enjoyable for both heterosexual men and nature's bachelors," she wrote. "Keeping a group of men—gay and straight—amused for a few hours should not be all that difficult."[16]

Interestingly, it was the second letter that the column featuring the term "nature's bachelors"—apparently a euphemism adopted by Howard to refer to gay men. Eventually, some readers took Prudie to task for her use of the term, including a gay man who wrote in April 2000 expressing his love of the column, but his irritation at the use of the term.

"I hate to gripe about such a small thing, especially when you seem to be so fair-minded and refreshingly gay positive," he wrote, "but there's

Chapter 10. "Dear Prudence"

just something about that term that rankles. I think my problem with the term is that we're not *nature's* bachelors, we are, unfortunately, *society's* bachelors. If I could, I'd marry my partner right now." He urged Prudie to abandon the term.[17]

Howard, writing as Prudence, explained she had introduced the term because it was "suggestive of the belief that gay people are born that way, that homosexuality is hard-wired rather than chosen or developed." She suggested her loyal reader was being "rather literal" in his interpretation of the term and said the matter would have to remain "a small interpretive disagreement among friends." She signed the reply, "Prudie, interpretively."[18]

Regardless of the moniker she was using, Prudie was serious in her reply to a gay man who wrote concerned that an online relationship was going nowhere because his love interest was only interested in dating other bodybuilders.

She wrote, "Your cybercrush sounds like a muscle-bound moron" and questioned the compatibility between the two men. She urged the young man to think carefully about being attracted to someone he clearly could not satisfy and figure out "why you want what you can't have. Prudie hopes you will refocus, consider yourself lucky, and move on to another chat room. Or better yet, start going out!"[19]

The inclusion of letters regarding gay-related topics prompted a year-end letter in 1999 from a reader stating, "I am not completely sure what your views are on sexual orientation" and wondered whether "Prudie" was accepting or damning of gay people. It mattered to the writer who identified himself as a 20-year-old gay man engaged to be married to another man. The pending nuptials meant both men would be wearing wedding rings and as a result, questions would be prompted about his "bride" from co-workers and acquaintances.[20]

"I really see no need to come out at work," he wrote, "as it could well alter my career for the worse. What should I say to those nosey people who ask for details?"[21]

Prudie seemed to delight that the young man's fiancé was named Chris—a gender-neutral name—and suggested he tell others, "I am engaged to a fine person named Chris, and I make it a practice to keep my work and my personal life separate. I know you will respect my wishes."[22]

Regarding the preface of the question seeking Prudie's views on sexual orientation, she stated she thought "everyone ought to have one ... a sexual orientation, that is." She added that she hoped for a time when gay people could "live in the open with no expectation of career-damaging consequences or disapproval."[23]

Demonstrating she clearly was Ann Landers' (Eppie Lederer) daughter and possessed the same sharp wit, she added that she did not believe in the concept of "Satan" except she did occasionally wonder if he had shown up at her first wedding—as the groom.[24]

Navigating the workplace as a gay or lesbian person was a topic raised more than once, including a 2001 letter from a lesbian woman who said whenever she attempted to befriend a co-worker, her sexual orientation became an issue for her straight peers. "I have dealt with people teasing me, making remarks about my sexual orientation in front of others, hetero guys who get excited at the thought and talk to me as if I were a porno actress they would want to watch, or hetero women who can't decide if I am a child molester or simply an abomination," the woman wrote.[25]

Prudie suggested off the top that the woman likely was working in a hostile work environment, whether she understood or recognized that or not. She urged the woman to be completely honest with others, discarding any ambivalence about whether she was gay or not by "declaring your major and trusting that, in time, even the bigots will regard you simply as the person you are."[26]

Just a week later, however, another reader wrote to complain about feelings of disgust and annoyance they had with "the gay people who feel the need to tell everyone about their lifestyle." The reader declared themselves "a fair-minded person" who believed in treating others equally, but, "the point is, I don't care about their personal life. When I go to work, I work. That is what I am paid to do."[27]

The writer revealed, however, some tension with living with gay people by chastising homosexuals who "come out, for whatever reason" and by doing so "publicly define themselves by a sexual criterion." She suggested the world adopt a variation of the U.S. military's "Don't Ask, Don't Tell" policy to be one of "Don't care!"[28]

Replying as "Prudie, wistfully," Howard declared the writer's position as "a utopian view" and that her emphasis on the word "should" was revealing. "If everyone were as rational and right-thinking (as in correct, not politically right), we would be part of a healthier, better culture. Alas, we live in this one."[29]

As was the case with almost every advice column ever penned, "Dear Prudence" dealt with letters from married women who had "discovered" their husband to have interest in gay sex. One letter writer

Chapter 10. "Dear Prudence"

reported finding a large stash of gay pornography on her husband's computer, and when confronted, he admitted he desired to have sex with men, but did not want to end his relationship with his wife.

Prudence quickly zeroed in on the incongruity of the woman's husband noting that he was claiming he was not gay, but that he would enjoy having sex with men. "That is like saying he's not an exhibitionist, just that he likes to expose himself in public," Prudie wrote. She suggested the married father of two was simply trying to "manage" the fact that he had been discovered without "blowing apart his marriage."[30]

"A pretty good definition of being gay is wanting to have sex with people of your same gender," Prudence wrote. She said the focus must switch to how the matter affects this woman, and not her husband (including health risks introduced if he were to have outside sexual relations with others). Not surprisingly, Prudence urged consulting a psychotherapist immediately.[31]

Another writer—labeled a "gay magnet"—was urged to seek therapy as she was ending her second relationship in a row with a man who later declared he harbored secret homosexual desires. She wrote asking for Prudence's advice on how to avoid getting involved with another man who was secretly gay.[32]

Prudie suggested that if a man seems to avoid sexual encounters or is "more into clothes and hair than you are," that these were the "little hints" she needed to discern whether he was a closeted or latent homosexual. She urged, "Do not become gun-shy because of your history, or you will be come immobilized by the fear of hooking up with yet another *friend of Dorothy*" (emphasis added). She submitted, "Chalk it up to two wrong picks, dust yourself off, and start all over again."[33]

One couple that had married—and later divorced—when the man decided he needed to stop hiding and act on his homosexual feelings, faced a sad reality. The man reported that he and his ex-wife had divorced amicably, parented their one child as best they could, and exchanged cards and phone calls with one another. Both mates had remarried, but the gay man's ex-wife was now terminally ill with cancer. He was seeking advice on how involved he should be as his ex-wife's life drew to a close.

"This is a woman with whom you shared a life and had a child, and your parting was friendly to boot," Prudence wrote, urging the man to continue to reach out to his ex. "Your presence will surely be appreciated, and is appropriate."[34]

Heterosexuals—or at least ones who had declared themselves

such—navigating gay issues was a familiar theme. One variation came from a straight man asking for advice on how to handle serious sexual advances from his friend—and golfing buddy—and whether he should tell the man's wife what her husband was up to. Prudie was firm in her reply urging the man to keep his mouth shut.

"Chances are, she already knows," Prudence wrote. "And if not, why would you want to be the one to tell her that her spouse may not have declared his major? Think, man. You do not need to be The Enlightener. It would serve no purpose."[35]

She did, however, compliment the man who said he was not freaked out about the sexual advances and felt equipped to rebuff them appropriately. "[Prudie] thinks it admirable that you are secure enough not to have a problem with this chap's overtures. A lot of men couldn't deal with it."[36]

Another angle on the same story came from a gay man who called to task Prudence's analysis of a woman's concern that she smelled cologne on her truck-driving husband's collar after he returned from long over-the-road trips. "You shouldn't be so quick to think he's got a girlfriend," the reader declared. "He may just have a boyfriend, or just like the quickies he can get from men at rest areas and truck stops."[37]

The gay man asserted himself an authority on such matters—noting that "just because a man is married to a woman, while he is on the road he does not necessarily have an aversion to sex with a man or men." He suggested Prudie become more "enlightened to the real world." Prudie's reply was simple, noting she was "fanning herself" and expressed surprise that the letter from the truck driver's wife had generated so much interest among her readers.[38]

Another interesting letter came from a gay man who had been chastised by a cousin after he had married his partner after dating for many years. The cousin, who made it clear that she disapproved of gay marriage, subsequently invited her gay cousin (but not his new husband) to attend her son's upcoming wedding. The hypocrisy went so far as the cousin sending a wedding gift registry list and requesting that a wedding gift be sent as soon as possible. Prudence was incredulous, noting that his cousin had basically declared that a gay man was not welcome at the wedding, but his gift was.

Prudie said the gay man had no obligation whatsoever to send a gift, even though it was unknown if the young man getting married shared his mother's homophobic views. She suggested sending his cousin a

Chapter 10. "Dear Prudence"

special "mother's gift"—Jonathan Rauch's book *Gay Marriage: Why It Is Good for Gays, Good for Straights, and Good for America*.[39]

As the frequency—and legality—of gay marriage emerged, Prudence began handling queries from readers not unlike those from straight couples. A July 2013 letter raised the rather pertinent question of when two men are marrying one another, who pays for the wedding? Traditional heterosexual weddings meant the family of the bride bore most of the cost of weddings, though that tradition was fading in favor of shared expenses. One gay man wrote saying it seemed logical that his fiancé's parents, who were wealthy, should pay for the nuptial ceremony.

"The Supreme Court, in its historic decision about gay marriage neglected to address the pressing issue of just who is going to pay for the bashes," she wrote just one week after the court's affirmative ruling for gay marriages. "I will provide the lone opinion that whatever the gender of the couples involved, the precedent should be that if your dreams and your finances are at odds, then it's your dreams that need modification."[40]

She advised against "pressuring aging parents" to pay for the wedding that the couple themselves could not afford. "If your future in-laws offer to contribute, accept what they give without telling them you consider it a starting offer," she added.[41]

Acceptance—or lack of it—from family members could cause significant tension. A 2012 letter came from a father who believed it was likely his effeminate 8-year-old son would likely grow up to be gay. The man's father, grandfather to the boy, disapproved wildly of gay people and frequently urged the boy to "man up" and to "stop acting like a sissy."[42]

Prudie was again in a feisty mood—chastising the father for ever allowing another adult, let alone the boy's grandfather—to "bully or humiliate your son." She said, "I understand your father is from a different generation. But that doesn't excuse someone from being so stupid as to think that if you slap some wrist splints on an effeminate boy and bellow at him to 'Man up, you sissy!' will turn him into a heterosexual."[43]

She urged the man to "address your father calmly but firmly" and remind him that the boy is still just a child and that "he deserves to be respected for who he is and for all his wonderful qualities."[44]

Shortly after Emily Yoffe began her duties as "Prudence," she handled a delicate issue from a reader who described themselves as "an admitted homophobe." The reader noted, "At my university, issues such as gay rights are brought up in discussion and, needless to say, my point

Dear Abby, I'm Gay

of view is not shared by many others." Adding that he had often been ridiculed for his beliefs he made it clear that "as much as I disagree with homosexuality, I do not ridicule anyone who engages in it, and I respect the fact that it is their belief. Is it too much to ask the same thing in return?"[45]

Prudie opened by acknowledging the writer was "entitled to your opinion" but quickly added, "being phobic about any category of people leaves you open to charges of being intolerant. Fair or not, your homophobia will make you unacceptable to quite a few people." She noted that being unaccepting of homosexuals often equated with "unkind, narrow and somewhat backward" thinking (even though many others likely shared these views).[46]

"You are wrong about one thing, however," Prudie added. "You refer to people's homosexuality as 'their belief.' It ain't a belief, cupcake, it is who they are. Perhaps with time and maturity your views will change, or at least soften."[47]

In contrast to a reader who openly admitted homophobic feelings toward gays and lesbians, Prudence took another letter in 2014 from a gay man who was alarmed that as soon as he came out to friends, the limits seemed to be off on personal disclosures.

"Following the heartwarming congratulations and affirmations of our friendships come the lurid questions," he wrote. "Am I a top or a bottom? These are deeply personal matters that I just don't feel comfortable discussing." Prudie supported the gay man's right to keep personal matters personal, but then added another perspective.[48]

A second letter on the same day came from a straight woman who had lived in two gay meccas—Washington, D.C., and West Hollywood—saying sexual topics never seemed to be off limits with her gay friends. "I don't think it's meant to be offensive, and it's often an important factor when I'm trying to set up a gay friend with another friend (goes to compatibility)," the woman wrote.[49]

Prudence was blunt in her reply: "At the risk of being labeled hopelessly heteronormative, I am grateful that during my dating years no one told me that they had a great guy for me, but first wanted to know if I liked it doggie style."[50]

She said discussion of sexual compatibility may indeed be different in the gay community, but it was not the issue at hand. The gay man was talking about his own personal privacy "and he was appalled [at the questions he received], and I say rightly so."[51]

Another reader wanted to know why gay men seemed to speak in a

Chapter 10. "Dear Prudence"

"somewhat high register and often with a subtle lisp." The reader wondered if this was due to a lack of testosterone "or a conscious effort they make to sound like what they think women sound like?"[52]

Prudie—responding "linguistically"—asked a gay friend to help with the answer—who confirmed it was an effeminate way of speaking, but "an effeminate gay way" where "everything is *absolutely fabulous*" and that "voice and mannerisms are a part of the presentation." He compared the speaking style of gay men to that sometimes seen in other cultures, such as among African American people.[53]

Faith and sexuality often collided in the "Dear Prudence" columns, especially so after Mallory Ortberg (later known as Daniel Lavery) took over the column. One mother wrote concerned that her daughter had agreed to a stipulation that she could have help paying for college as long as she remained active in church. The daughter, however, had selected only "openly affirming" congregations that welcomed LGBTQ members. Combined with her lack of a boyfriend, her Christian parents back home were in a sweat. "I'm worried that she might be gay and doesn't feel comfortable telling us because of some comments her father has made in the past," mother wrote. "I accept that I'm to blame too, because I never spoke up when her father said something derogatory."[54]

Prudie cut to the chase declaring, "You must realize you cannot make your daughter one whit less gay by wishing she were straight. Nor can you make her less gay by keeping quiet when her father or pastor says something homophobic."[55]

Suggesting that it is possible her daughter was either gay or bisexual, Prudence also offered that she may just be a straight person who is "disturbed by anti-gay sentiment." Bottom line: Prudie said "support your daughter by overtly telling her that you support her and love her" and leave out any reference to anything gay. "Be direct and affirming; your daughter deserves it."[56]

A 2018 letter from an aunt expressed grief and dismay after learning her sister-in-law had disowned her 13-year-old son after he disclosed he was gay. "His father and mother packed a bag, locked the door, and left him on the front porch homeless," the woman reported. "I drove three hours to pick him up and we have spent the summer getting legal custody and involving him in a LGBTQ-friendly school."[57]

Disturbing the situation now was that the boy's parents now seemed to want him back and continued to express interest in what he was doing and how his life was proceeding. "My husband doesn't understand why I can't be 'civil' to his sister, and I think he needs to focus on what is best for the child in our care rather than the bitch who abandoned her only child," the woman wrote.[58]

Prudie agreed that the young man was in need of more attention than the mother who had dumped her child—"it's his nephew who is actually vulnerable and in need of support." She added, "He's prioritizing civility over actual kindness—it's nice to be polite, but it's far more important to treat children like human beings who deserve love, safety and support, rather than yank that love and support away on the condition of their orientation."[59]

It was an issue Prudie—now written by Ortberg/Lavery had likely confronted personally as he reportedly remained estranged from his highly religious parents. This may have guided the reply ending with "Hope for the best but prepare for the worst."[60]

Acceptance of homosexuality was at the center of an emotional letter from a 70-year-old woman who was once married and raised several children and came out as a lesbian many years later. She was writing Prudence after being chastised by her daughter and her Christian fundamentalist husband who objected to a baby book she presented that included same-sex parents. The letter, she said, "felt like a stab in the heart."[61]

"Dear Prudence" cut through the issue and noted that her daughter and son-in-law were using the book to express disapproval of her being a lesbian. "They say they are writing to you out of religious conviction, but their nasty and gratuitous attack surely violates the commandment to 'Honor thy Father and thy Mother.'" Prudie recommended the woman reach out to her daughter and emphasize her desire to simply be a good grandmother to her granddaughter.[62]

Prudie was less understanding, however, when a gay couple wrote to express their disgust after a contractor they hired wore a hat with an American flag on it while working in their home. The gay man wrote they felt attacked by American culture and that the flag "was a sickening reminder of my childhood in rural America." They asked Prudence whether they should fire their contractor and hire another.[63]

"When did the American flag come to mean 'I want to assault gay people'?" Prudence asked. "You know nothing about this man's views except that he feels patriotic.... Do you really want to require that the person building your breakfast nook pass your political litmus test?" She added she found it unfortunate that people had sworn off friendships or interactions with those with varying political views. She suggested, "Let the guy with the American flag cap get to work."[64]

Chapter 10. "Dear Prudence"

Workplace issues arose, however, in a variety of ways including a troubling 2015 letter to "Dear Prudence" from a gay man who worked as a waiter in a restaurant. The man, who was half–Mexican, said the kitchen staff where he worked spoke almost exclusively in Spanish and often called him a "faggot" and other derogatory terms in Spanish in his presence. "I feel like I'm being bullied in grade school because nearly half the staff makes jokes about me in a language they think I can't understand," he wrote.[65]

He noted the difficulty of approaching management and "tattling" on co-workers, but, "I dread almost every shift I work because I know I'm going to hear them and I know there's little I can do about it."[66]

Prudence admitted the situation was "a lousy dilemma" but surprisingly noted, "Resign yourself to being called names at work, or face subtle (or overt) resistance from a group of people whose cooperation you need to do your job."[67]

She noted the man was "not being hypersensitive" and that "no one should have to hear people making cruel and homophobic jobs at their expense at work" but she offered a new alternative. Short of telling management of the problem, or quitting the job, she suggested telling the offending kitchen staff (in Spanish) "that you understand what they're saying and tell them to knock it off."[68]

In the end, if the bullying did not stop, Prudence said either the man would have to quit or the kitchen staff should be fired.

Transgender issues were raised in the "Dear Prudence" column before Ortberg/Lavery took over and took her readers along as he transitioned from female to male. A 2012 letter (handled by Emily Yoffe who was in the "Prudie chair" at that time) came from a woman whose open attitudes toward transgender people was challenged by her husband's disclosure that he wanted to become a woman.

"Initially I promised to remain married (to my spouse) during her transition and for some time afterward," the woman wrote, "to give our marriage a chance to adjust to her transition and sex change." Three months later, however, the letter writer proclaimed, "I am miserable."[69]

She said the transition had helped her to see that much of her love for her husband was "rooted in his manhood" and as the transition to becoming a woman went forward, she felt less and less romantic feelings for her. "Everyone commends me for supporting her and sticking with our marriage, so I feel like a fraud now," she confessed, asking whether it was still acceptable to leave the marriage.[70]

In the understatement of the world, Yoffe wrote that "people change and grow during the course of a marriage" but added, "If your husband confesses to you he plans to start growing breasts, he has so materially changed the contract of your marriage that I completely understand that you feel the husband you knew has died."[71]

Prudie praised the fact that the woman had tried—and still loved her spouse—but said it was perfectly acceptable to move on from the marriage, remain friends and support her spouse emotionally, and accept that "realizing your husband's change of life requires you to make your own."[72]

Ortberg/Lavery handled a sensitive issue involving a transgender issue in 2018 when a woman wrote concerned that her 28-year-old heterosexual daughter had begun dating a transgender man. The mother—using the "they" and "their" pronouns to refer to her daughter's boyfriend—said the entire matter confused her and she was uncomfortable at the "flamboyant and attention-getting behavior" the new love interest displayed. "I feel like my daughter is being used as a testing ground," she wrote.[73]

Prudence skipped past the transgender issue at hand and noted that there was not much a parent could—or should—try to do about who their 28-year-old child was dating. In standard form, she suggested that she let her daughter "make her own mistakes, enjoy things you find baffling, and generally [let her] wind her way through life."[74]

To conclude, however, Prudie decided to offer some help in discussing matters of gender. She noted the woman's "genuine lack of familiarity with terms, identities and what's within the limits of polite discussion" and encouraged her to refer to PFLAG "to learn the basics."[75]

"I think the person you should be asking 'gently probing questions' of in this case is *you*.... What am I really afraid of here? Why do I want to control what I can't, and how will I maintain inner peace and calm if my daughter continues to date someone who makes me feel so off-guard?"[76]

CHAPTER 11

"Ask Amy"
—Amy Dickinson

The name selected for the "Ask Amy" advice column was not an original creation by the editors of *The Chicago Tribune* as they went looking for a replacement for their franchise star, Ann Landers, who died in 2002. *The Atlanta Constitution* and eventually other newspapers (via syndication) ran a column under the name "Ask Amy" for their "women's pages" and was "geared to problems of teenagers."[1] The column, penned by an author known as Amy Adams, was syndicated between 1959 and 1971.

The new incarnation of "Ask Amy" columnist Amy Dickinson, was born in 1959, the same year the previous column of that name was taking off. A farm girl raised in Freeville, New York, she attended Georgetown University, and married CBS News correspondent Anthony Mason shortly afterward. Their marriage ended after four years in 1990, and produced one child, daughter Emily Mason. She later married an upstate New York builder named Bruno Schickel in 2008, and in between pursued more than two decades as a successful journalist and columnist.

Dickinson established a notable career in journalism, working for NBC News, *Esquire* magazine and the Oprah Winfrey magazine, *O*. She even launched one of the earliest "online" advice columns soon after the arrival of America Online. She has written two personal memoirs, *The Mighty Queens of Freeville: A Mother, a Daughter, and the Town That Raised Them*, published in 2009, and *Strangers Tell Me Things: A Memoir of Love, Loss and Coming Home*, published in 2017.

The Chicago Tribune marketed Dickinson's new column under the theme of "ask Amy anything" and informed readers that Dickinson was the great-granddaughter of the warden of the Sing Sing Prison, the great niece of an uncle who ran off to join the circus, and a distant relative of

Dear Abby, I'm Gay

author Emily Dickinson—"so our new advice columnist is not inclined to judge your family's problems too harshly." In selecting Dickinson, *The Tribune* touted that "we looked for someone with a no nonsense attitude and a voice as fresh as today."[2] The column debuted on Sunday, July 20, 2003.

Successful from the start, it wasn't until Dickinson was 10 years into her column that she permanently solidified herself among the hearts and minds of a legion of gay readers. Her response to a November 2013 letter from a parent expressing embarrassment about their gay son gained national attention—"went viral"—after it was retweeted by out-actor George Takei (followed by more than 10 million people).

Reporter Gregg Shapiro, writing for ChicagoPride.com, observed that Dickinson's open dealing with the parents and their repressed feelings demonstrated her "embrace of the LGBT community, which differs greatly from her late-to-the-table predecessor, Ann Landers."[3]

Dickinson told Shapiro that prior to becoming an advice columnist she was not naturally someone that others sought out for advice. "I'm the youngest in a large family, and I'm more likely to take advice and ask for advice than to offer it," she said. She believes the need for advice never diminishes, however. "I think that is because modern lives are fragmented and people are really looking for a sense of community," she said. "People share so many of the same problems and concerns."[4]

Dickinson said "Ask Amy" is committed to running the letters she receives worded just the way they came into her "because I really like the way people express their own problems. I think they are revealing in the way they choose to write to describe their own problem.... I don't want people to get burned by their own indiscretions, but otherwise, I do very little editing."[5]

Admitting that she feels a bit "trapped" by the Q&A format of the advice column that is typically limited to 700 words or less each day, she is pleased *The Tribune* offers an online option. "My answers tend to be longer than in other advice columns in newspapers, and one of the great things about [publishing it also] online is that you don't have length constraints," she said.[6]

Regarding her positions on the "place" of gay people in society and the family, she proclaims, "I have not changed my stand, so to speak, on LGBT issues in 10 years. I've been saying the same thing over and over and over again." She offered that her relationship with the gay community "is hard for me to describe," but adds, "I feel like the gay community is just looking for people to love, in a way. I feel that I have been

Chapter 11. "Ask Amy"

embraced, honestly, for no particular reason, just because I'm a decent human being. I would say that this is the most significant cultural issue in my professional life.... The LGBT community has just grown, blossomed changed and come into his own. It's really a beautiful thing."[7]

The "viral" letter that helped cement Dickinson's place among many LGBTQ readers was published on November 18, 2013, from the parent of a 17-year-old young man whom they had "discovered" was gay. "We are part of a church group and I fear that if people in that group find out, they will make fun of me for having a gay child," the parent wrote. "He won't listen to reason, and he will not stop being gay. I feel as if he is doing this just to get back at me for forgetting his birthday for the past three years."[8]

Dickinson seemed to view the letter as ridiculous from the start, first offering that the parent "could teach your son an important lesson by changing your own sexuality to show him just how easy it is." She suggested the "betrayed parent" try being homosexual for at least a year "to demonstrate to your son that a person's sexuality is a matter of choice—to be dictated by one's parents, the parents' church and social pressure."[9]

Dickinson noted that her ridiculous suggestion likely struck at the base of the parent's problem who seemed to understand their own sexuality "is at the core of who you are. The same is true for your son." She added, "He has a right to be accepted by his parents for being exactly who he is." She ended the matter by suggesting the parents find a new group—one that could assist them in learning to accept their son as he is.[10]

In the weeks that followed, Dickinson reported to her readers that "the outpouring of response tells me that this is a situation that is sadly familiar to many gay people." She ran another letter on December 27, 2013, from a gay reader who cautioned that that the "abuse" of a gay child by their parents can pose "an emotional threat" to gay teens for years to come. A January 2014 letter under the pen name "It Got Better" posed the question of whether a gay child should seek reconciliation with parents who had rejected them earlier. Readers and Amy noted it was appropriate to "set limits for yourself when it comes to family relationships" and that biological families don't always fit, but families one creates do.[11]

As did other advice columnists, "Ask Amy" took a fair share of letters from heterosexual readers seeking how to understand or "deal" with friends or family they suspected were gay. A January 2004 letter

Dear Abby, I'm Gay

from one reader wondered about her female friend who spent time with both heterosexual and homosexual friends. "In today's day and age, is it acceptable to ask a good friend what their sexual connotation is?" Amy clarified that the correct term to use was "sexual orientation" and that while it was really none of anyone's business, it was probably OK to gently ask if her friend had a girlfriend or a boyfriend. "If she gives you an ambiguous answer, consider it the beginning of your education into human sexuality. Some people are this, some are that, some both or neither."[12]

Another writer, a gay man, lamented that his heterosexual friends never seemed to approve of the men he chose to date. Amy considered the case presented and noted, "It's hard when the people who love you don't love your choices, and it's especially hard to face the fact they might be right." Amy said her read of the situation indicated the potential beau was "a relationship train wreck," but advised if the reader decided to go forward, to always practice safe sex.[13]

A married heterosexual couple wrote to disclose that the ongoing political debate about gay marriage had caused them to realize they did not "really understand what makes a person homosexual." Amy reported she had never been "flummoxed by this thorny issue" accepting that sexuality existed on a continuum and that "no two people are exactly alike, sexually or otherwise." She advised to stop worrying about why a person was gay, and to focus more on accepting them as they are.[14]

In August 2009, Amy reported that no topic featured in her column had raised as much response as did a letter from a parent upset that her son's college would not allow him to request an alternate roommate because of his concern about sharing a room with a gay student. The original letter detailed how university officials had told the young man and his parents that a room change would "persecute" the gay student and that if they did not want to accept the room assignment, the young man was free to attend college elsewhere.

"I was taken aback," the boy's mother wrote. "The university is a Jesuit school and has no policy for gay-straight roommates, other than that they don't permit discrimination." The mother said she did not view it as discrimination (and boasted her older children had shared dorm rooms with people of different races, religions and nationalities). She asked Amy if she agreed the university was handling the matter in the wrong manner.[15]

Amy pointed out that the mother seemed to be "drawing the line at sexual orientation" when it came to discrimination and said she agreed

Chapter 11. "Ask Amy"

with the university. "You could help your son by assuming that he will have a successful roommate experience," and that many factors could determine that (including getting a compatible roommate, or one who stays out late, drinks, smokes, etc.). "Saying 'my roommate is gay' is not a valid reason in and of itself to switch roommates any more than saying 'my roommate is Asian' would be. This is your son's issue to sort out on his own."[16]

Dickinson said letters poured in reflecting a "heated response" to her reply to the mother—another writer likening forcing a straight young man to room with a gay man as the same as forcing a young woman to room with a young man. Amy noted the letter she chose to print in reply was "among the more civilized expressions of the most commonly held view" but that those views seemed to come from older readers, and not college-age students.

While not backing down from her answer, Dickinson explained she was responding to what she viewed as a discriminatory response from the letter writer which was based on stereotypical assumptions. "Colleges give students the opportunity to switch roommates," Amy noted. "This enables incompatible people to make changes." With that, she closed the subject.[17]

The contrast between the views of younger and older readers was often on display in the column, reflected in a May 2008 letter from a man claiming to be a high school teacher who held fast to the idea that "homosexuality is a choice and a very bad and unnatural one at that. It is moral perversion, and it is sex outside of marriage. I have two daughters 12 and 10, and they won't ever hear me say it is OK to be gay." Amy showed no pause, replying that it was quite likely a good portion of the students where he taught were gay "and whether or not they are foolish or naïve enough to admit it to you.... I can only hope that your thinking evolves and that you learn to withhold judgment of people based on such an elemental issue as their sexuality."[18]

Not surprisingly, the exchange drew response letters, but almost entirely in support of Amy's position. One heterosexual man wrote to say, "I can state unequivocally that I do not have a choice to be gay. It is against my nature. To me, those who say it's a choice are either bisexual or are repressing their own feelings of homosexuality." Amy agreed, noting that those who think sexual orientation is a choice were wrong—"it's a choice I, for one, never remember making."[19]

Reflecting the era in which "Ask Amy" has existed, salient political issues related to LGBTQ Americans have repeatedly surfaced in the column, most notably gay marriage. As expected, letters appeared both in support and opposition to same-sex unions. One devoted reader wrote, "I find it repulsive that you would praise [gay marriage], something Christians and moralists view as a sinful and shameful lifestyle." The writer said that as a syndicated columnist, "you have a duty to the reading public to exhibit high ideals." Amy offered a dismissive and uncharacteristically brief reply: "OK, I reconsidered. And I still feel the same way. You're welcome."[20]

Another reader wrote worried that his mother refused to attend his marriage to another man because she "doesn't believe in gay marriage." Amy took a lighter tone in replying, noting that "gay marriage isn't like Santa Claus—it's not something you 'believe in.' It simply is."[21]

The gay marriage debate could strike deep, however, with a straight man writing to report his brother had accepted, and then refused an invitation to be best man in his wedding. The gay brother had alienated many of his family members by refusing to be a part of his brother's wedding (or to participate in any other heterosexual weddings) until or unless his family openly accepted his need and desire to marry his partner. Amy seemed to struggle with which side to be on but offered that the gay man was "driving a political stake through the heart of an institution he aspires to be part of" (while urging the brother to select another best man).[22]

As the proposal to ban marriage (Proposition 8) battle raged in California during the 2008 election cycle, another gay man wrote in with an all-or-nothing response noting that he had researched online petition drives for and against same-sex marriage. He was hurt and offended to find the names of some of his friends on opposing lists. "It is important to me to know that I have their support of gay marriage" and that without it, "it will be impossible for me to continue these friendships."[23]

Amy seemed circumspect in her response noting that she understood how important the issue was for gay people wishing to be married, but "your friends are already in your corner, that's what makes them your friends. Demanding that your friendship hinge on what people choose to do in the privacy of the voting booth is offensive.... I'd suggest that you tread very lightly."[24]

Some relationships, however, couldn't be saved—as Amy noted in response to a gay man who asked about the idea of "divorcing his family" after their open rejection of him and his partner. Amy noted that there was no provision in law that allowed one to officially "divorce" one's family, but "you are going to have to lead with your heart. Do what you are

Chapter 11. "Ask Amy"

going to do, accept that which you cannot change, and get on with your life." She acknowledged the sheer pain involved with such rejection but urged the man to "release your pain and resentment and choose to move forward." This included plans to marry his partner—"That's the beauty of marriage. You finally get to choose whom you will be related to!"[25]

In a letter that could have been written decades earlier, one of Amy's readers asked for advice about her fiancé who had waffled in the past on whether he was gay or not. Her question was a simple one: Should she proceed with the marriage? Amy noted that her male friend's sexuality seemed little in doubt—that any straight man would never leave the question of their sexuality in play—but that "at some point, your waffling over your boyfriend's sexuality is as vexing as his own" and added, "If you are aiming for a straight forward marriage with a fully heterosexual guy, I think you'd better look elsewhere. If you want a life of sexual game playing, you've got it."[26]

An organization known as the "Straight Spouse Network" was touted by Dickinson on more than one occasion to readers—mostly women—writing in to report they had discovered or come to know that their spouse was actually homosexual. One woman wrote that when she learned of her husband's gay desires, "There were no words to describe the degree of devastation to our marriage and our children. Everything that I thought was real became undone." But the woman wanted others to know that "a lifeline" existed—via the Straight Spouse Network—including in-person support and talk groups, focus on mental and physical health, and keeping families close amidst separation or divorce.[27]

Another familiar trope was introduced by a single man in his 30s who had grown weary of people assuming he was gay. He wondered whether in contemporary times whether it was impossible for a man to live as a single heterosexual man. "Ask Amy" assured him that it was.[28]

One gay man revealed that his brother was suddenly making life difficult following his marriage to a fundamentalist, conservative Christian woman who viewed homosexuality as "mortal sin." Amy acknowledged the pain that went with the situation, but added, "All of us lucky enough to be in a family are also saddled with the fear of being judged by them." She encouraged him to be polite to his brother, and not to assume his nieces and nephews would inherit similarly bigoted views.[29]

Use of the word "bigoted" prompted a few complaint letters, one reader writing she was offended that it was "arrogant" to assume that religious people who struggled with accepting gay people were automatically bigoted. "Having differing opinions and world views does not automatically make a person a bigot," the reader wrote. "It makes them diverse."[30]

Amy seemed to back down from her "bigot" remark saying that upon further review, the original letter did not seem to indicate a high level of bigotry aimed at the gay man. She noted her use of the word may have been in conflict with "the thrust of my answer—that tolerance comes in many forms and few of us receive unqualified endorsement from our family." She then apologized for the word "bigot."[31]

Not all family interactions were fraught with hurt and pain—Amy sharing one letter from a gay man who said he and his partner got a good laugh over the greeting cards coming from his mother-in-law addressed to "My Son and His Wife." The addled mother-in-law meant no harm, charmingly noting that she couldn't find a card for "My Son and His Husband." The gay men said they remembered the now departed loved one with a smile over her frequent cards.[32]

"Modern family problems" were at the center of a March 2004 letter from a gay man who said he caught his allegedly straight father and brother-in-law having sex together in the family swimming pool while their wives were away. The gay man's father begged his son not to tell anyone, an abuse of their relationship, Amy surmised. "This behavior is particularly despicable" and she noted she hoped the betrayed women would find out the truth on their own. If not, Amy suggested the man present his father with an ultimatum to tell the truth, or he would.[33]

Unusual family problems arose again for Amy when a mother wrote concerned that her daughter had married a man she knew was gay, and subsequently they both had decided to pursue homosexual sexual relationships outside of their marriage. To complicate matters, the woman's daughter was seeking permission to bring her female lover with her—along with her husband bringing his male lover—to the family's Thanksgiving dinner.

Amy seemed to understand the odd nature of the query, offering, "Your openness and liberal attitude about diversity are beautiful. Now your daughter is whacking you over the head with it. Don't let her." She recommended mom "stop bending over backward to understand and accommodate" the "chaotic" nature of the open relationships her daughter and son-in-law pursued.[34]

"This isn't a gay thing," Amy insisted. "This is a question of your daughter stepping way over the line.... Let's agree that this sort of

Chapter 11. "Ask Amy"

arrangement isn't quite what the Indians and Pilgrims had in mind when they sat down together for their first feast."[35]

Another modern family issue came from a gay man writing to complain that his long-term partner's teenage children were driving a wedge between them by living with them instead of their mother. The gay man wrote he had newfound respect for "breeders," but added: "I am not cut out to be a stepmom; nor did I envision that in my 40s I'd be dealing with adolescents.... I am torn between the need to help these kids and the desire to have my old life back."[36]

Amy took umbrage to the term "breeders" saying it "sticks in my craw and I wish you and others wouldn't use it." With that, she dispensed with offering that a gay stepparent's responsibilities were the same as a straight stepparent. She advised counseling, but noted, "Thoughtful stepparents sometimes find that the wisest course of action is to concentrate less on the kids and more on supporting the partner—if you watch his back, he can focus on his children."[37]

The "gay discovery" conundrum was at the center of an unusual letter from a few "Florida snow birds" who reported the 17-year-old boy they had hired to "pet sit" with their dog had, on occasion, used his access to their home to visit gay porn sites on their computers. The elderly couple fired the young man, changed their locks but still wanted to know if they should tell the young man's parents about his less-than-discrete online habits.

Amy advised talking to the young man before involving the parents. "Start by focusing on the computer usage," she said, and forget other issues they had. "You don't need to focus on the content of his surfing or make all sorts of assumptions about this young man's sexuality." She endorsed changing the locks and advised them to find another dog sitter.[38]

Homophobia could present itself in a variety of formats in "Ask Amy," one mother writing expressing concern about an invitation her 16-year-old son had received to travel with one of his art teachers to see soccer games in Manchester, England, over summer break. The mother admitted the man was a married father, "but that doesn't guarantee his sexual orientation" or his intentions with their son.

Amy believed it was inappropriate for a high school teacher to invite a teenaged student on such a long and elaborate trip. "This teacher's sexuality has nothing to do with it," she wrote. "He could be gay, your son could be gay, but as you may know, homosexuals are no more likely to be predators than anybody else." For Amy, the issue was that a teenager had no business traveling so far from home with adults other than his parents. She further advised the parents to report the teacher to the school so that he could be "reminded of the boundaries" that need to exist between teachers and students.[39]

In 2004, a high school girl wrote in to ask for advice on whether she should take her girlfriend with her to the high school prom. Amy skipped past the question about the dance and noted that the young woman's letter seemed to indicate a personal struggle with coming out. She urged her to work on getting help to feel stronger about her sexuality and noted that if her concerns about bullying or gay bashing were severe, she should notify school authorities of such risks.[40]

A follow-up letter from another gay reader suggested the young woman form a group of four friends to go to the dance together. "Dance as a group and nobody raises an eyebrow," the reader noted. Amy added, "This solution is perfect for people who feel as they do."[41]

"Coming out" remained an issue for young and older readers alike—many teenagers writing to express concern about whether to disclose their sexuality—and even an 85-year-old man writing to say he had finally decided to come out. National Coming Out Day, observed annually in October by LGBT activists, did not, however, win endorsement from Amy when a teenage boy wrote asking whether he should use that day to come out to family and friends. "I understand the concept behind National Coming Out Day," she wrote, "but what I don't like is the pressure it might put on you to come out on a specific day. Coming out is a process that doesn't follow neat guidelines or timetables."[42]

The voice of the "Ask Amy" column could be quite conversational at times, perhaps reflecting the new two-way, mediated nature of the dialogue because of its online component. The conversation was often direct, but always polite, Amy addressing one reader noting: "Regular readers of my column will notice that I don't generally make assumptions at all about people—gay or straight. If there's one thing I've learned in this job, it's that inappropriateness knows no sexual identity.... Cultural stereotypes, however, seem to hang on and on, especially when they are perpetuated by the very people to whom they are directed. Doesn't that get tired?"[43]

Sadly, numerous letters came in from gay men, lesbian women and transgender individuals reporting painful and sad encounters where they were openly ridiculed or criticized on the basis of their being. One man wrote that he even faced epithets such as "faggot" following the

Chapter 11. "Ask Amy"

death of a beloved uncle. Amy was as incensed as the man was, noting: "In terms of the relative who gay bashes in your presence, it's simple: You shouldn't tolerate it. There are times to keep your mouth shut and times to speak up. Shutting down an ignorant and offensive bully might be one way to honor your uncle's memory."[44]

"Ask Amy" took up a variety of topics that reflected the changing nature of society, including readers trying to decide whether to use the term "significant other," "partner," or some other term to describe gay couples. Another issue was a continued argument among straights about whether two gay friends could just be friends without being sexually involved with one another.[45]

Straight reactions to two gay men parenting a child also seemed to cause a lot of concern, with gay readers reporting that straight people tended to ask obnoxious questions such as "Where did you get her?" or "Where's her mother?" or, even more personal, "Did you two mix your sperm?" Amy addressed "two dads" reporting such instances that the most important thing they must remember is that in front of their child, they must communicate firmly to everyone that they were her parents, and she was your child.

"I think it's wise never to ask probing questions of parents—or pregnant women," Amy wrote. "In your case, just say, 'Heather has two dads and we're thrilled.'" She advised against giving such questioners any pause, and to shut them down succinctly.[46] Her answer reflected a broader philosophy Dickinson employed—and often referenced—telling readers: "You shouldn't wonder how to treat some people with dignity and respect—you should treat everyone equally well, just as you wish to be treated by others."[47]

The letter about the increased curiosity of heterosexuals about gay parenting had an impact, prompting Dickinson to contact pollsters with Zogby International to ask them to include a question about existing opinions on the reality of gay parents. She noted the first results were not promising—a slight majority of Americans (42 percent) indicated they believed same-sex couples were not prepared to be effective parents to children. Lower percentages thought gays could be effective parents or were unsure.

To accompany the results from the Zogby poll, Dickinson ran a series of letters on both sides of the issue, with gay parents telling of their experiences and others attacking the concept. One writer wrote, "No matter how clever the verbal responses are to questions, it will never make the situation normal for children of gays. It's one thing to

Dear Abby, I'm Gay

tolerate gays, but it's a different matter when defenseless children are put into such an unnatural setting."[48]

There were signs of hope—however—one flummoxed gay parent reporting being questioned about why two men had a child with them while waiting in line at the grocery store. Before the gay man could decide how to respond, from the background came another voice offering, "She has two parents who love her more than life itself"—a response met with applause.[49]

The letters kept coming in and Amy expressed pride that her column had been used to help educate people about the concept of gay parents. She noted, "I don't get a ton of hate mail for my neutral treatment of gay issues. I take the lack of anti-gay mail to be a sign that gays are swimming in the mainstream now."[50]

Mainstream or not, Amy still fielded rather "basic" questions about gay issues, one gay man wondering why he couldn't still call himself a "homosexual" rather than gay, difficulties inside relationships between partners separated by 15 or 20 years in age, and another from a lesbian woman who was approaching her 40s and still struggling to tell anyone about her sexual orientation. Teenagers struggling with whether to declare themselves "gay" or "bisexual" also seemed to hit on familiar themes—the ongoing struggle for young women and men to understand and accept their own sexuality.

Manifesting the dramatically changed nature of human relationships, one reader wrote expressing concern that his wife had been asked by two gay friends to serve as a surrogate for their new baby. "I have several big problems with this," the husband shared and worried he could never again be intimate with his wife if she went forward with such an idea.[51]

"While I fully believe in a woman's right to control what she does with her own body, your wife's choice to bear another man's child has a potentially huge impact on your whole family, and she doesn't have the right to do that," Amy wrote. She asked questions about what would happen if there were health complications during the pregnancy or after, who would pay for the medical bills involved, and what would happen if his wife decided she could not give up the child once it was born?[52]

"You must get your wife into a counselor's office to discuss this with the input of a neutral party," Amy said. "You should also contact a lawyer right away to see what your rights and obligations are."[53]

As expected, such a controversial issue drew a variety of responses,

Chapter 11. "Ask Amy"

including one from a reader who objected to Amy's response. "Putting aside for the moment that the husband's attitude toward his wife's rights is not only possessive but downright misogynistic, his and your practical concerns are easily circumvented," the writer noted. "In this day and age, when so many gay couples are maligned for not wanting to have children, I am shocked that you would deny them, and the surrogate mom, for that matter, this wonderful opportunity."[54]

Amy was not moved—noting she was unaware that gay couples were "maligned for not wanting to have children" and that many options existed for all couples, including adoption. "While I believe in a woman's right to choose, I don't necessarily believe in her right to choose to have her neighbor's baby, enduring a pregnancy that will have an impact on her family, and giving birth to and then relinquishing a child that will be genetically related to her."[55]

A February 2006 letter in "Ask Amy" was a spinoff from one of "Dear Abby's" most famous replies to a heterosexual couple concerned about home values after a gay couple moved onto the block. Amy's version of this letter came from a woman pleased with how the two gay men had renovated a rundown home, kept their property immaculate, and even voluntarily shoveled snow from the sidewalks and driveways of elderly neighbors nearby. The deal breaker? The two men kissed each other goodbye as one of them left for work—"I was appalled they would do something like that in plain view of everyone."[56]

Beyond being appalled, the letter writer who liked the way her gay neighbors kept their home, consulted her pastor and on his advice circulated a letter to most of the other neighbors asking the gay men to refrain from any public displays of affection. The topper came with the heterosexual woman complaining that the gay men had now become unfriendly and uncommunicative.

Amy seemed to struggle to control her aghast at the ugly turn of affairs, rating the woman's actions as "spiteful" and hoping that other neighbors would be more kind. "You basically stated that while you valued [these men] when they are raising the standard of your street ... [but] you loathe them for being who they are." Amy said it seemed unlikely, but she told the letter writer she owed the man an apology or should otherwise accept the fact she was rightfully being ignored.[57]

While the issues Amy Dickinson tackled varied dramatically from what Ann Landers took on—as did her viewpoints—her wit and charm was equal to her predecessor. Such wit was on full display for a March 2012 letter from a gay man who had caught his boyfriend cheating using ads on Craigslist. Amy questioned why the man would stay in such a relationship when he stated he valued monogamy.

"There is no such thing as 'mostly monogamous'—although it does make a great title for a Broadway musical," Amy wrote. "Monogamy, like pregnancy, is not a mostly/almost state of being. You are, or you are not."[58]

CHAPTER 12

"Since You Asked"
—Cary Tennis

Although *Salon* magazine and salon.com have struggled and never made money since their start in 1995, its "Since You Asked" advice column remained popular during its 12-year run from 2001 to 2013.

Started as an online magazine by San Francisco journalist and author David Talbot, despite its financial struggles Salon has become a major force online with a decidedly progressive/liberal outlook. Even after Salon "went public" seeking an infusion of resources from investors, it continued to roll up considerable debt. The site was saved by members and others who have kept it limping along—with salon.com at one time boasting as many as two million readers.

The "Since You Asked" column represented the work of journalist Cary Tennis, who, like other advice columnists, held no particular expertise in psychology or social work. Instead Tennis relied upon life experiences (including battles with cancer and alcoholism). Tennis does possess an interesting "life story," having earned undergraduate and graduate degrees in journalism and literature and starting his career as a part-time bike messenger, new wave band member, and rock journalist for *SF Weekly*. He joined salon.com as a copy editor in 1999, and in 2001 was selected to write the "Since You Asked" column.

Salon.com, like other online publications, refers to its "advice column" as a "digital help column" (sounding a bit like something out of the IT department). The column not only featured responses from Tennis to the letters received, but also occasionally feedback from readers who have an opinion.[1]

Calgary Herald writer Steve Burgess described the letters to Tennis as long and complex, and his answers to his readers as "multi-layered" because Tennis "takes his job seriously."[2]

Tennis said he believes "all advice is selfish. That doesn't mean we're

Dear Abby, I'm Gay

not trying to help, or that we don't genuinely want the person to be out of pain, to improve, to be happy. But advice is selfish. It makes us feel better. And it is cheap to give, much cheaper than actual help.... Advice is cheap. It doesn't require sacrifice. On the contrary, there's a net gain when we're giving advice. We feel bigger and stronger and smarter."[3]

Tennis has won fans—and a few enemies. Siobhan Welch, in reviewing Tennis' 2008 book featuring the best of his "Since You Asked" columns, declared: "Cary Tennis has resurrected the advice column into a relevant, even thriving literary form. He is the anti–Dear Abby, with a style more reminiscent of an essayist's ruminations than the pat responses usually found in print."[4]

Author Cary Tennis was the impresario of "Since You Asked" on Salon.com from 2001 to 2013 and continues his own independent advice column (© Amber Wolf, Penguin Random House. Used by permission).

Like many of his compatriots in the advice column business, Tennis has a lot of opinions (even some seemingly in conflict with themselves). He told one reporter that writing the column had caused him to conclude: "It's actually quite amazing to me what passes for knowledge in the oral culture. People actually canvass their friends for advice on things like water purifiers. What do their friends know?"[5]

But in an interview published just a month later, Los Angeles Times reporter David Sarno seemed to find Tennis taking a different tact. Sarno, reporting about the emerging nature of "digital help columns" that were supplanting their in-print ancestors, took note of the fact that Tennis' column

Chapter 12. "Since You Asked"

typically ran at least 1,000 words—something impossible to do in print. He noted that for Tennis "the way the Internet has truly redefined advice writing is by changing it from a simple two-way exchange to a sprawling many-way conversation. In a typical 'Since You Asked,' dozens of readers grapple over how to best advise the letter writer—and whether Tennis' answer was any good."[6]

"There are people writing in that are much smarter than me," Tennis said. "A lot of readers are really well-informed" (contradicting his earlier claim that a person's friends don't know anything). He referred to this phenomenon as "open source wisdom."[7]

The gay-related letters coming in to the "Since You Asked" column took similar forms to those offered in other advice columns. A 2005 letter from a mother presented an interesting take on having a gay son. The letter detailed how her son was "more than a good kid" and was "a bit of a phenom. Very bright, high-achieving, athletic, popular, good-looking, yadda, yadda." Her son, however, has had no romantic relationships with girls and spent most of his time with other "bright guys not unlike himself." Mom wanted to know, "Am I totally overstepping to even wonder?"[8]

Tennis replied that talks about intimate topics were often difficult. He recommended that instead of asking her son outright if he was gay, "take some time, a good amount of time, to ask him about his dreams for the future. He'll be better able to answer you if he understands what you want." He noted, "The trick is to give him enough room to talk … and to apply gentle pressure if he becomes afraid to speak."[9]

Tennis said it was not unusual for mothers and fathers to hold dreams for their children's futures—but have to wait for life to play out. "Sons also dream about the future," Tennis wrote. "They do not want to deceive their mothers. But neither do they wish to be labeled."[10]

In March 2006, Tennis fielded a letter from the "amused" heterosexual husband of a woman who apparently was fashion-challenged. The man wrote to detail an incident in a bar where two gay men approached him, bought him drinks and "were soon all over me." He noted his wife "was not amused, but I just laughed it off." Rather than deal with his wife's feelings about the incident, the man asked whether he should confront his wife and suggest that "she take the trouble to dress up more" and speculated that "a gay guy would be less likely to hit on me if my wife were dressed up more and even had on makeup."[11]

Tennis took the letter writer to task about the absurd nature of his query, a letter that provided more confusion than resolution. He wondered if the man's sentence, "gay guys hitting on me" was a metaphor for "something, a displacement of desire perhaps, an erotic frustration, something" and added, "Perhaps you do have homoerotic desires that are playing out here. Or perhaps they are only a metaphor."[12]

Getting more specific, Tennis added that he likely would not have handled the situation the same if it had been two women who had bought him drinks and come on to him in a bar. "So I think the homoerotic represents something that you cannot have or are not allowed to want." He recommended holding off on criticizing his wife's apparel asking, "Do you really understand what you're doing? And does your wife? Does she really know what you're asking for? Do you?"[13]

The parent of a male-to-female transgender youth wrote to ask for help coping with the life changes at hand. The mother detailed all of the ways they had tried to raise their son to be a good person but "then, in his late teens, he told us he was transgendered [sic] and was a girl. We coped.... I'll say that I accept her, though, I think this is going to be a hard life. Other family members, including her dad, have been very, very accepting."[14]

The issue rising to the top appeared to be how to motivate her daughter to do better in college—reporting that she attended less than half of her classes and seems to have lost all motivation for pursuing life. "I can love her, I'm there for her, I can send her to college, keep her in health care until she's 26, but I can't make her functional," mom wrote.[15]

Tennis replied stating the obvious that her daughter was "undergoing a miraculous transformation" and that it likely was taking all of her strength. "This is an existential task," Tennis wrote. "Think of her as pregnant with herself. Think of her as heavy and bloated with her own future, which she must assemble blindfolded."[16]

In advice he knew ran counter to a parent's normal inclination, he suggested she do nothing. "I suggest that in the midst of this miraculous transformation your role is to do nothing," he said. "Nothing is the most wonderful thing you can do right now. It is also the hardest.... Let this fact into your heart: You are now the observer. You have brought this being into the world, you have done everything asked of you to nurture and care for this being, and now you are witnessing the miracle of autonomy.... Trust in what comes next."[17]

In a rather unusual letter in August 2012, a young albino woman wrote describing herself as a "pansexual" who was struggling to deal with a heterosexual boyfriend who did not understand. "Upon discovering I was pansexual, I became suicidal and stooped into depression that lasted through middle school into high school," she wrote. "Coming out

Chapter 12. "Since You Asked"

made me feel alienated and like there was no hope. I was always under a microscope ... so I've felt 'othered' (because of being albino) as well."[18]

Tennis' reply, which included religious references to understanding "the idea of the son of God coming down and healing the souls of humans," urged acceptance. "Here is my bottom line: You are who you are and you have the right to be who you are and other people's degree of acceptance is out of your control."[19]

Religion was a factor in another letter from a gay man of Muslim faith who was suicidal over the turns his life had taken. The letter—and Cary Tennis' response—covered an amazing 3,500 words and likely lost most readers. The original letter, rambling and repetitive, detailed a troubled childhood in a Muslim home where the young man had endured being ridiculed for suspected of being homosexual, and threatened by his parents to be returned to Saudi Arabia where he could be fatally punished for his sexuality. In addition, the man reported having been raped by a gay man and holding repressed memories of incidents of molestation as a young boy.

"I just want to be free," the young man wrote. "My freedom is in death."[20]

The response from Tennis was equally rambling, asking almost as many rhetorical questions as answering—but emphasized the basic value in human life. One of his questions asked why adult men, such as the letter writer and himself, no longer believed in crying over their grief? "The crying seems to help," he said. "We feel better afterward. Why don't you let this pain and fear come out and cry about it now?"[21]

Tennis stated his belief that "we have no capacity to heal our own wounds" and that we must wait for "the animating force of life" that can heal us. "Our sole purpose when injured is to find, within our routines of work and family, a setting in which we can heal."[22]

Like every advice column, "Since You Asked" received its share of letters from closeted gay men and lesbian women struggling with how or whether to "come out" to family and friends. One such letter came from a young man who had dated the same woman for several years but could no longer deny his growing sexual interest in men. "I was thinking, maybe, I could just tough it out and marry her and have some kids and not ever have to tell," he told Tennis. "I know that if I break up with her that is the last chance I will ever have at a 'normal' lifestyle and the rest of my life, I will be lost in oblivion."[23]

Cary Tennis tried to reassure the young man to try and step back and breathe a little and added, "You are going to learn to live as a gay man and know happiness as a gay man. You don't have to become a screaming stereotype of a gay man and you don't have to be 'out and proud.' You can come out as quietly as if you had just ducked into the closet for a moment to choose a shirt."[24]

He cautioned that the only thing he should not do is "to pretend you are straight and get married to this beautiful woman and have kids with her and live 20 miserable years in secret.... That you just cannot do. That's a 1950s thing."[25]

The wife of a gay or bisexual man who had decided to go ahead with marriage wrote—18 years into their matrimony—reporting her dismay at her husband's recent sexual interludes with men he had solicited and met via Craigslist. After STD tests "came back clean," the wife reported she had taken her husband back trying not to disrupt the lives of their two teenage children. The woman, who had never worked outside the home, feared the financial struggle a divorce would bring but also remained annoyed that her "bisexual" husband continued "his virtual presence in the gay community through porn" and other online activities. "I do realize that his orientation is not a choice, but his behavior is," she added.[26]

Tennis said the woman needed the help of both a therapist and a lawyer in order to sort out what to do. "Because you are human you will seek meaning in what happened," he wrote. "We seek meaning in misfortune whether we get cancer or have an accident or are bombed out of our houses by unseen jets." He suggested she faced a "one day at a time" future where continuing to live with him, or leaving him, would create the need for many decisions, and good days and bad days. "One way or another, you will arrive in a future that was not the future you imagined," he shared.[27]

Adding a dash of hope, Tennis told the woman he saw "a wiser woman" in her future, one "who finds new strength in herself to protect her daughters and make a new life. I see a woman who ... learns that when disaster happens, you're capable of more than you realized."[28]

In a twist on the same issue, seven years earlier Tennis offered a letter from the daughter of a married couple who had divorced after 18 years. She reported that years of turmoil, alcohol abuse and fighting ended when her father moved out. What was bothering the young woman was the fact that at the time her parent's divorce became final, her mother disclosed that the reason for the divorce was not the fighting or drinking, but because their father was a homosexual.

The young woman was filled with questions: "Did he not know that

Chapter 12. "Since You Asked"

he was gay? If he did know, then why did he get married to my mom? Was he just trying to make it go away? What was he doing?"[29]

Tennis acknowledged that it was possible her father knew he was a homosexual at the time he got married and later had children but had repressed or pushed aside his feelings. "As you suggest, he may have thought that getting married would make the homosexual feelings go away," Tennis added.[30]

The father in question was not seeking forgiveness, as many might think, and he noted that it was not a child's responsibility to forgive her father in this instance. He encouraged her to let her father into her life and work on finding new ways to relate to him. "You may feel angry and sad all at the same time," he said. "But that's alright ... your emotions won't hurt you. They are not your enemy."[31]

Another gay man wrote in to ask whether sending a carefully worded email to his girlfriend disclosing that he was gay and wanted to just be friends was an acceptable approach. Tennis acknowledged that "sometimes when we want people to be happy, we tell them the things we wish to be true," but "you are ending the romantic part of the relationship" and he must be sensitive. Surprisingly, Tennis did not shoot down the idea of sending an email or letter to break the news rather than in person. He simply edited the letter and offered, "Good luck, and congratulations on taking a courageous and important step. I hope that you and she will remain lifelong friends."[32]

A lesbian woman wrote to ask for help in dealing with her feelings of doubt infiltrating her relationship. Admitting that she met her current girlfriend while she was dating another woman, she reported her partner "has a serious history of cheating." She was particularly concerned that her partner did not defend what she has done, "but she's also never volunteered a promise that she'd never do it again."[33]

Tennis replied in a philosophical manner suggesting that the woman "take seriously the proposition that the legacy of our parents' world, the restrictive, monogamous, marriage model, just may not be the most realistic model" and that "you don't have to do it the way it's always been done." He furthered the argument by noting that younger people, such as his writer, should challenge the idea of "blindly accepting the romantic myths and oppressive practices of an older and increasingly irrelevant social order" and change the world.[34]

"So why not be large of heart? Why not be large of spirit?" Tennis asked. "Why not be courageous and tell your girlfriend, OK, let's face it might happen and let's agree to talk about it if it does happen, and let's try to live as loving human beings, accepting each other.... And that what we have is beautiful, but fragile, and that life is short and the challenges are great, so let's do our best to be kind, and wise, and true to ourselves."[35]

In April 2013, Tennis dedicated his column to an apology to readers who had written in offended at his response to letters where he essentially equated bisexuality with being polyamorous. "I seem to have made an error that was offensive to many people who identify as bisexual, and I apologize," Tennis wrote. "I can really fall in love with my own nonsense sometimes. And to those who have written agreeing with me, I appreciate it, but I think I was wrong."[36]

Just five months later, Tennis announced via his Facebook page that he had been fired by salon.com but did not specify the reason for his termination. Leaving salon.com ended the column he had written for a dozen years and opened up opportunities for Tennis to move the column to his own site with a new name. He encouraged readers to send in letters and to "tell your friends. The more people who get involved the more likely we'll be able to keep the column running for the long haul. It turns out that giving advice is a hard habit to break."[37] He has continued the column and transformed it into a podcast.

CHAPTER 13

"Savage Love"
—Dan Savage

Dan Savage's successful "Savage Love" column, now almost three decades old and an internationally read sensation, started as a joke. The joke was on heterosexuals and those who had come to count on the advice of established advice columnists, such as Ann Landers or Dear Abby.

"I grew up reading Ann Landers, Abigail Van Buren, [and] the "Happy Hooker" column in *Penthouse* magazine," Savage said. "My brothers had *Penthouse* as a kid. I read them for the articles!" With that background, Savage (with no prior journalism or advising experience), took advice columns in a direction never before seen.[1]

The "joke" of the column was "I was a gay person giving straight people sex advice. This was a new experience for straight people." He noted, "I was going to treat straight people with the same contempt that heterosexual columnists traditionally treated gay people with. They loved it. They didn't take it as the insult it was intended to be at first. It turned into a real advice column. I got real questions and it became an advice column under my feet."[2]

In 1991, Seattle's new alternative weekly newspaper, *The Stranger*, became the home to "Savage Love" when Savage himself suggested to his friend, Tim Keck, that his new newspaper needed an advice column. Keck, a co-founder of the satirical masterpiece *The Onion*, agreed and "Savage Love" was born.

Timing was to Savage's benefit, he believes, when the column started. "You couldn't be out and gay if you hadn't given yourself permission to be out, to tell your parents you were gay, it was difficult to do," Savage said. As a result, from the beginning Savage decided to "own" the language of his column, the first several years of the column featuring letters that opened with the salutation "Hey Faggot."[3]

Dear Abby, I'm Gay

Beyond the controversial use of the term "faggot"—Savage's attempt to disarm the use of the most commonly used epithet used against gay men—subject matter for "Savage Love" was admittedly controversial from the start. The libertine nature of the sexual discussion in "Savage Love" is by design. "It is written in sexual vernacular," Savage said. "The whole idea was to let people use the language they used when they talked about sex and relationships with their friends which was fun and humorous using slang and sometimes profanity. That was the kind of juice that drove the column and continues to drive the column."[4]

Savage is now married to his long-term partner, Terry Miller, and the father of an adopted son. His backstory was on display for two seasons via ABC's primetime comedy *The Real O'Neals*, the story of a close-knit Catholic Chicago family dealing with their gay son. Savage served as executive producer of the show and has written five books, including two award-winning memoirs, *The Kid: What Happened After My Boyfriend and I Decided to Go Get Pregnant* (2000) and *The Commitment: Love, Sex, Marriage and My Family* (2006).

Savage has readily expanded his role beyond advice columnist, most notably launching the It Gets Better Project in 2010 following the suicide of Greensburg, Indiana, youth Billy Lucas who succumbed to relentless bullying at school from homophobic classmates. Savage said he started the organization on "a helpful impulse to get in a time machine and talk to that kid [Lucas] five minutes

Dan Savage made history as the first openly gay advice columnist, taking his sex advice column "Savage Love" from the pages of Seattle's alternate newspaper *The Stranger* to worldwide prominence. The co-founder of the "It Gets Better" project, Savage remains an active LGBTQ advocate (courtesy *The Stranger*).

Chapter 13. "Savage Love"

before he committed suicide. I struggled with that, this desire to speak to the kids who were harming themselves because they were in such despair about being bullied and feeling things would never get better."[5]

It Gets Better was necessary, Savage said, because "queer kids" need to speak to "queer adults" but have parents "who would never let their kid interact with a queer adult. The queer kid is being bullied at the hands of their peers, but the worst is being at the hands of the parents. I wanted to speak to those kids, but the parents wouldn't allow it."[6]

The project, which has attracted a massive worldwide response with testimonials from a diverse group of individuals (including President Barack Obama) served as "an end run around the preachers, teachers and parents of queer kids" via social media. "A queer kid doesn't have a queer parent to share with them on the path, so it's queer adults talking to queer kids about the strategies we employed.... The ways we made it better for ourselves so they too have the tools."[7]

Launched on September 23, 1991, Savage's "Savage Love" column was meant to be a pure contrast with the existing advice column faire offered by Ann Landers and others. In 1992, Savage (referring to himself as "Dan Landers") asked his readers to help upend a project launched by Landers to determine whether being gay was "a curse" or "a gift." Landers asked her readers to help "settle the question once and for all" and encouraged readers to send in cards indicating, "Yes, I'm glad I'm gay" or "No, I would rather be straight." Savage wrote, "Ann is a fellow advice monger, and out of professional courtesy, I've decided to help her out" by tilting the outcome toward "I'm glad I'm gay."[8]

A few years later Savage had some more fun with another famous advice columnist, Judith Martin and her well-liked etiquette column, "Miss Manners." The question at hand, for which Savage asked for Martin's help in replying to, concerned the propriety of discussing the sexual activities of others spotted in a gay sex club. Savage said he forwarded the letter, titled "If You See a Prude Eating Ass in a Sex Club, Are You Obligated to Keep Quiet About It" to Martin, but not surprisingly, "Miss Manners has not, as of this writing, done me the courtesy of responding." Savage addressed what he thought was appropriate, noting that having sex in a public space had a rather limited expectation of privacy. Performing oral sex "in front of 30 men is a remarkably sleazy thing to do—and it is Mr. Prig's own fault his sex-club tableau was so remarkable."[9]

The very first letters also reflected the frank nature "Savage Love" would always employ, one writer asking for help deciding between two men because he was "intensely horny." Another letter, from a straight woman, lamented her continued attraction to gay men. "I know it's crazy, but straight guys just don't do it for me," she wrote. "I don't find them nearly as sensitive, thoughtful, creative or sexy as many of the gay hunks I know." Savage answered that long-term relationships were possible between straight women and gay men—but "you just won't get laid much." He joked that he had met "some straight guys that were okay, if a little slow."[10]

Interactions between the straight and gay worlds was at the center of a 2009 letter from a newly married straight man frustrated that his new bride seemed to be taking Katy Perry's hit song "I Kissed a Girl" literally and became flirtatious with other women and gay male friends after a few drinks.

Savage believed the man was overreacting (calling him "an insufferable prick") to what he had witnessed and should forgive his wife and "cease being such a fucking douchebag about the flirting and the fucking kiss already." He added, "A successful marriage is basically an endless cycle of wrongs committed, apologies offered, and forgiveness granted ... all leavened by the occasional orgasm."[11]

Another straight man won Savage's scorn writing in to complain that his new roommate failed to disclose that he was gay prior to the two men deciding to split the rent on an expensive New York City apartment. The straight man noted, "I think he should have told me he was gay before I moved in. Who's the asshole?" Savage was crisp: "Unless your big gay roommate threatened to rape your tiny, straight butthole, you're the asshole." He advised the young man that living in New York meant he certainly was going to encounter gay people: "You can run from your gay roommate, you can't hide from the rest of us. Sooner or later you're gonna have to get a haircut or eat in a restaurant or ride on a subway, and guess what? When you do, there are gonna be gay men checkin' out your butt. Why not stay put and get used to it?"[12]

One gay male couple wrote in to complain that some of their straight friends seemed entirely too comfortable asking them personal and often awkward questions. One such question—whether the gay men enjoyed buttplugs or recommended them—seemed a particularly odd topic to raise at a dinner party.[13]

Another straight male apparently had questioned his gay friends about the fact that he liked digital manipulation of his anus during sex with his girlfriend. The young man was worried that his girlfriend would think he was gay, "and girls talk" and he worried "I may never get laid

Chapter 13. "Savage Love"

again." Savage discussed the concept of prostate stimulation for all men (and women) but gave rather tame advice. "Get a girlfriend," he said, noting, "you might benefit from opening up to one person, someone you can trust with your secret, but that will require an investment of time and emotional energy. But the payoff could be huge. Imagine having sex with someone you didn't have to hide from, someone who you didn't have to worry about judging you because she understood."[14]

Interestingly, he added, "get over yourself, you're a heterosexual guy who needs to be on the receiving end of a little heterosexual anal play.... Your sexuality isn't the problem; your need for prostate stimulation isn't the problem. The problem is your shame and desire to hide this aspect of your sexuality.... You may not be gay, but you *do* need to come out."[15] Seemingly no topic was off-limits for Savage, including letters from men distressed about the small size of their penis, a gay man upset that his short stature and adolescent looks seemed to attract "pedophile" like affections from older men, a transgender man who wanted surgery to have large breast implants, whether a straight man was actually gay based on his desire to have sexual relations with a hermaphrodite, whether Republicans or Democrats were more sexually adventurous, and a lengthy discussion about a scientific study about whether penis size differed dramatically between straight men and gay men.

Savage's column would often breach topics normally reserved by daytime TV schlock such as *The Jerry Springer Show*, with more than one writer asking for help on how to disclose to a partner or lover that they are transgender, or a person dressing and presenting as someone of a gender other than their own. One writer disclosed, "I've been living a lie. My girlfriend thinks I'm a guy, and I'm not a guy. I am really a female" and added, "I hate myself for doing this to her. She always talks about having kids and getting married as soon as we complete our last year of college.... Give me some advice and criticism. I know I deserve it."[16]

The query was shared with three outside experts—identified by Savage as "female-to-male transsexual" author Spencer Bergstedt, female-to-male author Loren Cameron, and male-to-female author Kate Bornstein. All three experts recommended getting more honesty into the relationship quickly and take a chance that the feelings between the two could overcome such a surprise disclosure. Bornstein was the most direct: "You are sincerely stupid," she replied, "but you are not a bad person. You were afraid to say things for fear of losing love, but who hasn't felt that? Now you have to make it right."[17]

An outside expert, Dr. Pepper Schwartz from the University of

Dear Abby, I'm Gay

Washington, assisted Savage in answering questions about incompatible sex drives between two lesbian women, as a result of Schwartz's concept of "the lesbian death bed." Savage used Schwartz's ideas to promote the concept that either the two women find a way to be on the same wavelength sexually, accept a sexless relationship, or break up.

Savage used the occasion of the letter to publicly comment on the announced break-up of TV celebrity Ellen DeGeneres and her film actress mate, Anne Heche, in 2000. Savage said the break-up was a wonderful opportunity to offer "I told you so" noting that he predicted the relationship wouldn't last, and had endured a stream of "hate mail" from "thousands of angry lesbians all over the world [who] wanted to know why I was so cynical."[18]

Savage denied he was falling into the hands of anti-gay bigots who wanted the relationship to fail as evidence that successful gay coupling was impossible. "I wasn't being bitchy, just honest," Savage said. "Anne and Ellen were running around the country acting like a couple of spot-faced teenagers. They couldn't keep their hands off each other, wouldn't shut up about their beautiful relationship." He noted they bought a house together a month before they exchanged rings. "Are there any bigger signs that a relationship is doomed?" He deemed their relationship caught in the "infatuation stage" and that gay versions of such infatuation shouldn't be taken any more seriously than straight ones.[19]

Seemingly offering an olive branch to his perhaps irritated lesbian readers (who undoubtedly noted Savage's trumpeting of the breakup of singer Melissa Etheridge and her girlfriend, Julie Cypher). "Listen, lesbians," Savage wrote, "relationships are delicate, perishable things, and no relationship should be used to make points about the visibility, validity, or stability of gay and lesbian love."[20]

Not all the topics were so serious, Savage devoting column space in September 2000 for his "very special" How Sleaze Is Lived in America series. This time focused on "gay sleaze," the columns examined issues such as gay men who still sought sex in bathhouses, porn store video booths or public restrooms, and masturbation parties. Savage noted that his "sleaze" columns were a perfect counterbalance to Ann Lander's "we met cute" columns.[21]

A "sleaze" or "kink" related topic answered by Savage gave him an opportunity to cut to what he believed to be the real problem underneath. One writer wrote to express frustration with his desire to be humiliated sexually by his partners, only to put aside such interests,

Chapter 13. "Savage Love"

but to fall back into them once again. The problem, Savage said, was not a troubled childhood or his love of kink. "The problems, plural, are self-loathing and attempts to swear off kink (which leads to binge-and-purge cycles), and reckless ways the kink is indulged when bingeing."[22]

Sexual relationships between gay men are featured often in "Savage Love" covering every type of concern imaginable. One 40-something gay man wanted to know how to handle a relationship with an 18-year-old Latino young man who was deeply closeted—with Savage explaining to his readers the concept of "bear" and "cub" love relationships. Savage advised his closeted friend "will have to risk a conversation now and then, and maybe even watching a movie together sometime at your apartment," he wrote. "Tell him you can't be friends-with-benefits with someone who isn't a friend." Another unusual relationship was revealed by a 25-year-old gay man who wrote to detail how he was into "puppy play" where he had "joined a pack with a Sir and several puppies."[23]

As expected, all of the column space dedicated to discussion of gay men and male genitalia irritated female readers, particularly gay women. One writer, calling herself "Frustrated Femme," took Savage to task: "We realize you're gay and everything, Dan, but whatever happened to pussy? You used to write about women's genitals once in a while.... I still have the column you wrote about the importance of the clit, and I give it to every new boyfriend. But I don't think you've written one word about pussy in, like, two whole years! Your column is all cock!"[24]

Savage took the bait and replied in language not often found on newspaper pages: "If it's pussy you want, FF, then pussy you shall have" and noted letters that followed took up direct conversations of "pussy wet, pussy drive, pussy bored, and pussy squirts."[25]

The often blunt language used by Savage created frequent controversy, something the columnist seems to revel in. Savage's 1999 response to a gay man wondering whether he should bother with a relationship with a bisexual man prompted angry replies from those identifying as bisexual. One complaint letter, from Jennifer Coderre, co-founder of an organization known as "Bisexual Insurgence," noted that Savage had "condemned all bisexuals as poor relationship material" and engaged in prejudiced "biphobic" behavior. Savage was unapologetic: "Sorry, but avoiding bi guys is a good rule of thumb for gay men looking for long-term relationships," and added, "when a guy is closeted, as most bi guys are, he can't really be there for his boyfriend."[26]

"I'm not saying bi guys are bad people, or they don't make great one-night stands.... But if a guy wants more, he'll have an easier time getting it from another gay man," Savage wrote. To support his view, he ran a companion letter from a gay man who said he had tried dating bisexual men and said "they just plain suck. They sneak out on wifey at home, then look for quick fixes with men, paranoid about being caught stiff-dicked with a guy. They want a straight life and its perks, and a cock when they can manage to squeeze it in. The bi guy's 'boyfriend' is always the disposable one."[27]

Savage was consistent in his view on this subject—in answering a letter from a gay man about whether he should remain sexually involved with his married male friend, Savage replied: "Don't mess around with bisexuals [and] don't mess around with married men." He noted the letter writer knew what he was getting into at the start, and the man has clearly resigned his gay lover to a secondary role. He suggested, either "resign yourself to that or, hey, here's an idea: Dump your bi boyfriend and find yourself a soul mate who's capital 'G' gay, just like you."[28]

The issue of whether Savage's "It Gets Better" campaign was of any help to bisexuals did bring a somewhat more kindly exchange. Savage said he believed that the coming out process for bisexuals could be "highly problematic" and that "it is not always safe or better for bi folks to come out, just as it is not always safe for anyone to come out." He added, though, that "nothing would more effectively combat bisexual invisibility and ignorance than for bisexuals to come out" to most or all of the important people in their lives. Savage said polling showed only 28 percent of bisexuals admitted they were open about their sexual orientation to loved ones.[29]

For bisexual or gay readers, Savage advised planning the coming out process carefully "and have a back-up plan." He noted younger people should "think long and hard about how their parents might react" given the risk of being tossed from the family home or cut off financially. He cautioned, however, that overblown fears about coming out sometimes keep closeted people from taking important steps forward.[30]

Savage's views on the ability of men to maintain monogamous relationships likely also won him some enemies. One gay man—who had broken up with his boyfriend over his desire for an "open" sexual relationship asked Savage for his advice. "When one makes generalizations about three billion people, like say, 'men are bad at monogamy,' one should keep in mind that there will be tens of millions of exceptions," Savage wrote. "However, men are bad at monogamy, and gay men are especially bad at it." Savage suggested the two men were incompatible

Chapter 13. "Savage Love"

based on their varying desires for their relationship and suggested, get an agreement for an "open" arrangement, move on to someone new, or try to pull off cheating behind his boyfriend's back.[31]

Such direct advice was a strong departure from other advice columnists—but it still seemed some readers didn't get it. One letter writer named "Jason" in 1999 wrote to thank Savage for being a "wonderful, caring, considerate and realistic straight" source of support. Savage chuckled his way through his reply, "Don't be thankin' God for me and 'all the other straight people' ... maybe it's been a while since I've mentioned it, but I'm a cocksucker, dude, just like you."[32]

Although he quickly became the nation's most famous openly gay advice columnist, he did not necessarily win the blind support of gay activists. AIDS and HIV activists seem to often take Savage to task for his sometimes-frank replies to queries he received. Savage seemed particularly focused on calling attention to HIV positive gay men who still engaged in irresponsible sexual behavior. Savage noted that current prevention efforts were failing—HIV infection rates were on the rise in 2001 as a result of "stupid guys" who refused to use condoms and otherwise protect themselves and others.

"Lifelong condom usage during casual and/or anonymous sexual encounters is not some horrible burden that gay men alone have to bear," he wrote. "It's a fact of life for all responsible sexually active adults, gay and straight."[33]

To further clarify his role in the discussion, Savage challenged a reader who said Savage, as an advice columnist, held a responsibility to help save lives from HIV and AIDS. "I'm not trying to save any lives," he responded, adding that HIV infection was no longer "a death sentence" but a part of a larger discussion about sexual responsibility.[34]

He drew a parallel between advice Ann Landers or other advice columnists would give to women who have sex with men without protection. "We order women not to sleep with them, and we tell them these men are assholes," Savage wrote. "Color me self-righteous, but I don't see much difference between some straight asshole who doesn't care how many girls he knocks up and some HIV-positive gay asshole who doesn't care how many guys he infects."[35]

There was little compassion in place in June 2000 when an HIV-positive man wrote in complaining the other gay men he met were "freaked out" as soon as they learned of his status, and typically didn't want to date anymore. "Why can't other gay men have more compassion?" he asked. Savage recommended getting involved in HIV support groups, a suggestion another HIV-positive reader took issue with. He told Savage, "What kind of advice is that?" offering that he went to a support group once only to find it was full of "a bunch of old barf bags. No thanks!"[36]

Savage replied, "Look, fuckbrain, meeting guys who already know you're positive is the only way to avoid 'What? You're positive?!' weirdness. If you are too ashamed to be out about your status, well you have no right to complain when guys react badly."[37]

He ended the strongly worded retort with the prediction that the letter writer would likely "not get off your ass" and "like a lot of other shit-for-brains poz guys out there, you'd probably be happier complaining. And hey, where does someone who calls older gay men 'barf bags' get off asking for compassion?"[38]

"Gay-centric" issues remained a Savage staple, including addressing a rarely discussed aspect of gay culture regarding highly effeminate or "sissy" gay men. Savage participated in the groundbreaking 2014 documentary by filmmaker David Thorpe, *Do I Sound Gay*, that explored nature of femininity and masculinity among gay men. One gay man wrote in April 2000 seeking advice about why he was not attracted to "femmy men."

"Some guys are sissies, and will be sissies all their lives," Savage said. "And more power to them, I say. I adore sissies, especially big, muscle-bound sissies who make straight guys feel uncomfortable using showers at the gym." He noted that some men go through a "sissy phase" when they are younger, "but most of these guys calm down by the time they're 30."[39]

Savage said he hated the term "straight-acting" for gay men and said it actually made meeting other gay men more difficult. "The fastest way to let other straight-actors know you're gay is by acting a little less straight yourself, or by nailing a fag flag, or a button, or a T-shirt, to your chest."[40]

In the days following the September 11, 2001, terrorist attacks in the United States, Savage admitted to his readers that "my heart wasn't in it" to write his weekly column. "Sometimes what I do for a living seems pretty silly and believe me, I've never felt quite as silly about being an advice columnist as I do today," he wrote. "The very last thing on my mind right now is sex.... Surely none of my readers are thinking about their sex lives at a time like this!"[41]

His assumption, however, was incorrect as he noted he received one letter from a reader just as the World Trade Center towers were

Chapter 13. "Savage Love"

collapsing in New York City. He blasted the reader: "Thousands of people in New York City, Washington, D.C., and Pennsylvania had died or were dying horrifying deaths, and all you could think about were gay men who liked to fist? What the hell is wrong with you?"[42]

In the aftermath of 9/11, the purpose or appropriateness of prayer was also on Savage's mind. Savage was a young man raised in the Catholic church who once considered becoming a priest, and posed the provocative question "Who could be against prayer at a time like this? Or against God? Well, I am." He said certainly the doomed victims of 9/11 surely engaged in tremendous prayers, as did those watching the scenes unfold, but Savage asked: "What good did all that prayer do?"[43]

"On September 11, suicidal Islamic radicals, their heads stuffed with absurdities, committed the most appalling atrocities," he added. "And what are we told to do in response? Trot out our own absurdities. Turn to God. Pray to God. God listens. God cares. Does He really? If so, I'd like to see Him get off his ass and prove it once in a while."[44]

Another political issue that raised Savage's ire was the abuse and danger homosexuals faced in some countries of the world, including Saudi Arabia and Egypt. Savage detailed carnage committed against gays in those nations and encouraged his readers to support the International Gay & Lesbian Human Rights Commission.[45] His open engagement of gay political issues could win him criticism, some of which seemed to sting as Savage detailed a sad news conference held by "pro-family groups" at the National Press Club where his marriage and parenting of his adoptive son were openly criticized. "My family being attacked from the podium of the National Press Club—*that* was a new experience.... But there are things straight people can learn from gay people and also I think gay people can learn from straight people."[46]

The politics of "Savage Love" gave rise to a vocabulary of specific terms regular readers of the column came to know—some of them tame, such as "GGG" meaning "good, giving and game" for being generous in intimate relationships; "breeders" to refer to heterosexuals; "the campsite rule" meaning older partners leave their younger mates better off than they found them; "tea and sympathy rule" meaning younger partners speaking positively about their older partners after it's over or they're gone; "DTMFA" for "dump the Motherfucker Already"; "CPOS" for "Cheating Piece of Shit"; "Monogamish" for "mostly monogamous" relationships; and HTH for "How'd That Happen?"

Two of the most controversial terms in Savage's glossary were political shots fired back at anti-gay conservatives, including former U.S.

Dear Abby, I'm Gay

senator Rick Santorum, a Pennsylvania Republican opposed to gay marriage rights, and conservative mega-church Pastor Rick Warren.

Via a 2003 reader poll, Savage launched the term "Santorum" which officially refers to "the frothy mixture of lube and fecal matter that is sometimes the byproduct of anal sex." Savage said he believed Santorum deserved to be infamously preserved in this manner because the former Senator had "compared consensual gay sex to incest, bigamy, adultery and man-on-dog sex."[47]

Pastor Warren's Saddleback Community Church was the subject of a 2009 reader poll prompting the term "Saddlebacking" which represented "the phenomenon of Christian teens engaging in unprotected anal sex to preserve their virginities."[48]

Politics is never far from Dan Savage's mind, and his column. During the historically close 2000 Presidential contest between George W. Bush and Al Gore, Savage took up the issue of Dick Cheney, Bush's Republican running mate, being the father of an openly gay woman, Mary Cheney. He noted that her father had defended George H.W. Bush's ban on allowing gay men and lesbian women to serve openly in the military, but Mary was still actively involved with the Bush-Cheney campaign.

"Mary Cheney was exposed as a carpet-munching sodomite by reporter/fellow barbarian Matt Drudge," Savage reported, "but some of us knew Mary Cheney was a lesbian before we read Matt's scooplet (asserting that taking one look at her photo convinced him she was gay)."[49]

Apparently unconcerned about insulting anyone, Savage added, "Not all dykes look like dykes, of course, but the picture [(of Cheney] gave it away. Cheney is one of those looks-likes-a-dyke-quacks-like-a-dyke triple threats: she has the lesbian hairdo, the lesbian polo shirt, and tasteful lesbian makeup." Savage spotted hypocrisy—the Bush campaign saying Dick Cheney was "a good family man" and that Mary's sexual orientation presented no concerns. This was, Savage noted, despite Bush's promise to fundamentalist TV icon, the Rev. Pat Robertson, that Bush would not knowingly appoint any gay or lesbian people to his administration.[50]

In February 1999, Savage retired the "Hey Faggot" salutation for letters to his column, explaining, "When I started writing this column in 1991, there was a debate raging in hellish homosexual circles about words like faggot. The idea was that if we used these words ourselves ... straights couldn't use them as hate words anymore." Using "Hey Faggot" was Savage's joke about the lively debate about reclaiming hate words. A

Chapter 13. "Savage Love"

decade later and the debate over, Savage noted, "Unless someone comes up with a better salutation, you don't have to address me as anything at all."[51]

After nearly three decades of writing the column—and hosting spin-off radio, TV and podcast versions of "Savage Love"—Savage predicts, "Oh my God, I'll keep doing my column, and [just like it was with] Ann Landers, I think it will have to be pried out of my cold, dead hands one day." Writing the column remains an "honor," Savage believes. "People trust me with their secrets and their problems … they trust my judgment, value my insight and trust me with their dilemmas. That's a real honor."[52]

CHAPTER 14

Other Columnists
—*The Rev. Dr. Martin Luther King, Jr., Miss Manners (Judith Martin), Cullen Moore, Dr. Walter C. Alvarez, Lew and Joanne Koch, the Rev. Billy Graham, Dr. Michael Fox, Dr. Lawrence E. Lamb and Lori Gottlieb*

Giving advice—and commentary on homosexuals—was not limited to the most popular or well-known writers. From psychics, to evangelists, medical doctors, astrologists, etiquette experts, and even from veterinarians, opinions about homosexuality and its "causes" and how to deal with it were widespread on newspaper pages across America. A sampling of columns on LGBT-related topics follows:

"Advice for Living"—The Rev. Dr. Martin Luther King, Jr.

Among the myriad number of advice columnists to emerge was one unlikely candidate, the Rev. Dr. Martin Luther King, Jr., who in 1957–58 accepted the invitation of the editors of *Ebony* magazine to write a column "Advice for Living." An advertisement for King's new column urged readers to "let the man that led the Montgomery boycott lead you into happier living."[1] Letters to King covered a wide range of personal, religious and personal issues—letters one might expect to be written to a minister and civil rights leader.

One letter King answered on the pages of Ebony in 1958 (before King relinquished the column following an incident in which he was wounded in a stabbing attack in September 1958) came from a young boy wrestling with issues related to his sexuality. The boy did not

Chapter 14. Other Columnists

identify his race in the latter, but presumably was African American which made up most of *Ebony's* readers at the time. In his letter, the boy told King, "My problem is different from ones most people have. I am a boy, but I feel about boys the way I ought to feel about girls." Beyond that, the boy's letter revealed he was reaching out to an advice column for much the same reason most did—"I don't want my parents to know about me. What can I do? Is there any place where I can go for help?"[2]

The Rev. Dr. Martin Luther King, Jr., briefly wrote an advice column entitled "Advice for Living" for *Ebony* magazine in 1957–58. He gave up the column as his civil rights efforts continued to grow (Library of Congress Image LC-USZ62-111165).

King's response, though polite and lacking any sense of disgust or condemnation, reflected the "problem perspective" that existed in 1958 about homosexuality. In fact, King referred to the boy as having "a problem" and commended him for starting "on the right road toward a solution, since you honestly recognize the problem and have a desire to solve it." King acknowledged that the boy's "problem" was "not at all an uncommon one" (which may have helped relieve the writer's sense of isolation), but noted, "it does require careful attention. The type of feeling that you have toward boys is probably not an innate tendency, but something that has been culturally acquired."[3]

The reply indicated King viewed homosexuality, perhaps, as a "habit" adopted by the boy and suggested that "to deal with this problem ... get back to some of the experiences and circumstances that led to the habit." As most other advice columnists would do, King urged the boy to

185

"see a good psychiatrist who can assist you in bringing to the forefront of conscience all of those experiences and circumstances that led to the habit."[4]

"Miss Manners" (Judith Martin)

Washington, D.C., socialite Judith Martin started her writing career as a journalist covering social events at the White House and other exclusive locales in the nation's capital. The daughter of a United Nations economist, Martin lived in many countries as a child and began to value the importance of social etiquette. She launched her "Miss Manners" column in 1978 and it quickly grew in popularity.

While often referred to as unnecessary and outdated, the idea of etiquette had everyday application, according to Martin (who always referred to herself in third-person voice): "When people complain about the rudeness of others, they like to generalize.... Miss Manners keeps being alerted to two categories of rude people: 'people who should know better,' and 'people like *that*.' Etiquette crimes committed in both categories are pretty much the same. It is reported that these people don't know the basic decencies of how to eat, dress or talk, respond, reciprocate or thank, but have mastered infinite ways of enraging decent folk."[5]

Miss Manners' readers seemed, at first, quite befuddled on how to respond to gay people they encountered. Two early letters to her column asked very basic questions, such as "Is a patron of a gay bar supposed to tip the bartender?" and "What am I supposed to say when I am introduced to a homosexual couple?" Miss Manners was crisp in her reply to her "gentle readers"—to the first question she answered with her own question: Did you think etiquette is affected by the sexual preference of a bar? And to the latter question, she replied, "Just say, 'How do you do?'"[6]

The rise of gay couples had lent a useful term to etiquette, Miss Manners noted in 1980. A reader asking what name she should use in introducing her lover or partner, Martin credited gay couples with helping find a proper name for such arrangements. "The most useful term I know is one that the feminist and homosexual movement have given us, the term is 'significant other,'" Miss Manners wrote. "This is an especially good phrase as it may be used for heterosexual or homosexual couples and implies nothing more than the 'significant other' is the most important person in one's life at that time."[7]

Chapter 14. Other Columnists

A gay couple wrote to "Miss Manners" in December 1980 asking for her help on getting over the inclination of dinner and reception hosts of seating the two men separately—despite their desire to sit together. "It seems there is a limit to society's acceptance," the writer complained. "Could you please give further etiquette rules governing the behavior of gay couples in the family, social and business functions, and also the behavior that should be extended by the host, hostess and other guests."[8]

Miss Manners—the advice column persona of real-life etiquette expert Judith Martin—continues to offer her perspectives on a variety of social issues (photograph by Daniel Lake).

Martin addressed her "gentle reader" with pointed questions: "What is it that you want? To be introduced as lovers, with some explanation provided to the company at large about your feelings for each other? To sit together and chat, if not hold hands, instead of socializing with other people?"[9]

Miss Manners was firm—"The rule is that those who wish to be accepted in conventional society must accept the conventions of the society. This has nothing whatever to do with your private emotions, activities or living arrangements, but everything to do with society's failure to recognize non-legal relationships, homosexual or heterosexual."[10]

She ended the matter with suggesting gay and straight couples be treated the same—and challenged the idea that couples needed to be seated together at all times. Couples who insisted upon sitting together at social events caused her to wonder: "People who live together should be prepared to mix with others when they go out, and their pleas of being in love only makes Miss Manners wonder why, then, don't they refuse all invitations and stay home and enjoy themselves."[11]

The frank nature of Miss Manners and her responses could cause concern—one writer complaining about her position that homosexual couples should not dance together at formal parties and occasions. The writer, a gay man, noted: "My friend and I do not wish to offend anyone, but we are, as you say, a couple, and feel we have as much right as ordinary married couples to show it on the dance floor."[12]

Miss Manners said she wanted to "explain the difference between social form and romance." She acknowledged that couples like to be close to one another, but noted "conventionally, ballroom dancing is done in mixed couples. If some couples happen to be in love, that is not society's fault. But neither is it society's intention to pair partners on the basis of such attachment." She noted that a married couple that danced exclusively with one another at such an event would be considered rude—as male guests would be expected to ask the hostess, or a mother or grandmother, for at least one dance. "To suggest that such conventions are based on sexual proclivity would be outrageous," she wrote. "Please do not take this as intolerance on the part of Miss Manners. It is simply recognition that society would be impossible if its symbolic forms clearly and accurately corresponded directly with the emotions of its members."[13]

"Stars and Lovers"—Cullen Moore

Cullen Moore was the wife of a successful paper company executive and so perhaps it was not surprising that her "Stars and Lovers" astrology columns made their way into more than 50 newspapers across the United States in the 1960s and '70s. While she normally enjoyed discussing the alignment of the stars and what they meant to readers, she did take a question or two along the way about homosexuality.

A 1961 letter from a young woman disclosed that she was in love with another woman and "felt toward her the way you are supposed to feel about a boy. But I hear everywhere people saying that what we feel for each other means something terrible and ugly.... Is there any cure for us? I can't sleep at night and feel guilty, but I also can't live without my girlfriend."[14]

Moore replied, "There is nothing wrong with your mind" and said she receives "hundreds of similar letters from distraught teenagers. Apparently parents and teachers shy away from the painfully misunderstood subject of adolescent crushes between members of the same sex. They are embarrassed by degrading slang terms for adults who form unwholesome homosexual alliances."[15]

She urged parents to answer their "duty to help children understand" such emotional relationships of adolescence and said "a delicate

Chapter 14. Other Columnists

understanding by the parent of counselors and parents" is needed. She predicted "most young people pass through such periods when love is directed towards the same sex without catastrophe."[16]

Using language that reflected she viewed a homosexual lifestyle as problematic, Cullen cautioned that "tragedies occur only when distorted thinking or debauchery from an adult prevents the personality of the young person from evolving into a natural stage of love for the opposite sex." She warned of instances where homosexual adults "deliberately take advantage of a younger's innocent enchantment and attempt to turn this into abnormal and unwholesome ties. Sad to say we find these depraved people often at top levels of society or leadership."[17]

"Medical Advice"—Dr. Walter C. Alvarez

Noted physician Dr. Walter C. Alvarez was entering retirement in 1951 when a newspaper editor approached him about writing a regular medical advice column. Alvarez, the father of Nobel Laureate physicist Luis Alvarez, wrote the "Medical Advice" column for more than 20 years. It was carried by more than 100 newspapers.

A native of San Francisco, Dr. Alvarez enjoyed a long career with the Mayo Clinic of Rochester, Minnesota, and was noted as having treated injured persons following the devastating 1906 San Francisco earthquake (just one year after graduating medical school at Stanford University). As one reported, via his column, Alvarez offered "his opinions about everything from medicine to sex, evolution to the importance of genes and heredity, and was contemporary and

Dr. Walter C. Alvarez of the Mayo Clinic wrote the "Medical Advice" column for 20 years, starting in 1951. He often provided affirming and supportive advice for LGBTQ readers (used with permission of Mayo Foundation for Medical Education and Research. All rights reserved).

unstuffy for a physician who had enjoyed prestige for three-quarters of a century."[18]

Dr. Alvarez devoted an entire column in December 1972 to a review of the Rev. Troy Perry's new book, *The Lord Is My Shepherd and He Knows I'm Gay*. Alvarez praised Perry for the brave story he told and added, "I wish everyone could read this book to better understand what homosexuality can do to a fine man." He detailed Perry's struggles—losing his wife and family—but also his successes (starting one of the nation's first and largest gay-affirming churches, the Metropolitan Community Church).[19]

"Although Troy tried hard to get over his homosexuality, he finally had some homosexual relationships," Dr. Alvarez noted. "Then he got a great idea. Lacking the comfort of religion, he decided to start a new type of church, one in which homosexuals would be so welcome that they could even take part in the services."[20]

Alvarez displayed an openness to discussing homosexuality as early as 1953 when he wrote, "We doctors have usually refused to learn enough about the subject to help the poor, unhappy persons—men and women who were terribly gypped by some freak of nature. I remember a medical editor who once refused to let me even mention homosexualism in an article on serious neuroses. He said he was proud of the fact that he had never permitted the use of 'that vile word' in his journal."[21]

In another column in 1971, Alvarez wrote, "I wish I could convince people that just the knowledge of the fact that homosexuality exists has never made a person homosexual. What impresses me most about homosexuals is that according to the world's best students on the subject, the homosexual has inherited an odd nervous system that is made the moment he is conceived."[22]

"Family Lib"—Lew and Joanne Koch

Building off the idea of women's, black and gay liberation of the 1970s—Lew and Joanne Koch offered a unique column that purported to view the world from the perspective of the nuclear family. As advertised, the couple planned to offer "a very special kind of column that has quite a bit to do with the liberation of the family."[23]

They made clear, however, they would NOT dispense professional family counsel. "We're not preaching to anybody," Lew Koch said. "We're not ideologues in any way." *The Chicago Tribune* boasted

Chapter 14. Other Columnists

that "the young family today is like none that has gone before" and that "the best way to view the new family is through the eyes of a couple who make up one" allowing them to "present, from a personal viewpoint the story of one liberated family, theirs."[24]

The "laboratory" for the Koches' "Family Lib" column was their suburban home and their three children, ages seven, five and three when they started the column in 1972 in *The Chicago Tribune* (eventually distributed twice a week by the Newspaper Enterprise Association [NEA] syndicate).

Presumably written by both Lew and Joanne, some columns were offered under the byline of just one of them. One such column was a broadly written offering in July 1974 under Lew Koch's byline in which he took up the issue of whether gay men and lesbian women should be allowed to be parents.

"In the past few years, a number of divorce cases have arisen where the wife-mother has decided to reject a heterosexual relationship with her husband," Lew wrote. "In many of these cases, the lesbian mother has petitioned the court for custody of the children on the grounds that her sexual preference has nothing to do with her ability to be a good mother."[25]

Lew wrote that "a lesbian may, in fact, be a good mother, loving, nurturing, caring for the child" but that the bigger issue was the home in which the child would be placed. "A lesbian mother with custody of her child forces that child into two conflicting environments—the home where homosexuality is 'normal' and the world of school mates and friends where heterosexuality is 'normal.'"[26]

It was clear to Lew Koch that "a child, even a very young one, will quickly perceive the conflict" and that despite "emotional rationalizing" by "militant Gay Liberation Front forces," a child would be bound into uncertainty and trauma. "Adults must be allowed the freedom of choice," he wrote. "But that freedom comes with the responsibility of accepting the consequences of that choice. The adult's freedom must not become the child's repression."[27]

Lew Koch took up a similar issue, a plan in the New York foster care system that would allow gay men to become foster parents for self-identified gay boys between the ages of 12 and 18. The rationale for the approach, Lew noted, was to keep these foster care boys from the street where they may be subject to exploitation.

"At first glance, the idea appears to have merit," he wrote. "But on closer inspection, the concept is actually counter-productive to the needs of both the boy and society. First, society should not be prepared to accept the sexual judgments of a 12-year-old boy as something final and irreversible."[28]

He noted that "society should be involved in continuing attempts to secure a sound heterosexual environment for such a youth—despite his protestations to the opposite. Finally, we must acknowledge that society still regards homosexuality as a sickness, as deviant behavior and unacceptable." He acknowledged the rightful place of homosexuals to live lives free of violence and harassment, but noted, "To acquiesce, in fact, even to aid a young boy in choosing this path is unwittingly condemning him to a sexual lifestyle which will be filled with sadness and loneliness."[29]

A few weeks later it was Joanne Koch's turn to take on the subject and she rejected not only the idea that anyone would "choose" to be homosexual, but also her husband's argument that a lesbian woman or gay man may not be a suitable parent. "I cannot accept Lew's opinion that lesbians should invariably be denied custody of their children," she wrote. "Lew's judgment would prevent society from responding to individuals by judging all lesbian mothers as unfit to continue as parents."[30]

She openly questioned "how the current sexual activity of a man or a woman tell us everything we need to know about the kind of parent they have been or will be?"[31] She juxtaposed the option of having a gay parent raise a child against the option of having an alcoholic father, or physically abusive mother. She further doubted the state foster system could in any way match the love and nurturing a natural parent—gay or otherwise—could provide a child.

"I refuse to single out lesbianism as a trail so reprehensible, so psychologically damaging that is it inimical to being a parent," she concluded. "We hardly take a step forward when we exchange the Scarlet Letter 'A' to a brand of 'L.'"[32]

"My Answer"—The Rev. Billy Graham

Although his "My Answer" column dealt mostly with issues of faith and scripture—and as a vehicle to evangelize readers to his brand of Christian faith—the Rev. Billy Graham occasionally received letters asking about homosexuality.

Started in 1952, Graham's column reached a reported five million readers nationwide, according to the Billy Graham Evangelistic

Chapter 14. Other Columnists

Association. Graham, who died at the age of 99 on February 21, 2018, offered one last column before his death. Graham wrote, "By the time you read this, I will be in heaven," as he answered one final question about how he would like to be remembered. He replied: "I hope I will be remembered as someone who was faithful—faithful to God, faithful to the Gospel of Jesus Christ, and faithful to the calling God gave me not only as an evangelist, but as a husband, father and friend."[33]

His earliest "My Answer" column regarding homosexuality appeared in January 1961 in which a wife wrote to report her husband was a homosexual, had deserted the family at times and at other times "becomes very cruel and unreasonable, mistreating me terribly." Asking for help, the woman said, "My husband said he has a sickness and that God cannot judge him for an affliction of this kind."[34]

Christian evangelist the Rev. Billy Graham took letters on gay-related topics for his newspaper column, "My Answer." Graham's "answers" closely followed his literal biblical interpretations, and often called on homosexuals to "repent of their sin"—an early version of the "pray the gay away" movement (Library of Congress Image LC-DIG-ppmsc-03261).

The Rev. Graham replied that "many people who become thoroughly entrenched in a vicious habit are apt to make it appear as if it is either a sickness or a general weakness of some sort. This is their best way of justifying what they are doing." Graham criticized psychiatrists and psychoanalysts who "tend to equate all conduct of this kind, and even criminal conduct, with some kind of mental illness. When all is said and done, they can almost prove that no one is bad, only sick."[35]

He countered, "The Bible teaches that [homosexuality] is sin! While it started as a sin it soon became a disease." He added there was hope based on his evangelistic crusades across the globe in which he had seen homosexuals, alcoholics and narcotics addicts shed their afflictions via faith in Jesus Christ. "Your husband has no excuse," Graham concluded.[36]

Another letter suggested Graham needed to update his views, given that God had created homosexuals and even kleptomaniacs. The writer suggested it was unwise to judge any part of God's creation. Graham was having none of it: "Let's set the record straight, God did not create the pervert, the kleptomaniac, or the homosexual. He created man as a perfect being that He might have unbroken fellowship with man. But man elected to become dependent and to make his own choices."[37]

Graham said psychiatrists such as Sigmund Freud and others have provided "an excuse to man for his sinful practices saying that man cannot help himself"—but Graham disagreed and noted, "Man can help himself! He is responsible for his moral acts, and God will hold him accountable."[38]

"The Pet Doctor"—Dr. Michael Fox

Homosexuality was a rather regular feature of "The Pet Doctor" column of Dr. Michael V. Fox that was nationally syndicated by United Features Syndicate. Dr. Fox, who served as director of the Institute for the Study of Animal Problems in Washington, D.C., took the concerns of dog and cat owners seriously.

One writer told Dr. Fox, "If I didn't see it with my own eyes, I wouldn't have believed it, but several times our male cats have behaved homosexually." The cat owner said she was both confused and offended by the activity and wondered what to do.[39]

Dr. Fox advised, "Your cats are not gay and are not perverse. Many animals, including cats, will appear to act homosexually, even mounting each other. But the behavior is not what it seems and carries strong elements of dominance." The good vet recommended the woman "ignore the behavior" and assured her that the cats would "outgrow this behavior."[40]

Another reader told Dr. Fox that it was "hogwash" that a dog or cat could be prone to homosexual behavior, or mental depression, as the doctor had suggested. Regardless, one dog owner still insisted his dog had committed suicide by purposefully running in front of a car in traffic. The doctor said it was unclear if animals could feel suicidal, and the death may have just been accidental. Regarding homosexuality in dogs, Dr. Fox said, "Many species of animals—swans, geese, dogs and humans—do enjoy homosexual relationships. These occur especially in young animals, but they normally grow out of them. Actually, such relationships are more social and emotional rather than sexual, although some sexual behavior may occur occasionally."[41]

Whether her letter was intended to be funny or not, one letter writer to Dr. Fox complained about her female dog that not only seemed to act like "a hussy" with all male dogs she met, but also with female dogs. Dr. Fox assured the reader "not to worry" that it was common for spayed female dogs to engage in sex-like activities while playing with other dogs—and was likely related to a hormonal imbalance.[42]

"Ask Dr. Lamb"—Dr. Lawrence E. Lamb

In his position as Chief of Medical Sciences for NASA, Dr. Lawrence E. Lamb reportedly examined every American who ever went to the moon. A respected cardiologist, Lamb wrote medical textbooks, and treated President Lyndon B. Johnson throughout his public life, but also found time to write a syndicated newspaper column beginning in 1970 that lasted for 24 years. His "Ask Dr. Lamb" column appeared in more than 700 newspapers nationwide and reported receiving as many as 400,000 letters a year from readers.

The Newspaper Enterprise Association (NEA) distributed the column and touted it to readers as written by "an uncommon doctor who writes an uncommon medical column.... A brilliant physician, highly honored and uniquely qualified, he has agreed to write a newspaper column designed to help the average person protect his health. Dr. Lamb will answer all questions of general interest but will not practice medicine in his column."[43]

"I believe that the general public really shouldn't be inflicted with two-dollar medical words when explanations can be made in clear, concise English," Dr. Lamb said in 1970. "My job, as I see it, is to shed some light on what is surely a person's most prized possession, his health."[44]

A 1974 letter from a Mormon woman who said she had "battled" lesbian feelings throughout her life allowed Dr. Lamb to expound upon his views on homosexuality. "I have said many times before in this column that homosexual feelings or acts are only symptoms. They may be a normal fantasy or even in some cultures of the world, part of the normal culture."[45]

Lamb said it was important that "we always keep in mind that people, both male and female, are capable of a wide range of sexual responses and behavior. The culture and the training dictates what is normal and what is not for that particular culture."[46]

Not surprisingly, as the advent of AIDS swept the nation, Dr. Lamb fielded many questions from readers trying to understand the disease and how to avoid becoming infected. Lamb quickly dispensed with one concern: "AIDS is not a disease of homosexuals, rather, it is a disease of people. Homosexual activity is not the cause of the disease at all."[47]

Many letters would ask specific questions—one writer wanting to know if the fact they had once been diagnosed with herpes, would that make them more susceptible to getting AIDS? Dr. Lamb assured that having herpes "does not mean you are going to get AIDS" but cautioned that "if you already have the AIDS virus in your body, having herpes could stimulate the AIDS virus infection."[48]

The cause of AIDS was frequently on readers' minds, including one who asked whether AIDS was caused by an ape having sexually molested a human being. Dr. Lamb cautioned against "letting our imagination get the best of us" and noted, "The human species is capable of a lot of things, but I don't think that ape-rape has occurred. The truth is that we really do not know how the AIDS virus developed, although it appears to be a variant of less harmful viruses."

He acknowledged, however, one idea that the virus was passed from animal to man via a monkey's bite. He suggested readers write and request a copy of his newest booklet, "Sex and AIDS," for $1 and added: "Readers should know that this booklet is very explicit about sexual practices in case that should bother anyone."[49]

As he ended his column in 1994, Dr. Lamb asked his readers to "keep learning. Knowledge is the key to improving your health. Follow a healthy lifestyle. I shall miss you, and my wish for all of you is that you may live as long as you want to, and want to as long as you live."[50]

"Dear Therapist"—Lori Gottlieb

Psychotherapist and author Lori Gottlieb is a bit of a household name to regular listeners of NPR and viewers of *The Today Show, Good Morning America* or *Dr. Phil*. But Gottlieb believes her most significant credential is that "I'm a card-carrying member of the human race. I know what it's like to be a person."[51]

Chapter 14. Other Columnists

Gottlieb sees key connections between her role as a therapist and a writer. "In both of these roles, I believe that our stories form the core of our lives and give them deeper meaning," she said. "As a therapist, I ask the same questions. In both the therapy room and at my writing desk, I do a lot of editing of these stories. What material is extraneous? Is the story advancing or is the protagonist going in circles? Do the plot points reveal a point?"[52]

In 2018, *The Atlantic* brought Gottlieb aboard as a contributing writer for their new "Dear Therapist" advice column that reaches the magazine's nearly one million print and online readers. Because of the column's presentation in a longer-form publication such as a magazine, and its online companion, Gottlieb's responses are usually between 700 and 1,200 words—far beyond what most advice columnists offer. Gottlieb's books, however, tend to draw as much attention as does her column.

Her 2019 book, *Maybe You Should Talk to Someone: A Therapist, Her Therapist, and Our Lives Revealed*, has received wide attention because she openly discusses not only her own clients, but also her own therapy experiences. She described her book as "sharing stories" as part of "one person saying to another: This is who I am. Can you understand me?"[53] Hollywood has come calling with the idea of turning her book into a movie or TV series.

"I thought it was important to put myself out there with this book," Gottlieb said. "Therapists are real people, and we have our own struggles. We're all members of the human race."[54]

The book has won praise and criticism, the latter mostly based on the idea of disclosing information about clients (which is apparently aggregated and presented with their approval). As *Jewish Journal* columnist Melanie Chartoff noted, "Certainly, patients and therapists are guilty of Googling one another all the time, but knowing too much about your therapist is a little like reading the last page of a mystery thriller before you've read the rest of the book." She added, "For those considering therapy, her book is very educational, moving, inspiring and entertaining. For those considering Lori Gottlieb as a therapist, it could be a problem."[55]

Gottlieb's words have drawn controversy before, especially her 2010 book, *Marry Him: The Case for Settling for Mr. Good Enough*—a title and subject that rubbed many readers, especially women, the wrong way. As *The Chicago Tribune* noted, Gottlieb, a 40-plus mom of a son conceived via a sperm donor, "exhorts twenty- and thirty-somethings to strike while the marital iron is still hot" and settle in the husband hunt.

Dear Abby, I'm Gay

"We're way too hard to please, and we need to get over it," *The Tribune* summarized Gottlieb's contentious argument.[56] The book sparked criticism that she was "everything from being anti-feminist to provoking anxiety"[57]

Stick Figure: A Diary of My Former Self, an edited version of Gottlieb's personal diary beginning in 1978 as she battled with anorexia and body image challenges, was published in 2000 and first won her fame.

For the advice column, the editors of *The Atlantic* post an advisory that the column is offered "for informational purposes only, does not constitute medical advice, and is not a substitute for professional medical advice, diagnosis or treatment."[58]

Letters to "Dear Therapist" are, as expected, mostly relationship based and include an even smattering of letters on LGBT topics. This included a letter from a lesbian woman who was not sure she wanted children as much as did her girlfriend. As the woman reported, "I had, to a certain extent, made peace with not being a parent" and was concerned she was being pushed too much to consent to becoming a parent, something that could cause resentment.

Gottlieb said she understood the need to take time to decide, as the decision to have a child was "truly irreversible." She noted her girlfriend was given ambivalent information about having a child and likely would not have proceeded if she had made it clear she would not have children. She urged seeing a therapist, "because if you do ultimately become a family together, the self-awareness you'll gain will give you a much stronger foundation to weather the challenges of raising kids."[59]

A 65-year-old gay man who had never come out to anyone sought Gottlieb's counsel after a lifetime of "pretending." The man noted he had often engaged in unrequited crushes on other men, the most recent involving his male boss. "I will probably take my secret of my sexuality to the grave and everyone will just think I was a nice guy. But my heart aches. I've pretended for so long. Then again, what benefit would it be to my boss, my elderly mother, or my friends to know the truth?"[60]

Gottlieb replied, "I can only imagine the depth of your pain after more than six decades of pretending to be someone you're not. After all, it's a basic human need to be who we really are—and for others to know us as we really are—and the ache you're experiencing is the ache of an incarcerated self, a self that's been held in solitary confinement."[61]

She said she often asks her patients what brought them to her at

Chapter 14. Other Columnists

this particular time—and wondered the same about this man who had kept his secret for decades. She suggested he may be a person who forms "a second self to protect their original self" and then "distinguishing between the two becomes difficult." She underlined that his crushes were on heterosexual men "which means that even if you were to share your romantic interest, it wouldn't be reciprocated."[62]

"Once you step out of your jail, you'll be free to pursue relationships with available men. Your friends, who might already suspect that you're gay, will get to know you on a deeper level and likely feel much closer to you.... You'll quickly discover who matters in your life, who is worth your time. The people who care about you will want to know you, not an edited version of yourself. Those who care about you will want you to be happy."[63]

A September 2019 letter mirrored the topic of Gottlieb's book about the "back story" of her own role as a therapist. A 20-year-old gay man wrote to report he had done his own "research" on his therapist. The research yielded a revealing profile on Grindr, a gay male dating app, that surprised and "unsettled" the young man. "While I understand that my therapist, also an out gay man, is an adult with his own life outside of his office, I was deeply unnerved by learning so much explicit information."[64]

Gottlieb explained that curiosity about one's therapist was natural and normally patients know little about the lives of this person they share their most vulnerable details of life with. "Unintended encounters between therapists and patients happen out in the world," she replied. "What patients may not realize is that these unexpected encounters, as innocuous as they may seem, can be uncomfortable for the therapist as well."[65]

She encouraged the man to openly discuss the topic with his therapist and determine whether resolution was possible, or whether the therapy relationship needed to end. "Either way, the experience of talking about sex in such a courageous way will push you forward—both in therapy and in life."[66]

Gottlieb fielded a similar question from a gay couple in March 2018 who had grown fond of their female therapist who had "fundamentally changed our lives." Reporting they believed she would make a good personal friend in another setting, they were unnerved after doing some checking to find that she was the daughter of a prominent community figure who took strongly anti-gay political positions.

Gottlieb confessed that she herself had "Googled" background information on her own therapist and eventually told him so. "When I finally confessed my Google-stalking to my therapist, all the air returned to the room," she wrote. She encouraged an open discussion with the therapist because "therapy cannot be effective with a secret whirring in the background."[67]

Chapter Notes

Introduction

1. Ann Landers column, June 10, 1974.

2. Hevesi, Dennis. (2011, Oct. 28). "Elizabeth Winship dies at 90; advised youths in 'Ask Beth.'" *The New York Times.* Retrieved June 8, 2020. online at: https://www.nytimes.com/2011/10/28/us/elizabeth-winship-advice-columnist-for-youths-dies-at-90.html.

3. Anderson-Minshall, Diane. (2011, Oct. 28). "LGBT folks mourn the death of 'Ask Beth' columnist." *The Advocate.* Retrieved June 8, 2020, online at: https://www.advocate.com/news/daily-news/2011/10/28/lgbt-folks-mourn-death-ask-beth-columnist.

4. McHenry, F.A. (1941). "A Note on Homosexuality, Crime and the Newspapers." *Journal of Criminal Psychopathology* 2(2), pp. 533–548.

5. Time magazine, Jan. 21, 1966.

6. Durham, Grey. (1971, Dec. 31). "Homosexuals in revolt: The year that one liberation movement turned militant." *Life Magazine.*

7. Scutts, Joana. (2018, Aug. 10). "The evolution of the advice column: Private questions, answered in public, are a window into the great anxieties of our times." *Medium.* Retrieved Dec. 22, 2019, online at: https://medium.com/s/story/the-evolution-of-the-advice-column-4676167c4317.

8. Scutts, Joana. (2018, Aug. 10). "The evolution of the advice column: Private questions, answered in public, are a window into the great anxieties of our times." *Medium.* Retrieved Dec. 22, 2019, online at: https://medium.com/s/story/the-evolution-of-the-advice-column-4676167c4317.

9. Coleman, Marilyn J., & Ganong, Lawrence H. (eds.). (2014). *The Social History of the American Family: An Encyclopedia.* Thousand Oaks, CA: Sage.

10. Coleman, Marilyn J., & Ganong, Lawrence H. (eds.). (2014). *The Social History of the American Family: An Encyclopedia.* Thousand Oaks, CA: Sage.

11. Scutts, Joana. (2018, Aug. 10). "The evolution of the advice column: Private questions, answered in public, are a window into the great anxieties of our times." *Medium.* Retrieved Dec. 22, 2019, online at: https://medium.com/s/story/the-evolution-of-the-advice-column-4676167c4317.

12. Whitt, Jan. (2008). *Women in American Journalism: A New History.* Champaign: University of Illinois Press; Vaughn, Stephen L. (ed.). (2007). *Encyclopedia of American Journalism.* New York: Routledge.

13. Douglas, George H. (1999). *The Golden Age of the Newspaper.* Westport, CT: Greenwood Publishing Group.

14. Lord Alfred Douglas poem, "Two Loves," first published December 1894, *The Chameleon*, Oxford University. Retrieved Dec. 21, 2019, online at: https://www.bl.uk/collection-items/the-chameleon; Douglas, George H. (1999). *The Golden Age of the Newspaper.* Westport, CT: Greenwood Publishing Group.

15. *San Rafael Daily Independent Journal*, April 8, 1967.

16. Finnie, Hannah. (2015, Dec. 15). "How the Internet changed advice columns." *The Atlantic.* Retrieved Dec. 22, 2019, online at: https://www.theatlantic.

Notes—Chapters 1 and 2

com/technology/archive/2015/12/how-the-internet-changed-advice-columns/420579/.
17. Brammer, John Paul. (2019, Winter). "The advice column renaissance." *Columbia Journalism Review*. Retrieved Dec. 19, 2019, online at: https://www.cjr.org/special_report/the-advice-column-renaissance.php.
18. Brammer, John Paul. (2019, Winter). "The advice column renaissance." *Columbia Journalism Review*. Retrieved Dec. 19, 2019, online at: https://www.cjr.org/special_report/the-advice-column-renaissance.php.

Chapter 1

1. *Chicago Tribune*, June 22, 2002.
2. *Life Magazine*, April 7, 1958.
3. *Life Magazine*, April 7, 1958.
4. *Life Magazine*, April 7, 1958.
5. *Life Magazine*, April 7, 1958.
6. *Life Magazine*, April 7, 1958.
7. *Life Magazine*, April 7, 1958.
8. *Chicago Tribune*, June 22, 2002.
9. *Chicago Tribune*, June 22, 2002.
10. *Chicago Tribune*, June 22, 2002.
11. United Press International, Jan. 1, 1980.
12. Ann Landers column, July 21, 1996.
13. Ann Landers column, Aug. 3, 1976.
14. Ann Landers column, Aug. 3, 1976.
15. Ann Landers column, Oct. 22, 1959.
16. Ann Landers column, Feb. 7, 1961.
17. Ann Landers column, Feb. 7, 1961.
18. Ann Landers column, March 9, 1961.
19. Ann Landers column, March 9, 1961.
20. Ann Landers column, March 9, 1961.
21. Ann Landers column, March 9, 1961.
22. Ann Landers column, March 10, 1961.
23. Ann Landers column, March 10, 1961.
24. Ann Landers column, March 12, 1961
25. Ann Landers column, Dec. 24, 1962.
26. Ann Landers column, Dec. 24, 1962.
27. Ann Landers column, Feb. 12, 1963.
28. Ann Landers column, Oct. 10, 1965, and Jan. 4, 1966.
29. Ann Landers column, Oct. 10, 1965, and Jan. 4, 1966.
30. Ann Landers column, Nov. 19, 1972.
31. Ann Landers column, Nov. 19, 1972.
32. Ann Landers column, Oct. 8, 1973.
33. Ann Landers column, Jan. 11, 1971.
34. Ann Landers column, Jan. 11, 1971.
35. Ann Landers column, April 4, 1971.
36. Ann Landers column, March 11, 1964.
37. Ann Landers column, March 11, 1964.
38. Ann Landers column, June 21, 1972.
39. Ann Landers column, April 22, 1964.
40. Ann Landers column, April 22, 1964.
41. Ann Landers column, April 22, 1964.
42. Ann Landers column, April 12, 1964.
43. Ann Landers column, April 12, 1964.
44. Ann Landers column, April 12, 1964.
45. Ann Landers column, April 12, 1964.
46. Ann Landers column, April 12, 1964.
47. Ann Landers column, April 12, 1964.
48. Ann Landers column, March 12, 1965.
49. Ann Landers column, May 5, 1965.
50. Ann Landers column, Aug. 29, 1969.
51. Ann Landers column, July 8, 1965.
52. Ann Landers column, Jan. 2, 1971.
53. Ann Landers column, June 10, 1974.
54. Ann Landers column, June 10, 1974.
55. Ann Landers column, March 1, 1973.
56. *Chicago Tribune*, June 22, 2002.

Chapter 2

1. Gudelunas, David. (2017). *Confidential to America: Newspaper Advice Columns and Sexual Education*. New York: Routledge.
2. Gudelunas, David. (2017). *Confidential to America: Newspaper Advice Columns and Sexual Education*. New York: Routledge.
3. Gudelunas, David. (2017). *Confidential to America: Newspaper Advice Columns and Sexual Education*. New York: Routledge.
4. Associated Press, Jan. 18, 2013.
5. "Dear Abby," Sept. 23, 1966.
6. "Dear Abby," May 3, 1972.
7. "Dear Abby," May 3, 1972.
8. "Dear Abby," May 3, 1972.
9. "Dear Abby," Oct. 20, 1969.

Notes—Chapter 3

10. "Dear Abby," Dec. 30, 1969.
11. "Dear Abby," May 22, 1967.
12. "Dear Abby," May 22, 1967.
13. "Dear Abby," July 21, 1979.
14. "Dear Abby," Nov. 7, 1967.
15. "Dear Abby," Nov. 7, 1967.
16. "Dear Abby," Nov. 7, 1967.
17. "Dear Abby," Nov. 20, 1969.
18. "Dear Abby," Feb. 2, 1970.
19. "Dear Abby," Feb. 2, 1970.
20. "Dear Abby," Feb. 2, 1970.
21. Marcus, Eric. (Producer/Host). (2016). *Pauline Phillips, founder of the "Dear Abby" column.* [Audio podcast] Retrieved from: https://makinggayhistory.com/season-one/.
22. "Dear Abby," Feb. 27, 1970.
23. "Dear Abby," Dec. 31, 1967.
24. "Dear Abby," Dec. 31, 1967.
25. "Dear Abby," Feb. 12, 1970.
26. "Dear Abby," Feb. 12, 1970.
27. "Dear Abby," April 13, 1970.
28. *Greenwood (MS) Commonwealth*, Dec. 17, 1973.
29. *Decatur (IL) Herald*, Feb. 9, 1978, and *Staunton (VA) News-Leader*, Feb. 24, 1980.
30. *Albany (OR) Democrat-Herald*, Feb. 27, 1980
31. Marcus, Eric. (Producer/Host). (2016). *Pauline Phillips, founder of the "Dear Abby" column.* [Audio podcast] Retrieved from: https://makinggayhistory.com/season-one/.
32. Marcus, Eric. (Producer/Host). (2016). *Pauline Phillips, founder of the "Dear Abby" column.* [Audio podcast] Retrieved from: https://makinggayhistory.com/season-one/.
33. "Dear Abby," Feb. 9, 1971.
34. "Dear Abby," May 29, 1972.
35. "Dear Abby," May 29, 1972, and June 18, 1973.
36. "Dear Abby," May 29, 1972, and June 18, 1973.
37. "Dear Abby," Oct. 20, 1973.
38. "Dear Abby," Sept. 22, 1977.
39. "Dear Abby," Jan. 11, 1971.
40. "Dear Abby," June 14, 1979.
41. "Dear Abby," Oct. 28, 1987.
42. "Dear Abby," Oct. 28, 1987.
43. "Dear Abby," July 29, 1979.
44. "Dear Abby," Sept. 23, 1983.
45. "Dear Abby," June 5, 1974.
46. "Dear Abby," June 5, 1974.
47. "Dear Abby," March 15, 1972.
48. "Dear Abby," Jan. 28, 1978.
49. "Dear Abby," Nov. 27, 1978.
50. "Dear Abby," Jan. 27, 1983.
51. "Dear Abby," Jan. 30, 1978.
52. "Dear Abby," Sept. 23, 1986.
53. "Dear Abby," Sept. 23, 1986.
54. "Dear Abby," Aug. 16, 1971.
55. "Dear Abby," Dec. 22, 1975.
56. "Dear Abby," March 10, 1972.
57. "Dear Abby," June 22, 1975.
58. "Dear Abby," April 23, 1982.
59. "Dear Abby," Aug. 6, 1982.
60. "Dear Abby," Aug. 6, 1982.
61. "Dear Abby," Oct. 20, 1971.
62. "Dear Abby," Oct. 30, 1974.
63. "Dear Abby," Dec. 8, 1982.
64. "Dear Abby," Dec. 8, 1982.
65. "Dear Abby," Dec. 8, 1982.
66. "Dear Abby," Oct. 16, 1987.
67. "Dear Abby," Oct. 16, 1987.
68. "Dear Abby," Nov. 10, 1986.
69. "Dear Abby," Nov. 10, 1986.
70. "Dear Abby," May 6, 1987.
71. "Dear Abby," May 6, 1987.
72. Marcus, Eric. (Producer/Host). (2016). *Pauline Phillips, founder of the "Dear Abby" column.* [Audio podcast] Retrieved from: https://makinggayhistory.com/season-one/.

Chapter 3

1. *San Rafael (CA) Independent-Journal*, April 8, 1967.
2. *San Rafael (CA) Independent-Journal*, April 8, 1967.
3. *San Rafael (CA) Independent-Journal*, April 8, 1967.
4. "Helen Help Us," Feb. 8, 1966.
5. *San Francisco Examiner*, July 15, 1979.
6. *Los Angeles Times*, June 7, 1988.
7. *Los Angeles Times*, June 7, 1988.
8. *Los Angeles Times*, June 7, 1988.
9. *Los Angeles Times*, June 7, 1988.
10. *San Francisco Examiner*, July 15, 1979.
11. *Los Angeles Times*, June 7, 1988.
12. "Helen Help Us," Jan. 11, 1968.
13. "Helen Help Us," May 31, 1968.

Notes—Chapters 4 and 5

14. "Helen Help Us," May 31, 1968.
15. "Helen Help Us," May 31, 1968.
16. "Helen Help Us," April 4, 1977.
17. "Helen Help Us," March 20, 1970.
18. "Helen Help Us," May 13, 1970.
19. "Helen Help Us," May 26, 1972.
20. "Helen Help Us," May 13, 1970.
21. "Helen Help Us," May 13, 1970.
22. "Helen Help Us," July 3, 1973.
23. "Helen Help Us," Dec. 28, 1973.
24. "Helen Help Us," Dec. 28, 1973.
25. "Helen Help Us," Oct. 25, 1974.
26. "Helen Help Us," Dec. 2, 1974.
27. "Helen Help Us," Dec. 2, 1974.
28. "Helen Help Us," Dec. 2, 1974.
29. "Helen Help Us," May 2, 1975.
30. "Helen Help Us," June 19, 1975.
31. "Helen Help Us," April 13, 1975.
32. "Helen Help Us," April 13, 1975.
33. "Helen Help Us," Dec. 12, 1972.
34. "Helen Help Us," Feb. 2, 1973.
35. "Helen Help Us," Dec. 28, 1978.
36. "Helen Help Us," May 20, 1977.
37. "Helen Help Us," May 20, 1977.
38. "Helen Help Us," Aug. 4, 1969.
39. "Helen Help Us," July 26, 1976.
40. "Helen Help Us," July 26, 1976.
41. "Helen Help Us," July 26, 1976.
42. "Helen Help Us," Sept. 13, 1976.
43. "Helen Help Us," Sept. 13, 1976.
44. "Helen Help Us," Sept. 13, 1976.
45. "Helen Help Us," Nov. 3, 1976.
46. "Helen Help Us," Nov. 3, 1976.
47. "Helen Help Us," Nov. 3, 1976.
48. "Helen Help Us," Feb. 26, 1970.
49. "Helen Help Us," Feb. 26, 1970.

Chapter 4

1. *Washington Post*, Dec. 14, 1989.
2. *Christian Science Monitor*, Oct. 14, 1959.
3. Associated Press, Nov. 16, 1955.
4. Associated Press, May 5, 1978.
5. Associated Press, Jan. 10, 1971.
6. *New York Times*, May 14, 2013.
7. Dr. Brothers column, Sept. 20, 1966.
8. Dr. Brothers column, Nov. 21, 1967.
9. Dr. Brothers column, Nov. 21, 1967.
10. Dr. Brothers column, Nov. 21, 1967.
11. Dr. Brothers column, Nov. 21, 1967.
12. Dr. Brothers column, Nov. 21, 1967.
13. Dr. Brothers column, Oct. 24, 1969.
14. Dr. Brothers column, Oct. 24, 1969.
15. Dr. Brothers column, Oct. 24, 1969.
16. Dr. Brothers column, Oct. 24, 1969.
17. Dr. Brothers column, Oct. 24, 1969.
18. Dr. Brothers column, June 30, 1981.
19. Dr. Brothers column, June 30, 1981.
20. Dr. Brothers column, Feb. 6, 1973.
21. Dr. Brothers column, Feb. 6, 1973.
22. Dr. Brothers column, Feb. 6, 1973.
23. Dr. Brothers column, June 28, 1968.
24. Dr. Brothers column, April 17, 1969.
25. Dr. Brothers column, Dec. 4, 1970.
26. Dr. Brothers column, April 26, 1971.
27. Dr. Brothers column, April 26, 1971.
28. Dr. Brothers column, April 26, 1971.
29. Dr. Brothers column, Dec. 29, 1971.
30. Dr. Brothers column, July 23, 1973.
31. Dr. Brothers column, Oct. 5, 1982.
32. Dr. Brothers column, Oct. 5, 1982.
33. Dr. Brothers column, Sept. 3, 1985.
34. Dr. Brothers column, Nov. 29, 1969.
35. Dr. Brothers column, Nov. 29, 1969.
36. Dr. Brothers column, May 19, 1972, July 31, 1972, Aug. 17, 1976, May 15, 1978, and May 16, 1980.
37. Dr. Brothers column, March 15, 1976, and July 5, 1976.
38. Dr. Brothers column, March 15, 1976, and July 5, 1976.
39. Dr. Brothers column, Feb. 17, 1977.
40. Dr. Brothers column, Feb. 17, 1977.
41. Dr. Brothers column, June 24, 1977.
42. Associated Press, Oct. 9, 1977.
43. Dr. Brothers column, Nov. 8, 1979.
44. Dr. Brothers column, Nov. 8, 1979.
45. Dr. Brothers column, July 14, 1981.
46. Dr. Brothers column, July 14, 1981.
47. Dr. Brothers column, Sept. 16, 1986, and May 21, 1986.
48. Collins, Kathleen. (2016). *Dr. Joyce Brothers: The Founding Mother of TV Psychology*. Lanham, MD: Rowman & Littlefield.

Chapter 5

1. Dr. Crane's "Worry Clinic," Aug. 14, 1968.
2. Dr. Crane's "Worry Clinic," Aug. 14, 1968.
3. Dr. Crane's "Worry Clinic," Aug. 14, 1968.
4. *Chicago Tribune*, July 24, 1995.

Notes—Chapter 5

5. *Chicago Tribune*, July 24, 1995.
6. *Billboard Magazine*, May 24, 1947.
7. *Billboard Magazine*, May 24, 1947.
8. Dr. Crane's "Worry Clinic," Dec. 31, 1936.
9. Dr. Crane's "Worry Clinic," Dec. 31, 1936.
10. Dr. Crane's "Worry Clinic," Dec. 31, 1936.
11. Dr. Crane's "Worry Clinic," Dec. 31, 1936.
12. Dr. Crane's "Worry Clinic," April 27, 1937.
13. Dr. Crane's "Worry Clinic," April 27, 1937.
14. Dr. Crane's "Worry Clinic," April 27, 1937.
15. Dr. Crane's "Worry Clinic," April 27, 1937.
16. Dr. Crane's "Worry Clinic," April 27, 1937.
17. Dr. Crane's "Worry Clinic," April 27, 1937.
18. Dr. Crane's "Worry Clinic," Jan. 13, 1938.
19. Dr. Crane's "Worry Clinic," Jan. 13, 1938.
20. Dr. Crane's "Worry Clinic," Jan. 13, 1938.
21. Dr. Crane's "Worry Clinic," May 12, 1938.
22. Dr. Crane's "Worry Clinic," May 12, 1938.
23. Dr. Crane's "Worry Clinic," May 12, 1938.
24. Dr. Crane's "Worry Clinic," May 12, 1938.
25. Dr. Crane's "Worry Clinic," June 23, 1938.
26. Dr. Crane's "Worry Clinic," June 23, 1938.
27. Dr. Crane's "Worry Clinic," June 23, 1938.
28. Dr. Crane's "Worry Clinic," June 23, 1938.
29. Dr. Crane's "Worry Clinic," Dec. 3, 1938.
30. Dr. Crane's "Worry Clinic," Dec. 3, 1938.
31. Dr. Crane's "Worry Clinic," Dec. 3, 1938.
32. Dr. Crane's "Worry Clinic," Feb. 14, 1939.
33. Dr. Crane's "Worry Clinic," May 8, 1941.
34. Dr. Crane's "Worry Clinic," May 8, 1941.
35. Dr. Crane's "Worry Clinic," May 8, 1941.
36. Dr. Crane's "Worry Clinic," May 8, 1941.
37. Dr. Crane's "Worry Clinic," Nov. 22, 1941.
38. Dr. Crane's "Worry Clinic," Nov. 22, 1941.
39. Dr. Crane's "Worry Clinic," Oct. 2, 1942.
40. Dr. Crane's "Worry Clinic," Jan. 16, 1943.
41. Dr. Crane's "Worry Clinic," Jan. 16, 1943.
42. Dr. Crane's "Worry Clinic," Jan. 16, 1943.
43. Dr. Crane's "Worry Clinic," June 6, 1967.
44. Dr. Crane's "Worry Clinic," Dec. 14, 1943.
45. Dr. Crane's "Worry Clinic," Dec. 14, 1943.
46. Dr. Crane's "Worry Clinic," Dec. 14, 1943.
47. Dr. Crane's "Worry Clinic," Nov. 5, 1949.
48. Dr. Crane's "Worry Clinic," Dec. 14, 1943.
49. Dr. Crane's "Worry Clinic," Feb. 28, 1944.
50. Dr. Crane's "Worry Clinic," Feb. 28, 1944.
51. Dr. Crane's "Worry Clinic," Feb. 28, 1944.
52. Dr. Crane's "Worry Clinic," Aug. 3, 1955.
53. Dr. Crane's "Worry Clinic," Feb. 28, 1944.
54. Dr. Crane's "Worry Clinic," May 17, 1945.
55. Dr. Crane's "Worry Clinic," May 17, 1945.
56. Dr. Crane's "Worry Clinic," Nov. 12, 1951.
57. Dr. Crane's "Worry Clinic," Nov. 12, 1951.
58. Dr. Crane's "Worry Clinic," Nov. 12, 1951.
59. Dr. Crane's "Worry Clinic," Nov. 12, 1951.

Notes—Chapter 6

60. Dr. Crane's "Worry Clinic," Nov. 4, 1954.
61. Dr. Crane's "Worry Clinic," Feb. 18, 1964.
62. Dr. Crane's "Worry Clinic," Jan. 25, 1965.
63. Dr. Crane's "Worry Clinic," Jan. 25, 1965.
64. Dr. Crane's "Worry Clinic," Jan. 23, 1953.
65. Dr. Crane's "Worry Clinic," April 9, 1955.
66. Dr. Crane's "Worry Clinic," April 9, 1955.
67. Dr. Crane's "Worry Clinic," April 9, 1955.
68. Dr. Crane's "Worry Clinic," April 9, 1955.
69. Dr. Crane's "Worry Clinic," April 11, 1955.
70. Dr. Crane's "Worry Clinic," March 10, 1958.
71. Dr. Crane's "Worry Clinic," March 10, 1958.
72. Dr. Crane's "Worry Clinic," March 10, 1958.
73. Dr. Crane's "Worry Clinic," March 10, 1958.
74. Dr. Crane's "Worry Clinic," Aug. 19, 1964.
75. Dr. Crane's "Worry Clinic," Jan. 5, 1965.
76. Dr. Crane's "Worry Clinic," Sept. 6, 1965.
77. Dr. Crane's "Worry Clinic," Jan. 18, 1965.
78. Dr. Crane's "Worry Clinic," June 2, 1967.
79. Dr. Crane's "Worry Clinic," June 2, 1967.
80. Dr. Crane's "Worry Clinic," May 17, 1968.
81. Dr. Crane's "Worry Clinic," July 9, 1971.
82. Dr. Crane's "Worry Clinic," Feb. 5, 1963.
83. Dr. Crane's "Worry Clinic," Feb. 5, 1963.
84. Dr. Crane's "Worry Clinic," Feb. 5, 1963.
85. Dr. Crane's "Worry Clinic," Dec. 16, 1963, and Sept. 6, 1965.
86. Dr. Crane's "Worry Clinic," Dec. 16, 1963.
87. Dr. Crane's "Worry Clinic," March 9, 1965.
88. Dr. Crane's "Worry Clinic," Dec. 16, 1963.
89. Dr. Crane's "Worry Clinic," April 22, 1969.
90. Dr. Crane's "Worry Clinic," July 18, 1969.
91. Dr. Crane's "Worry Clinic," July 18, 1969.
92. Dr. Crane's "Worry Clinic," May 17, 1968.
93. Dr. Crane's "Worry Clinic," Oct. 27, 1967.
94. Dr. Crane's "Worry Clinic," Oct. 24, 1973.
95. Dr. Crane's "Worry Clinic," July 9, 1973.
96. Dr. Crane's "Worry Clinic," July 9, 1973.
97. Dr. Crane's "Worry Clinic," July 9, 1973.
98. Dr. Crane's "Worry Clinic," July 9, 1973.
99. Dr. Crane's "Worry Clinic," July 9, 1973.
100. Dr. Crane's "Worry Clinic," July 9, 1973.
101. Dr. Crane's "Worry Clinic," July 9, 1973.
102. Dr. Crane's "Worry Clinic," Dec. 8, 1972.
103. Associated Press, July 16, 1983.

Chapter 6

1. *Chattanooga (TN) Daily Times*, Jan. 1, 1953.
2. *Chattanooga (TN) Daily Times*, Jan. 1, 1953.
3. *Chattanooga (TN) Daily Times*, Jan. 1, 1953.
4. Dalton, Joseph. (2018). *Washington's Golden Age: Hope Ridings Miller, the Society Beat and the Rise of Women Journalists*. Lanham, MD: Rowman & Littlefield. Conant, Jennet. (2005). *109 East Palace: Robert Oppenheimer and the Secret City of Los Alamos*. New York: Simon & Schuster.
5. McLearn quoted in *Congressional Record: Proceedings and Debates of the 80th Congress*, Second Session. Vol. 94, Part 11, p. 4073. Retrieved Dec. 20, 2019 at: https://books.google.com/books?id=-mCxUTFSj1-AC&pg=SL1-PA4073&lpg=

Notes—Chapter 7

SL1PA4073&dq=Frank+McLearn+Washington+Post+editor&source=bl&ots=NfQQTWNwGX&sig=ACfU3U1uCV4_Mndg6aRzpDxlBqXNp8WaA&hl=en&sa=X&ved=2ahUKEwjOyIL7ocrmAhXzJzQIHazODloQ6AEwAHoECAkQAQ#v=onepage&q=Frank%20McLearn%20Washington%20Post%20editor&f=false.

6. *Chattanooga (TN) Daily Times*, Jan. 1, 1953.
7. "Mary Haworth's Mail," April 9, 1953.
8. Associated Press, Nov. 2, 1981.
9. *Fortune* (2013, Aug. 11). "Rise of *The Washington Post*," originally published Aug. 5, 1944. Retrieved Dec. 20, 2019, online at: https://fortune.com/2013/08/11/rise-of-the-washington-post-fortune-1944/.
10. *Fortune* (2013, Aug. 11). "Rise of *The Washington Post*," originally published Aug. 5, 1944. Retrieved Dec. 20, 2019, online at: https://fortune.com/2013/08/11/rise-of-the-washington-post-fortune-1944/.
11. "Mary Haworth's Mail," July 24 and Aug. 21, 1944.
12. "Mary Haworth's Mail," July 21, 1945.
13. "Mary Haworth's Mail," July 25, 1946.
14. "Mary Haworth's Mail," Dec. 23, 1946.
15. "Mary Haworth's Mail," Jan. 11, 1947.
16. "Mary Haworth's Mail," Jan. 11, 1947.
17. "Mary Haworth's Mail," May 22, 1947.
18. "Mary Haworth's Mail," Aug. 6, 1952.
19. "Mary Haworth's Mail," Sept. 16, 1952.
20. "Mary Haworth's Mail," Oct. 30, 1952.
21. "Mary Haworth's Mail," March 10, 1953.
22. "Mary Haworth's Mail," April 9, 1953.
23. "Mary Haworth's Mail," April 9, 1953.
24. "Mary Haworth's Mail," April 15, 1953; Nov. 8, 1954.
25. "Mary Haworth's Mail," July 25, 1957.
26. "Mary Haworth's Mail," July 25, 1957.
27. "Mary Haworth's Mail," July 25, 1957.
28. "Mary Haworth's Mail," July 25, 1957.
29. "Mary Haworth's Mail," July 25, 1957.
30. "Mary Haworth's Mail," May 28, 1957, June 6, 1957, and June 24, 1957.
31. "Mary Haworth's Mail," June 24, 1957.
32. "Mary Haworth's Mail," June 24, 1957.
33. "Mary Haworth's Mail," June 24, 1957.
34. "Mary Haworth's Mail," June 24, 1957.
35. "Mary Haworth's Mail," April 16, 1959.
36. "Mary Haworth's Mail," April 16, 1959.
37. "Mary Haworth's Mail," April 16, 1959.
38. "Mary Haworth's Mail," April 16, 1959.
39. "Mary Haworth's Mail," Aug. 26, 1960.
40. "Mary Haworth's Mail," Sept. 7, 1962.
41. "Mary Haworth's Mail," Sept. 7, 1962.
42. "Mary Haworth's Mail," April 3, 1963.
43. "Mary Haworth's Mail," April 3, 1963.
44. "Mary Haworth's Mail," May 3, 1963.
45. "Mary Haworth's Mail," May 3, 1963.
46. "Mary Haworth's Mail," Sept. 18, 1963.
47. "Mary Haworth's Mail," Sept. 18, 1963.
48. "Mary Haworth's Mail," Sept. 18, 1963.
49. "Mary Haworth's Mail," Sept. 18, 1963.
50. "Mary Haworth's Mail," Oct. 3, 1963.
51. "Mary Haworth's Mail," Oct. 3, 1963.
52. "Mary Haworth's Mail," Oct. 3, 1963.
53. "Mary Haworth's Mail," Jan. 13, 1966.
54. "Mary Haworth's Mail," Feb. 16, 1966.
55. "Mary Haworth's Mail," July 17, 1968.
56. "Mary Haworth's Mail," July 17, 1968.
57. "Mary Haworth's Mail," Jan. 24, 1970.
58. "Mary Haworth's Mail," April 11, 1972
59. *Washington Post*, Nov. 2, 1981.

Chapter 7

1. *Hammond (IN) Times*, Feb. 19, 1982.
2. *Hammond (IN) Times*, Feb. 19, 1982
3. "Dear Meg," Dec. 13, 1982.
4. "Dear Meg," July 13, 1983.
5. "Dear Meg," April 29, 1983.
6. "Dear Meg," Sept. 18, 1983.
7. "Dear Meg," Sept. 18, 1983.
8. "Dear Meg," Nov. 29, 1987.
9. "Dear Meg," Nov. 29, 1987.
10. "Dear Meg," June 28, 1985, and July 23, 1985.
11. "Dear Meg," Dec. 7, 1984.
12. "Dear Meg," Dec. 7, 1984.
13. "Dear Meg," Dec. 9, 1987.
14. "Dear Meg," July 26, 1986.
15. "Dear Meg," Nov. 18, 1983.
16. "Dear Meg," May 15, 1984.
17. "Dear Meg," Oct. 4, 1983.
18. "Dear Meg," Oct. 4, 1983.
19. "Dear Meg," April 23, 1985.
20. "Dear Meg," Sept. 24, 1985.
21. "Dear Meg," Nov. 25, 1985.
22. "Dear Meg," Nov. 25, 1985.
23. "Dear Meg," Nov. 25, 1985.
24. "Dear Meg," Nov. 25, 1985.
25. "Dear Meg," April 7, 1986.
26. "Dear Meg," May 17, 1988.

Chapter 8

1. *The Advocate*, Oct. 28, 2011.
2. *Boston Globe*, Sept. 29, 1998.
3. *Boston Globe*, Sept. 29, 1998.
4. *Boston Globe*, Sept. 29, 1998.
5. *Boston Globe*, Sept. 29, 1998.
6. *Boston Globe*, Sept. 29, 1998.
7. *Boston Globe*, Sept. 29, 1998.
8. *Boston Globe*, May 26, 1985.
9. *Boston Globe*, May 26, 1985.
10. "Ask Beth," Sept. 14, 1972.
11. "Ask Beth," Jan. 3, 1974.
12. "Ask Beth," Jan. 3, 1974.
13. "Ask Beth," Jan. 3, 1974.
14. "Ask Beth," March 7, 1974.
15. "Ask Beth," March 7, 1974.
16. "Ask Beth," March 7, 1974.
17. "Ask Beth," June 19, 1975.
18. "Ask Beth," June 19, 1975.
19. "Ask Beth," June 19, 1975.
20. "Ask Beth," June 19, 1975.
21. Lane, Stephen. (2018). *No Sanctuary: Teachers and the School Reform That Brought Gay Rights to the Masses*. Lebanon, NH: University Press of New England.
22. "Ask Beth," Aug. 7, 1975.
23. "Ask Beth," Aug. 7, 1975.
24. "Ask Beth," Feb. 26, 1976.
25. "Ask Beth," Feb. 26, 1976.
26. "Ask Beth," Sept. 30, 1976.
27. "Ask Beth," Oct. 29, 1976.
28. "Ask Beth," Oct. 29, 1976.
29. "Ask Beth," June 12, 1977.
30. "Ask Beth," Aug. 17, 1978.
31. "Ask Beth," Aug. 17, 1978.
32. "Ask Beth," Sept. 28, 1978.
33. "Ask Beth," Sept. 23, 1980.
34. "Ask Beth," Sept. 23, 1980.
35. "Ask Beth," Sept. 23, 1980.
36. "Ask Beth," Feb. 25, 1991.
37. "Ask Beth," Aug. 29, 1976.
38. "Ask Beth," Aug. 29, 1976.
39. "Ask Beth," Aug. 29, 1976.
40. "Ask Beth," Aug. 21, 1981.
41. "Ask Beth," Nov. 23, 1977.
42. "Ask Beth," Nov. 23, 1977.
43. "Ask Beth," Dec. 22, 1977.
44. "Ask Beth," Dec. 22, 1977.
45. "Ask Beth," Dec. 30, 1978.
46. "Ask Beth," Dec. 21, 1979.
47. "Ask Beth," March 4, 1983.
48. "Ask Beth," Feb. 21, 1986.
49. "Ask Beth," Oct. 7, 1982.
50. "Ask Beth," Oct. 7, 1982.
51. "Ask Beth," Sept. 23, 1979.
52. "Ask Beth," Aug. 24, 1980.
53. "Ask Beth," Dec. 13, 1981.
54. "Ask Beth," Sept. 12, 1982.
55. "Ask Beth," March 6, 1988.
56. "Ask Beth," Jan. 15, 1984.
57. "Ask Beth," Jan. 15, 1984.
58. "Ask Beth," April 22, 1984.
59. "Ask Beth," Oct. 30, 1980.
60. "Ask Beth," Oct. 30, 1980.
61. "Ask Beth," July 30, 1981.
62. "Ask Beth," July 30, 1981.
63. "Ask Beth," July 30, 1981.
64. "Ask Beth," Oct. 28, 1982.
65. "Ask Beth," June 19, 1980.
66. "Ask Beth," June 19, 1980.
67. "Ask Beth," May 13, 1983.
68. "Ask Beth," May 13, 1983.
69. "Ask Beth," May 13, 1983.
70. "Ask Beth," March 7, 1986.
71. "Ask Beth," May 24, 1986.
72. "Ask Beth," April 19, 1987.
73. "Ask Beth," Oct. 22, 1988.

Chapter 9

1. Retrieved online at: https://www.washingtonpost.com/people/carolyn-hax/.
2. *Palm Beach (FL) Post*, June 27, 1999.
3. *Sunbury (PA) Daily Item*, Feb. 1, 1998.
4. *Philadelphia Inquirer*, Nov. 14, 2001.
5. *Tampa Bay (FL) Times*, Jan. 12, 2013.
6. *Tampa Bay (FL) Times*, Jan. 12, 2013.
7. *Tampa Bay (FL) Times*, Jan. 12, 2013.
8. *Palm Beach (FL) Post*, June 27, 1999.
9. *White Plains (NY) Journal-News*, April 12, 2001.
10. *White Plains (NY) Journal-News*, April 12, 2001.
11. *White Plains (NY) Journal-News*, April 12, 2001.
12. "Tell Me About It," March 20, 1998.
13. "Tell Me About It," March 20, 1998.
14. "Tell Me About It," Sept. 11, 1998.
15. "Tell Me About It," Feb. 21, 1999.
16. "Tell Me About It," June 25, 2000.
17. "Tell Me About It," June 25, 2000.
18. "Tell Me About It," May 14, 1999.

Notes—Chapter 10

19. "Tell Me About It," Jan. 12, 2012.
20. "Tell Me About It," Jan. 12, 2012.
21. "Tell Me About It," Dec. 28, 1999.
22. "Tell Me About It," Dec. 28, 1999.
23. "Tell Me About It," March 30, 2000.
24. "Tell Me About It," March 30, 2000.
25. "Tell Me About It," March 30, 2000.
26. "Tell Me About It," March 30, 2000.
27. "Tell Me About It," Jan. 3, 2001.
28. "Tell Me About It," Jan. 3, 2001.
29. "Tell Me About It," Dec. 11, 2003.
30. "Tell Me About It," July 27, 2010.
31. "Tell Me About It," July 27, 2010.
32. "Tell Me About It," Oct. 5, 2008.
33. "Tell Me About It," Oct. 5, 2008.
34. "Tell Me About It," Aug. 2, 2016.
35. "Tell Me About It," Aug. 2, 2016.
36. "Tell Me About It," Aug. 2, 2016.
37. "Tell Me About It," Aug. 2, 2016.
38. "Tell Me About It," July 23, 2019.
39. "Tell Me About It," July 23, 2019.
40. "Tell Me About It," Oct. 30, 1998.
41. "Tell Me About It," Oct. 30, 1998.
42. "Tell Me About It," Oct. 30, 1998.
43. "Tell Me About It," Aug. 9, 2002.
44. "Tell Me About It," Aug. 9, 2002.
45. "Tell Me About It," April 4, 2008.
46. "Tell Me About It," April 4, 2008.
47. "Tell Me About It," April 4, 2008.
48. "Tell Me About It," April 7, 2019.
49. "Tell Me About It," April 7, 2019.
50. "Tell Me About It," April 7, 2019.
51. *Palm Beach (FL) Post*, June 27, 1999.
52. *Palm Beach (FL) Post*, June 27, 1999.

Chapter 10

1. *Boston Globe,* May 22, 1998.
2. *Boston Globe,* Feb. 3, 2006.
3. *Red Deer (Canada) Advocate*, Feb. 19, 2006.
4. *Chicago Tribune*, March 25, 2015.
5. "Dear Prudence," Feb. 16, 2012.
6. "Dear Prudence," Feb. 16, 2012.
7. "Dear Prudence," Feb. 16, 2012.
8. "Dear Prudence," Feb. 16, 2012.
9. "Dear Prudence," Feb. 16, 2012.
10. "Dear Prudence," Feb. 16, 2012.
11. Autostradle.com, Feb. 28, 2018. Retrieved online at: https://www.autostraddle.com/mal-ortberg-merry-spinster-coming-out-trans-412246/.
12. "Dear Prudence," Feb. 27, 1999.
13. "Dear Prudence," Feb. 27, 1999.
14. "Dear Prudence," Feb. 8, 2001.
15. "Dear Prudence," Sept. 24, 1999.
16. "Dear Prudence," Sept. 24, 1999.
17. "Dear Prudence," April 26, 2000.
18. "Dear Prudence," April 26, 2000.
19. "Dear Prudence," Nov. 12, 1999.
20. "Dear Prudence," Dec. 31, 1999.
21. "Dear Prudence," Dec. 31, 1999.
22. "Dear Prudence," Dec. 31, 1999.
23. "Dear Prudence," Dec. 31, 1999.
24. "Dear Prudence," Dec. 31, 1999.
25. "Dear Prudence," July 5, 2001.
26. "Dear Prudence," July 5, 2001.
27. "Dear Prudence," July 12, 2001.
28. "Dear Prudence," July 12, 2001.
29. "Dear Prudence," July 12, 2001.
30. "Dear Prudence," July 26, 2001.
31. "Dear Prudence," July 26, 2001.
32. "Dear Prudence," Feb. 21, 2002.
33. "Dear Prudence," Feb. 21, 2002.
34. "Dear Prudence," Aug. 22, 2002.
35. "Dear Prudence," April 18, 2002.
36. "Dear Prudence," April 18, 2002.
37. "Dear Prudence," Nov. 24, 2002.
38. "Dear Prudence," Nov. 24, 2002.
39. "Dear Prudence," June 7, 2010.
40. "Dear Prudence," July 4, 2013.
41. "Dear Prudence," July 4, 2013.
42. "Dear Prudence," June 16, 2012.
43. "Dear Prudence," June 16, 2012.
44. "Dear Prudence," June 16, 2012.
45. "Dear Prudence," Feb. 2, 2006.
46. "Dear Prudence," Feb. 2, 2006.
47. "Dear Prudence," Feb. 2, 2006.
48. "Dear Prudence," Feb 18, 2014.
49. "Dear Prudence," Feb 18, 2014.
50. "Dear Prudence," Feb 18, 2014.
51. "Dear Prudence," Feb 18, 2014.
52. "Dear Prudence," Oct. 14, 2004.
53. "Dear Prudence," Oct. 14, 2004.
54. "Dear Prudence," Jan. 26, 2017.
55. "Dear Prudence," Jan. 26, 2017.
56. "Dear Prudence," Jan. 26, 2017.
57. "Dear Prudence," Aug. 28, 2018.
58. "Dear Prudence," Aug. 28, 2018.
59. "Dear Prudence," Aug. 28, 2018.
60. "Dear Prudence," Aug. 28, 2018.
61. "Dear Prudence," June 1, 2006.
62. "Dear Prudence," June 1, 2006.
63. "Dear Prudence," Aug. 31, 2006.
64. "Dear Prudence," Aug. 31, 2006.
65. "Dear Prudence," Dec. 3, 2015.

Notes—Chapters 11 and 12

66. "Dear Prudence," Dec. 3, 2015.
67. "Dear Prudence," Dec. 3, 2015.
68. "Dear Prudence," Dec. 3, 2015.
69. "Dear Prudence," Nov. 12, 2012.
70. "Dear Prudence," Nov. 12, 2012.
71. "Dear Prudence," Nov. 12, 2012.
72. "Dear Prudence," Nov. 12, 2012.
73. "Dear Prudence," April 16, 2018.
74. "Dear Prudence," April 16, 2018.
75. "Dear Prudence," April 16, 2018.
76. "Dear Prudence," April 16, 2018.

Chapter 11

1. *Atlanta Constitution*, Nov. 20, 1965.
2. *Chicago Tribune*, July 10, 2003.
3. GoPride.com, May 12, 2014. Retrieved online at: https://web.archive.org/web/20140512224132/http://chicago.gopride.com/news/interview.cfm/articleid/581401?ref=askamy.
4. *Chicago Tribune*, July 9, 2003.
5. GoPride.com, May 12, 2014. Retrieved online at: https://web.archive.org/web/20140512224132/http://chicago.gopride.com/news/interview.cfm/articleid/581401?ref=askamy.
6. GoPride.com, May 12, 2014. Retrieved online at: https://web.archive.org/web/20140512224132/http://chicago.gopride.com/news/interview.cfm/articleid/581401?ref=askamy.
7. GoPride.com, May 12, 2014. Retrieved online at: https://web.archive.org/web/20140512224132/http://chicago.gopride.com/news/interview.cfm/articleid/581401?ref=askamy.
8. "Ask Amy," Nov. 18, 2013.
9. "Ask Amy," Nov. 18, 2013.
10. "Ask Amy," Nov. 18, 2013.
11. "Ask Amy," Dec. 27, 2013, and Jan. 4, 2014.
12. "Ask Amy," Jan. 15, 2004.
13. "Ask Amy," Jan. 19, 2004.
14. "Ask Amy," March 11, 2004.
15. "Ask Amy," July 20, 2009.
16. "Ask Amy," July 20, 2009.
17. "Ask Amy," Aug. 8, 2009.
18. "Ask Amy," May 31, 2008.
19. "Ask Amy," June 28, 2008.
20. "Ask Amy," Sept. 27, 2004.
21. "Ask Amy," Dec. 3, 2010.
22. "Ask Amy," Nov. 24, 2009.
23. "Ask Amy," June 7, 2008.
24. "Ask Amy," June 7, 2008.
25. "Ask Amy," March 30, 2006.
26. "Ask Amy," Nov. 2, 2004.
27. "Ask Amy," Oct. 6, 2006.
28. "Ask Amy," May 7, 2005.
29. "Ask Amy," May 6, 2004.
30. "Ask Amy," May 24, 2004.
31. "Ask Amy," May 24, 2004.
32. "Ask Amy," Dec. 28, 2004.
33. "Ask Amy," March 10, 2004.
34. "Ask Amy," Nov. 21, 2005.
35. "Ask Amy," Nov. 21, 2005.
36. "Ask Amy," Aug. 25, 2004.
37. "Ask Amy," Aug. 25, 2004.
38. "Ask Amy," June 7, 2004.
39. "Ask Amy," June 16, 2004.
40. "Ask Amy," Oct. 4, 2004.
41. "Ask Amy," Nov. 15, 2004.
42. "Ask Amy," Oct. 6, 2009.
43. "Ask Amy," Dec. 23, 2004.
44. "Ask Amy," Jan. 23, 2008.
45. "Ask Amy," Jan. 1, and Jan. 3, 2005.
46. "Ask Amy," March 31, 2005.
47. "Ask Amy," May 3, 2005.
48. "Ask Amy," June 10, 2005.
49. "Ask Amy," June 10, 2005.
50. "Ask Amy," Aug. 3, 2005.
51. "Ask Amy," March 6, 2006.
52. "Ask Amy," March 6, 2006.
53. "Ask Amy," March 6, 2006.
54. "Ask Amy," April 8, 2006.
55. "Ask Amy," April 8, 2006.
56. "Ask Amy," Feb. 20, 2006.
57. "Ask Amy," Feb. 20, 2006.
58. "Ask Amy," March 13, 2012.

Chapter 12

1. *Los Angeles Times*, July 15, 2007.
2. *Calgary Herald*, June 15, 2007.
3. *Calgary Herald*, June 15, 2007.
4. Tennis book review, retrieved online at: https://www.popmatters.com/since-you-asked-by-cary-tennis-2496113437.html.
5. *Calgary Herald*, June 15, 2007.
6. *Los Angeles Times*, July 15, 2007.
7. *Los Angeles Times*, July 15, 2007.
8. "Since You Asked," July 5, 2005.
9. "Since You Asked," July 5, 2005.
10. "Since You Asked," July 5, 2005.
11. "Since You Asked," March 27, 2006.

Notes—Chapter 13

12. "Since You Asked," March 27, 2006.
13. "Since You Asked," March 27, 2006.
14. "Since You Asked," Nov. 17, 2011.
15. "Since You Asked," Nov. 17, 2011.
16. "Since You Asked," Nov. 17, 2011.
17. "Since You Asked," Nov. 17, 2011.
18. "Since You Asked," Aug. 3, 2012.
19. "Since You Asked," Aug. 3, 2012.
20. "Since You Asked," Nov. 1, 2012.
21. "Since You Asked," Nov. 1, 2012.
22. "Since You Asked," Nov. 1, 2012.
23. "Since You Asked," Dec. 16, 2011.
24. "Since You Asked," Dec. 16, 2011.
25. "Since You Asked," Dec. 16, 2011.
26. "Since You Asked," May 22, 2012.
27. "Since You Asked," May 22, 2012.
28. "Since You Asked," May 22, 2012.
29. "Since You Asked," April 22, 2005.
30. "Since You Asked," April 22, 2005.
31. "Since You Asked," April 22, 2005.
32. "Since You Asked," Feb. 23, 2012.
33. "Since You Asked," Sept. 26, 2011.
34. "Since You Asked," Sept. 26, 2011.
35. "Since You Asked," Sept. 26, 2011.
36. "Since You Asked," April 19, 2013.
37. Cary Tennis blog entry, Oct. 9, 2013, retrieved online at: https://www.carytennis.com/2013/10/09/cary-tennis-leaves-salon-now-it-gets-interesting-2/.

Chapter 13

1. KAET-TV interview, "Arizona Horizon," April 12, 2018. Retrieved online at: https://azpbs.org/horizon/2018/04/author-of-savage-love-dan-savage-shares-how-his-column-began/.
2. KAET-TV interview, "Arizona Horizon," April 12, 2018. Retrieved online at: https://azpbs.org/horizon/2018/04/author-of-savage-love-dan-savage-shares-how-his-column-began/.
3. KAET-TV interview, "Arizona Horizon," April 12, 2018. Retrieved online at: https://azpbs.org/horizon/2018/04/author-of-savage-love-dan-savage-shares-how-his-column-began/.
4. KAET-TV interview, "Arizona Horizon," April 12, 2018. Retrieved online at: https://azpbs.org/horizon/2018/04/author-of-savage-love-dan-savage-shares-how-his-column-began/.
5. KAET-TV interview, "Arizona Horizon," April 12, 2018. Retrieved online at: https://azpbs.org/horizon/2018/04/author-of-savage-love-dan-savage-shares-how-his-column-began/.
6. KAET-TV interview, "Arizona Horizon," April 12, 2018. Retrieved online at: https://azpbs.org/horizon/2018/04/author-of-savage-love-dan-savage-shares-how-his-column-began/.
7. KAET-TV interview, "Arizona Horizon," April 12, 2018. Retrieved online at: https://azpbs.org/horizon/2018/04/author-of-savage-love-dan-savage-shares-how-his-column-began/.
8. "Savage Love," March 16, 1992.
9. "Savage Love," March 22, 2001.
10. "Savage Love," Sept. 23, 1991.
11. "Savage Love," Dec. 15, 2009.
12. "Savage Love," Nov. 30, 2000.
13. "Savage Love," Dec. 12, 2012.
14. "Savage Love," Aug. 15, 2012.
15. "Savage Love," Aug. 15, 2012.
16. "Savage Love," May 13, 1999.
17. "Savage Love," May 13, 1999.
18. "Savage Love, Sept. 28, 1999.
19. "Savage Love," Sept. 28, 1999.
20. "Savage Love," Sept. 28, 1999.
21. "Savage Love," Sept. 12, 2000.
22. "Savage Love," Dec. 19, 2012.
23. "Savage Love," Feb. 18, 2015 and Aug. 13, 2014.
24. "Savage Love," Sept. 2, 1999.
25. "Savage Love," Sept. 2, 1999.
26. "Savage Love," Dec. 23, 1999.
27. "Savage Love," Dec. 23, 1999.
28. "Savage Love," Dec. 2, 1999.
29. "Savage Love," Feb. 27 and March 4, 2014.
30. "Savage Love," Feb. 27 and March 4, 2014.
31. "Savage Love," Dec. 2, 1999.
32. "Savage Love," Dec. 2, 1999.
33. "Savage Love," Sept. 13, 2001.
34. "Savage Love," Sept. 13, 2001.
35. "Savage Love," Sept. 13, 2001.
36. "Savage Love," June 15, 2000.
37. "Savage Love," June 15, 2000.
38. "Savage Love," June 15, 2000.
39. "Savage Love," April 13, 2000.
40. "Savage Love," April 13, 2000.
41. "Savage Love," Sept. 20, 2001.
42. "Savage Love," Sept. 20, 2001.
43. "Savage Love," Sept. 20, 2001.

44. "Savage Love," Sept. 20, 2001.
45. "Savage Love," Jan. 24, 2002.
46. "Savage Love," Feb. 25, 2014.
47. *The Stranger*, Oct. 12, 2016.
48. *The Stranger*, Oct. 12, 2016.
49. "Savage Love," Aug. 3, 2000.
50. "Savage Love," Aug. 3, 2000.
51. "Savage Love," Feb. 25, 1999.
52. KAET-TV interview, "Arizona Horizon," April 12, 2018. Retrieved online at: https://azpbs.org/horizon/2018/04/author-of-savage-love-dan-savage-shares-how-his-column-began/.

Chapter 14

1. Papers of Martin Luther King, Jr. The Martin Luther King, Jr. Research & Education Institute, Stanford University. Retrieved Dec. 21, 2019 online at: https://kinginstitute.stanford.edu/encyclopedia/advice-living.
2. Papers of Martin Luther King, Jr. The Martin Luther King, Jr. Research & Education Institute, Stanford University. Retrieved Dec. 21, 2019 online at: https://swap.stanford.edu/20141218230500/http://mlk-kpp01.stanford.edu/kingweb/publications/papers/vol4/580100-000-Advice_For_Living.htm.
3. Papers of Martin Luther King, Jr. The Martin Luther King, Jr. Research & Education Institute, Stanford University. Retrieved Dec. 21, 2019 online at: https://swap.stanford.edu/20141218230500/http://mlk-kpp01.stanford.edu/kingweb/publications/papers/vol4/580100-000-Advice_For_Living.htm.
4. Papers of Martin Luther King, Jr. The Martin Luther King, Jr. Research & Education Institute, Stanford University. Retrieved Dec. 21, 2019 online at: https://swap.stanford.edu/20141218230500/http://mlk-kpp01.stanford.edu/kingweb/publications/papers/vol4/580100-000-Advice_For_Living.htm.
5. Martin, Judith. (2005). *Miss Manners' Guide to Excruciatingly Correct Behavior*. New York: W.W. Norton & Co.
6. "Miss Manners," Jan. 29, 1990, and March 6, 1979.
7. "Miss Manners," Sept. 10, 1980.
8. "Miss Manners," Dec. 20, 1980.
9. "Miss Manners," Dec. 20, 1980.
10. "Miss Manners," Dec. 20, 1980.
11. "Miss Manners," Dec. 20, 1980.
12. "Miss Manners," Oct. 15, 1981.
13. "Miss Manners," Oct. 15, 1981.
14. Cullen Moore column, April 2, 1961.
15. Cullen Moore column, April 2, 1961.
16. Cullen Moore column, April 2, 1961.
17. Cullen Moore column, April 2, 1961.
18. *Philadelphia (PA) Inquirer*, June 20, 1978.
19. Dr. Walter Alvarez column, Dec. 1, 1972.
20. Dr. Walter Alvarez column, Dec. 1, 1972.
21. Dr. Walter Alvarez column, Sept. 12, 1953.
22. Dr. Walter Alvarez column, June 23, 1971.
23. *Gastonia (NC) Gazette*, March 3, 1973.
24. *Chicago Tribune*, April 16, 1972.
25. "Family Lib," July 8, 1974.
26. "Family Lib," July 8, 1974.
27. "Family Lib," July 8, 1974.
28. "Family Lib," July 9, 1974.
29. "Family Lib," July 9, 1974.
30. "Family Lib," July 22, 1974.
31. "Family Lib," July 22, 1974.
32. "Family Lib," July 22, 1974.
33. *Charlotte (NC) Observer*, Feb. 22, 2018
34. "My Answer," Jan. 10, 1961.
35. "My Answer," Jan. 10, 1961.
36. "My Answer," Jan. 10, 1961.
37. "My Answer," Feb. 1, 1961.
38. "My Answer," Feb. 1, 1961.
39. "The Pet Doctor," Oct. 28, 1987.
40. "The Pet Doctor," Oct. 28, 1987.
41. "The Pet Doctor," Nov. 15, 1977.
42. "The Pet Doctor," Dec. 17, 1986
43. *Lancaster (PA) Intelligencer Journal*, Oct. 5, 1970.
44. *Alexandria (LA) Town Talk*, Sept. 19, 1970.
45. "Ask Dr. Lamb," Oct. 5, 1974.
46. "Ask Dr. Lamb," Oct. 5, 1974.
47. "Ask Dr. Lamb," Oct. 17, 1987.
48. "Ask Dr. Lamb," Nov. 17, 1987.
49. "Ask Dr. Lamb," Dec. 29, 1987.
50. "Ask Dr. Lamb," May 30, 1994.
51. https://lorigottlieb.com/books/maybe-you-should-talk-to-someone/.

Notes—Chapter 14

52. https://lorigottlieb.com/books/maybe-you-should-talk-to-someone/.
53. *Times of Northwest Indiana*, April 7, 2019.
54. *Times of Northwest Indiana*, April 7, 2019.
55. *Jewish Journal*, April 10, 2019.
56. *Chicago Tribune*, March 19, 2010.
57. *London (UK) Daily Telegraph*, June 25, 2019.
58. "Dear Therapist," Dec. 2, 2019.
59. "Dear Therapist," Dec. 2, 2019.
60. "Dear Therapist," Nov. 25, 2019.
61. "Dear Therapist," Nov. 25, 2019.
62. "Dear Therapist," Nov. 25, 2019.
63. "Dear Therapist," Nov. 25, 2019.
64. "Dear Therapist," Sept. 23, 2019.
65. "Dear Therapist," Sept. 23, 2019.
66. "Dear Therapist," Sept. 23, 2019.
67. "Dear Therapist," March 21, 2018.

Index

Numbers in ***bold italics*** indicate pages with illustrations

ABC 172
Ackerman, Ken 125
acquired immune deficiency syndrome (AIDS) 36, 37, 61, 104–107, 119, 121–123, 179–180, 196
advice columns, history of 1, 3, 4, 5, 6, 7, 8, 9, 11, 23–25, 29–30, 38, 39–41, 48–49, 51–52, 61, 62–64, 66, 73, 74, 86, 87–90, 100–101, 102–103, 108–109, 118, 123, 124, 126, 135–136, 149–150, 163–165, 170, 171–172, 183, 184, 190–191, 195, 196–197
"Advice for Living" column 184, 185
"Advice to the Lovelorn" column 6, 7
The Albany Democrat-Herald 29
alcoholism (also alcoholic) 82, 90, 91, 92, 99, 163, 192, 194
Alvarez, Dr. Walter C. 184, 189–190
America Online (AOL) 149
American Psychiatric Association (APA) 13, 61
Anderson-Marshall, Diane 4, 108
Ann Landers Talks to Teenagers About Sex 19
The Annapolis Log 90
"Annie's Mailbox" column 22
applied psychology 64, 80
"Ask Amy" column 149–153, 155, 157–159, 161
"Ask Beth" column 108–112, 118–119, 121, 123
Ask Beth; You Can't Ask Your Mother 109
"Ask Dr. Brothers" column 50, 56
"Ask Dr. Lamb" column 195
Associated Press (AP) 50
The Atlanta Constitution 149
The Atlantic 197, 198

Baton Rouge, LA 48
Bergler, Dr. Edmund 94
Bergstedt, Spencer 175
Billboard magazine 64
Billy Graham Evangelistic Association 192–193

Bisexual Insurgence 177
bisexuals (bisexuality) 1, 17, 44, 61, 85–86, 106, 113, 126, 127, 138, 145, 153, 160, 168, 170, 177–178
Bornstein, Kate 175
Boston City Council 112–113
The Boston Globe 108, 110, 118, 123, 135
Bottel, Helen 39–41, 48, 49
Boy Scouts 85
Boys and Sex 116
Brammer, John Paul 8
Brisbane, Arthur 6
Brooklyn, NY 8
Brothers, Dr. Joyce 50, ***51***, 52–61
Bryant, Anita 60
Budget Rent-A-Car 11
Burgess, Steve 163
Burns, Tommy 50
Bush, George W. 182
The Business of Living 87

The Calgary Herald 163
The Call Girl: A Social and Psychoanalytic Study 53
Cameron, Loren 175
Casanova complex 92
"Case Files of a Psychologist" column 62
CBS (also CBS News, CBS Sports) 50, 51, 149
Centers for Disease Control (CDC) 37
Charlie's Angels 51
Chartoff, Melanie 197
Cheney, Dick 182
Cheney, Mary 182
Chicago, IL 10, 14, 17, 22, 63, 64, 68, 73, 75, 172
The Chicago Sun-Times 9, 10, 12
The Chicago Tribune 12, 64, 149, 150, 190, 191, 197–198
Chicagopride.com 150
Civil Liberties Union 45
Cleveland, OH 14

215

Index

closeted gays/coming out 4, 19, 27–28, 37, 43, 54, 57, 95, 96, 97, 104–105, 111, 113, 116, 126–127, 128, 132, 139, 145, 157, 166–167, 168, 169, 177, 178, 184–185, 198–199
Coderre, Jennifer 177
Cold War 52
Coleman, Marilyn 6
Collins, Kathleen 61
Columbia University 50
Commitment: Love, Sex, Marriage and My Family 172
Committee for Gay Youth 113
Communists/Communism 20, 92
Confidential to America: Newspaper Advice Columns and Sexual Education 23
Coolidge, Calvin 62
Council of Economic Advisers 135
Craemer, Jack 7, 39
Craigslist.com 162, 168
Crane, Daniel B. 86
Crane, Dr. George 62, **63**, 64–86, 114
Creators Syndicate 22
criticism of advice columnists 3, 21–22, 29–30, 43, 45, 90, 91, 99, 106–107, 110–111, 119–120, 123, 134, 138–139, 155–156, 158, 161, 177–178, 179, 187
cross-dressing/transsexuals 15–16, 21, 82, 103, 121
Cunningham, John 117
Cypher, Julie 176

The Daily Show 51
Dear Abby (person) 7, 10, 11, **24**, 38, 39, 50, 63, 126
"Dear Abby" column 11, 23, **24**, 29, 34, 36, 38, 41, 52, 161, 164, 171
"Dear Meg" column 102–106
"Dear Prudence" column 8, 135–137, 140, 145–147
"Dear Therapist" column 196–200
Decatur, IL 29
The Decatur Herald 29
DeGeneres, Ellen 176
Democratic National Convention **110**
Detroit, MI 13, 14
Dewey, Thomas 66
Dickinson, Amy 149–153, 159, 161
Dickinson, Emily 150
discrimination against gays 6, 25, 27, 30, 31, 35, 44, 46, 53–54, 58, 59, 60–61, 74, 111, 120–121, 129, 132–133, 140, 142 143, 144, 147, 152–153, 161, 190
divorce 12, 18, 26, 32, 46, 84, 89, 90, 104, 125, 130, 131, 141, 147, 168–169, 191
Dix, Dorothy 6, 7, 10
Do I Sound Gay? 180
Dr. Phil 196
"Dorothy Dix Talks" column 7

Douglas, George H. 7
Douglas, William O. 9
Drudge, Matt 182

Easter Seals 24
Ebony magazine 184, 185
Egypt 181
Erickson, Reed 48
Erickson Educational Foundation 36, 48
Esquire magazine 149
Etheridge, Melissa 176
European Republican Committee 102

Facebook.com 170
fag hags 104, 131–132, 138, 141, 174
Fairfax, Beatrice 6–7
"Family Lib" column 190–191
A Family Matter 117
Fanning, Larry 9
Feldman, Dr. M.P. 80
femininity/masculinity 15, 31–32, 56, 68, 76, 80, 81, 82–83, 85, 93, 94, 180
50 Plus magazine 102
Finnie, Hannah 8
Ford, Gerald R. 33–34, 135, 136
former homosexuals 14–15, 27, 28, 42, 44, 55, 77, 78, 80, 82, 94, 100, 118, 119, 120
Fox, Margalit 52
Fox, Dr. Michael 184, 194–195
Freeville, NY 149
Freud, Dr. Sigmund 87, 92, 194
Friedman Lederer, Esther Pauline "Eppie" 9, **10**, 11, 22, 23, 50, 135, 140; *see also* Landers, Ann
Friedman Phillips, Pauline Esther "Popo" 10, 23, **24**, 38, 50; *see also* "Dear Abby"; Van Buren, Abigail
friend of Dorothy 141

Galifianakis, Nick 124, 125
Ganong, Lawrence 6
gay celebrities 176
Gay Hotline 112, 113
Gay Liberation Front 111, 112, 191
gay marriage 104, 142, 143, 152, 154, 182
gay marriage 12, 34, 47–48, 139, 143, 152, 154–155, 172, 176, 187–188
Gay Marriage: Why It Is Good for Gays, Good for Straights, and Good for America 143
Gay Men's Health Crisis 106
gay monogamy 178–179
gay parents 47–48, 104, 129–130, 159–160, 191–192, 198
gay porn/pornography 16, 46, 83, 135–136, 141, 157, 168, 176
gay pride parade 17
gay rights 12, 13, 16–17, 36, 43, 58, 59–60, 84, 96, **110**, 111, 112, 114, 143

216

Index

gay senior citizens 105–106
gay teens 4, 19, 20, 26, 41–42, 45, 60, 61, 71, 73, 81, 85, 103, 105, 109, 111, 112, 113, 114, 116, 119, 151, 157–158, 172–173
gaydar 105
gays from problem perspective 5, 8, 13, 14, 15, 31, 42, 74, 97
gays in the military 20–21, 26–27, 75–76, 77, 92
"Generation Rap" column 40
"The Gentler Sex" column 88
Georgetown University 149
Girl Scouts 85
Glide Memorial United Methodist Church 83–84
Good Housekeeping magazine 51, 52
Good Morning America 196
Google.com 199–200
Gore, Al 182
Gottlieb, Lori 184, 196–200
Graham, the Rev. Billy 184, 192, **193**, 194
Greene, Bob 64
Greensburg, IN 172
Greenwald, Harold 53
The Greenwood Commonwealth 29
Grindr.com 199
Group for the Advancement of Psychiatry 53
Gudelunas, David 23–24

Hadar, Mary 126
Hanckel, France 117
"Happy Hooker" column 171
Harvard University 124–125
Haworth, Mary 10, 87, **88**, 89–101, 124
Hax, Carolyn 124–134
Hearst, William Randolph 7
Hearst newspapers 6, 7
Heche, Anne 176
"Helen Help Us!" column 39–40, 42–44, 48–49
Hoffman, Martin 57
Hollywood Squares 52
homophile movement 96, 119
homophobia/homophobic 128–129, 142, 144, 145, 147, 157, 172
homosexuality: in animals 21, 33, 194–195; cause 19–20, 29, 33, 35, 42, 46, 58, 67–68, 69, 70–71, 73, 75, 76, 84, 93, 94, 100, 111, 185, 194
Homosexuality: Disease or Way of Life? 94
homosexuals marrying heterosexuals 18, 25–26, 46–47, 68, 81, 84, 92–93, 96, 98, 104, 130, 131, 140–141, 155, 156, 168–169, 191, 193
Hopkins Syndicate 64
"Horse Sense" column 62
House Ethics Committee 86

Howard, Ken 135
Howard, Margo 135, 137–139, 140
"The Human Guinea Pig" column 135
human immunodeficiency virus (HIV) 37, 61, 106, 121–123, 179–180

incest 136–137
Institute for Study of Animal Problems 194
International Gay & Lesbian Human Rights Commission 181
It Gets Better 172–173, 178

Japan 49
The Jerry Springer Show 175
The Jewish Journal 197
Jewish sisters 63
Johnson, Lyndon B. 195
The Journal News (White Plains, NY) 126

Kahn, Joseph P. 108, 109
Keck, Tim 171
Kennedy, Edward M. "Teddy" 86
The Kid: What Happened After My Boyfriend and I Decided to Go Get Pregnant 172
King, the Rev. Dr. Martin Luther, Jr. 184, **185**
King Features Syndicate 7, 39, 41, 87, 89
The King of Comedy 51
Kinsey, Dr. Alfred 58, 78, 94
Kinsey Institute 115
Koch, Joanne 184, 190, 192
Koch, Lew 184, 190, 191

Lamb, Dr. Lawrence E. 184, 195–196
Landers, Ann 3, 7, 9, **10**, 11–15, 17, 19–22, 23–24, 29, 31, 39, 41, 50, 52, 63, 86, 120, 126, 135, 140, 149, 150, 161, 171, 173, 179, 183
Laurie, Peter 66
Lavery, Daniel (also Ortberg, Mallory) 8, 135, 137, 145, 146, 147, 148
lesbians 17, 28, 47–48, 69–70, 71, 74, 76–77, 78, 80–81, 83, 84, 85, 114–115, 116, 117, 118, 127, 140, 145, 146, 165, 169, 174, 182, 188, 191, 192, 195
Lesenvich, Gus 50
LGBT Youth Talkline 127
Life magazine 5, 10–11, 102
Look magazine 48
The Lord Is My Shepherd and He Knows I'm Gay 190
The Los Angeles Times 164
Los Angeles Times Syndicate 108
Lucas, Billy 172–173

MacCulloch, Dr. M.J. 80
Madison, WI 14
Mama's Family 51

217

Index

Manchester, England 157
Manning, Marie 6–7; see also Dix, Dorothy
Manson family 33
Marciano, Rocky 50
Marcus, Eric 38
Marry Him: The Case for Settling for Mr. Good Enough 197
Martin, Judith 173, 184, *186*, 187
Mary Queen of Scots 11
Mason, Anthony 149
Mason, Emily 149
Match Game 51
Maybe You Should Talk to Someone: A Therapist, Her Therapist, and Our Lives Revealed 197
Mayo Clinic 189
McHenry, F.A. 4
McNaught Syndicate 23
"Medical Advice" column 189
Meriwether Gilmer, Elizabeth 7
The Merv Griffin Show 51
Metropolitan Community Church (MCC) 190
Miami-Dade County, FL 60
The Mighty Queens of Freevillle: A Mother, a Daughter, and the Town That Raised Them 149
Milk, Harvey 33
Miller, Terry 172
"Miss Manners" column 173, 184, 186–188
Mitchell, Kathy 22
Moore, Cullen 184, 188
Moore, Sarah Jane 33–34
Moscone, George 33
Murdoch, Rupert 102
"My Answer" column 192–194

The Naked Gun: From the Files of the Police Squad 51
National Aeronautics and Space Administration (NASA) 195
National Coming Out Day 158
National Press Club 181
Naval Academy, U.S. 90
NBC News 149
Nebraska 27
New York, NY 50, 51, 52, 86, 102, *110*, 174, 180–181, 191
New York Post 7, 102
New York Times 52
Newspaper Enterprise Association (NEA) 191, 195
9/11 terrorist attacks 180–181
Nixon, Richard M. 102, 135
Northwestern University 62, 67

O magazine 149
Oh God! Book II 51

Olin, Bob 50
Onion 171
online advice columns 7, 163, 197
Oppenheimer, Robert 88–89
Ortberg, the Rev. John 137
Ortberg, Mallory *see* Lavery, Daniel M.
outing 33, 34

pansexual 166–167
Parents & Friends of Lesbians and Gays (PFLAG) 33, 118, 148
parents of gay children 15–16, 21, 28, 29, 31–33, 34, 43, 44–45, 55–58, 70, 77, 93–94, 97, 99, 103, 105, 117, 118, 128–129, 143, 145–146, 151, 165, 172, 188
Penthouse magazine 171
Peppers, Suzanne (Bottel) 40
Perry, Katy 174
Perry, the Rev. Troy 190
"The Pet Doctor" column 194–195
Phillips, Jeanne 24
polyamorous 170
Pomeroy, Wardell 116
Prentice-Hall 19
Project Lambda 112–113
Psychology in Action 64

Quincy, MA 110

Rauch, Jonathan 143
The Real O'Neals 172
Redbook magazine 87
The Regis Philbin Show 102
Reno, NV 60
Robertson, Rev. Pat 182
Rochester, MN 189

Sacramento, CA 41
Saddleback Community Church 182
Saginaw, MI 79
St. Louis, MO 14
Salon.com 163, 170
Salon magazine 163
The San Antonio Express-News 102
The San Diego Union 29
San Francisco, CA 26, 33, 34, 37, 52, 77, 83–84, 163, 189
The San Francisco Chronicle 10, 23
San Francisco earthquake 189
The San Francisco Examiner 23
The San Rafael Independent Journal 7, 39
Santorum, Rick 181–182
Sarno, David 164
Saturday Night Live 51
Saudi Arabia 167, 181–183
Savage, Dan 7, 171, *172*, 173–183
"Savage Love" column 7, 171–173, 177, 181, 183

Index

Schickel, Bruno 149
Schwartz, Dr. Pepper 175–176
Scientific Marriage Foundation 78–79
Scutts, Joanna 5, 6
Selective Service (also draft), U.S. 20, 21, 26, 27, 75, 77
Senior Action in Gay Environment (SAGE) 105–106
Senior magazine 49
SF Weekly 163
Shapiro, Gregg 150
Sharkey, Jack 50
Shustack, Mary 126
Silverman, Dr. Meryvn 37
Silverstein, Charles 117
The Simpsons 51
"Since You Asked" column 163
Sing Sing Prison 149
Sioux City, IA 10
Sipple, Oliver 33–34
The $64,000 Question 50, 51
Slate.com 137
Slate magazine 135
The Social History of the American Family 6
Sodom and Gomorrah 86
South Hamilton, MA 110
South Vietnam 20
Southeast Asia 20, 26
Stanford University 189
Star magazine 102
"Stars and Lovers" column 188
Staunton News-Leader 29
Stein, Ben 135
Stein, Herb 135, *136*, 137
Stick Figure: A Diary of My Former Self 198
Straight Spouse Network 131, 155
The Stranger 171
Strangers Tell Me Things: A Memoir of Love, Loss and Coming Home 149
Studds, Gerry 86
Sugar, Marcy 22
suicide 15, 172–173
Supreme Court, U.S. 9, 143

Taft, Robert A. 62
Takei, George 150
Talbot, David 163
The Tampa Morning Tribune 93
Tangent, OR 29
"Tell Me About It" column 124–125, 132–133
Tell Me About It: Lying, Sulking, Getting Fat and 56 Other Things Not to Do While Looking for Love 125
Tennis, Cary 163, *164*, 165–170

Thorpe, David 180
Time magazine 4–5, 10
"Toast" column 137
The Today Show 196
The Tonight Show 51
transgender 8, 36, 48, 130–131, 137, 147–148, 166, 175–176
Trevor Project 127
Trimbos, Dr. C.J. 100

Uganda 8
United Features Syndicate 194
United Press International (UPI) 50
Universal Press Syndicate 38
University of Washington 175–176

Van Buren, Abigail 23, *24*, 171
Vanguards 84
venereal disease (also sexually-transmitted diseases; STD) 4, 22, 28, 73, 81, 122, 168
Vietnam War 20, 26, 33

Walcott, Jersey Joe 50
Walker, Mickey 50
The Wall Street Journal 135
Warren, the Rev. Rick 182
Washington, DC 86, 144, 181, 186, 194
The Washington Post 87–89, 124, 126
A Way of Love, a Way of Life 117
Welch, Siobhan 164
West Hollywood, CA 144
WGN Radio 64
Whitcomb, Meg 102, 105
White Plains, NY 126
Winfrey, Oprah 149
Winship, Elizabeth 4, 108–110, 112–115, 117–119, 121–123
Winship, Peg 123
Winship, Tom 108
WMCA Radio 52
WNBC Radio 102
WNBC-TV 102
World Trade Center 180–181
World War I 7
World War II 75, 90, 92
"The Worry Clinic" column 62–64, 86

Yahoo 135
Yoffe, Emily 135, 136, 143, 147–148
Yomiuri Shimbun 49
Young, Mary Elizabeth Reardon 88, 124
"Your Problems" column 9, 12, 19, 23

Zogby International 159–160

www.ingramcontent.com/pod-product-compliance
Lightning Source LLC
Chambersburg PA
CBHW032042300426
44117CB00009B/1152